WOMEN AND THE MAKING OF BUILT SPACE IN ENGLAND, 1870–1950

In memory of Judith Attfield

Women and the Making of Built Space in England, 1870–1950

Edited by
ELIZABETH DARLING
and
LESLEY WHITWORTH

ASHGATE

Published by
Ashgate Publishing Limited
Gower House
Croft Road
Aldershot
Hants GU11 3HR
England

Ashgate Publishing Company
Suite 420
101 Cherry Street
Burlington, VT 05401-4405
USA

Ashgate website: http://www.ashgate.com

British Library Cataloguing in Publication Data
Women and the making of built space in England, 1870–1950 1. Women – England – Social conditions – 20th century 2. Women – England – Social conditions – 19th century 3. Women and city planning – England – History 4. Architecture and women – England – History
    I. Darling, Elizabeth II. Whitworth, Lesley
    305.4'2'0942'09034

Library of Congress Cataloging-in-Publication Data
Women and the making of built space in England, 1870–1950 / edited by Elizabeth Darling and Lesley Whitworth.
      p. cm.
   Includes bibliographical references and index.
   ISBN-13: 978-0-7546-5185-7 (alk. paper)
   1. Urban women—England—History—19th century. 2. Urban women—England—History—20th century. 3. Women and city plannin—England—History—19th century. 4. Women and city planning—England—History—20th century. 5. Architecture and women—England—History—19th century. 6. Architecture and women—England—History—20th century. I. Darling, Elizabeth. II. Whitworth, Lesley.

HQ1593.W543 2007
307.76082'0941—dc22

ISBN 978-0-7546-5185-7

2006032296

Printed and bound in Great Britain by TJ International Ltd, Padstow, Cornwall.

Contents

Figures

Contributors

Anne Anderson received her doctorate in English from Exeter in 2001. She is a Fellow of the Society of Antiquaries and Senior Lecturer in History of Art and Design at Southampton Institute. Her research has been published in *the Journal of Design History* and the *Journal of the History of Education*. Most recently she has edited a volume of the letters of Octavia Hill.

Elizabeth Darling is an architectural historian and Senior Lecturer in Art History at Oxford Brookes University. She researches on gender, housing and modernism, particularly in inter-war Britain, and has been published in the *Journal of Architectural Education*, *The London Journal* and *Planning Perspectives* as well as contributing chapters to *Negotiating Domesticity, Spatial Productions of Gender in Modern Architecture* (Routledge, 2005) and *Man-made Futures, Planning, Education and Design in mid-twentieth century Britain* (Routledge, 2007). Her monograph, *Re-forming Britain: Narratives of Modernity before Reconstruction* was published by Routledge in 2007.

Emma Ferry lectures at Worcester School of Art and Design, Bristol University and the School of Art and Design History at Kingston University, where she is attached to the Modern Interiors Research Centre (MIRC). Her research on Macmillan's 'Art at Home' Series (1876-83) has been published in the *Journal of Design History* (2003), *Intimus: Interior Design Theory Reader* (2006), *Women's History Magazine* (2006) and *Design and the Modern Magazine* (2007).

Karen Hunt is Professor of Modern British History at Keele University. She has published extensively on gender and the British Left. Her recent articles have been on socialist masculinity (*Labour History Review*, 2004) and women communists in the 1920s (*Twentieth Century British History*, 2004). She has also published *Equivocal Feminists: the Social Democratic Federation and the Woman Question, 1884–1911* (Cambridge University Press, 1996) and, with June Hannam, *Socialist Women. Britain 1880s to 1920s* (Routledge, 2002). She is currently writing a book exploring gendered politics in a life, that of the socialist, suffragist, communist and internationalist, Dora Montefiore (1851–1933).

Trevor Keeble is Head of the School of Art & Design History at Kingston University. He has contributed chapters to *Women's Places: Architecture and Design 1860–1960* (Routledge, 2003), and *Design and the Modern Magazine* (Manchester University Press, 2007). Most recently he has co-edited a collection of essays entitled *The Modern Period Room* (Routledge 2006).

Ruth Livesey is a lecturer in nineteenth-century literature and Deputy Director of the Centre for Victorian Studies, Department of English, Royal Holloway, University of London. Her work on gender, class and narratives of late nineteenth-century urban exploration has appeared in, among other publications, the *Journal of Victorian Culture* and *Women's History Review*. She is currently completing a monograph entitled *Socialism, Sex and the Culture of Aestheticism in Britain* and articles relating to this more recent project have appeared in various journals including *Victorian Literature and Culture*.

Helen Meller is Professor of Urban History and Director of the Centre of Urban Culture at the University of Nottingham. She has published widely on themes relating to leisure and cities, social aspects of planning history, women and cities, and most recently, European cities. Her books include *Patrick Geddes: Social Evolutionist and City Planner* (Routledge, 1990 and 1993); *Towns, Plans and Society in Modern Britain* (Cambridge University Press, 1997); and *European Cities 1890–1930s: History, Culture and the Built Environment* (Wiley, 2001). She is currently working on a history of green open spaces in European cities 1850–2000.

Gillian Scott is a Principal Lecturer in the School of Historical and Critical Studies at the University of Brighton. Her work on the Women's Co-operative Guild arises from an interest in the history of the relationship between feminist ideas and the organisation of working-class women. Her monograph was published in 1998, titled *Feminism and the Politics of Working Women: The Women's Co-operative Guild, 1880s to the Second World War* (UCL Press).

Jill Seddon is Principal Lecturer and Academic Programme Leader for History of Design, Decorative Arts and Visual Culture at the University of Brighton. Her long-standing research interest in the work of women designers between the wars has resulted in a co-curated exhibition, 'Women Designing: Redefining Design in Britain Between the Wars' (University of Brighton Gallery, 1994), its accompanying eponymous publication, and the commission to write entries on Sadie Speight and the furniture designer Betty Joel for the new *Dictionary of National Biography*.

Lesley Whitworth is Assistant Curator of the Design Archives, University of Brighton, and a Visiting Research Fellow at the Business History Unit, London School of Economics. She has recently completed a project funded within the ESRC-AHRC 'Cultures of Consumption' research programme. This investigated the consumer education work of the Council of Industrial Design and will result in a monograph. She edited a special issue of the *Journal of Design History* ('Anxious Homes', 2003), and has published in the area of gendered shopping and home-making practices, suburban transport, and aspects of Design Council and Mass-Observation history.

Acknowledgments

This volume has its origins in 'Women and Built Space, 1860-1960', the second Annual Workshop of the Centre for Urban Culture, University of Nottingham, held in summer 2002 and co-organised by Darling and Whitworth with Professor Helen Meller. The Editors would like to thank the Universities of Nottingham and Brighton for their support of this event.

The development of the present volume reflects the continuing involvement of the Faculty Research Support Fund of the Faculty of Arts and Architecture, University of Brighton. In particular this enabled a period of research leave (Darling), and administrative support of the book's production. In this connection, our heartfelt thanks go to Pamela Smith for her patience, tenacity and skill. Thanks are also due to Catherine Moriarty, Sirpa Kutilainen and Barbara Taylor of the Design Archives, University of Brighton, for their kind assistance with the production of the book's illustrations. The authoring of Whitworth's chapter was facilitated by award number RES-143-25-0037 granted through the jointly funded Economic and Social Research Council – Arts and Humanities Research Council 'Cultures of Consumption' Research Programme (www.consume.bbk.ac.uk).

The intellectual framing of this book owes much to the Gender and Built Space Research Group founded at Brighton by Darling, Whitworth, Jill Seddon and Gillian Scott in the wake of the Nottingham workshop. Through the organisation of a series of workshops, conference panels, seminars and closed symposia, the group's concern has been to produce and promote research which investigates and interrogates our concept of 'built space'. This has generated work whose subject matter encompasses architectural space, everyday space, designed objects, artefacts, and related discourses; that is, any material or social form which may be understood as playing a part in the production, reproduction, and contestation of gender identities. The Editors would like to thank the many contributors to and participants in Gender and Built Space's ongoing activities. Among our colleagues, we wish to acknowledge especially the engagement of Gail Braybon, Monica Brewis, Ine van Dooren, John McKean and Louise Purbrick.

At Ashgate we are grateful to our editor Ann Donahue, and her predecessor Erika Gaffney, for their interest and guidance in bringing the present volume to fruition. Finally, we thank our authors for their contributions and steadfast resolve.

The volume is dedicated to the memory of Judith Attfield, an inspirational presence in the field of Design History and beyond, with whom we shared the pleasure of a common interest in the interplay between the construction of gender and the gendering of constructions.

Elizabeth Darling and Lesley Whitworth
Brighton, 2006

Abbreviations

AAD	Archive of Art and Design
AEH	All-Europe House
BCMI	'Britain Can Make It' exhibition
BSI	British Standards Institute
CAI	Council for Art and Industry
CC	Central Committee (of the WCG)
COI	Central Office of Information
CoID	Council of Industrial Design
COS	Charity Organisation Society
DCA	Design Council Archive
DIA	Design and Industries Association
DMIHE	*Daily Mail* Ideal Home Exhibition
DRU	Design Research Unit
EAW	Electrical Association for Women
EEDC	East End Dwellings Company
EIU	Economic Information Unit
GPC	General Purposes Committee (of the SJC)
GWHA	Glasgow Women's Housing Association
HOMB	Head Office Monthly Bulletin
ILP	Independent Labour Party
KHT	Kensington Housing Association and Trust
LCC	London County Council
LHASC	Labour History Archive & Study Centre
MRC	Modern Records Centre
NFWI	National Federation of Women's Institutes
NUTG	National Union of Townswomen's Guilds
RIBA	Royal Institute of British Architects
SDF	Social Democratic Federation
SICLC	Society for Improving the Conditions of the Labouring Classes
SJC	Standing Joint Committee of Working Women's Organisations
TUC	Trades Union Congress
WAHC	Women's Advisory Housing Council
WCG	Women's Co-operative Guild
WGPW	Women's Group on Public Welfare
WLL	Women's Labour League
WNHC	Workmen's National Housing Council
WSPU	Women's Social and Political Union

Introduction: Making Space and Re-making History

Elizabeth Darling and Lesley Whitworth

The Book

More than thirty years ago, the case for the reappraisal of women's roles in the shaping of social and built environments was made irrevocably. Such a concern, as is well known, has its roots in the 1960s and the combined assault on historical epistemologies by the new discipline of social history and the resurgent Women's Movement. Since then, in discourses both popular and academic, a desire to return women to the historical record might even be considered to have become a commonplace. Within the academy, women's involvement as activists and producers has been unpicked and scrutinised by scholars from a variety of disciplines including the many branches of history, sociology and geography. This has resulted in a body of work which encompasses monographs, that is, reclamations of women protagonists,[1] proposals for new methodologies,[2] and studies which use gender as a category of analysis for understanding the nature of the material and spatial world.[3]

In the 1980s, the seismic shift inaugurated in the late 1960s was further effected by the revivifying influences of oral history, cultural theory, consumption studies, the new art history, anthropology, psychoanalysis, and the turn towards the literary. These made possible and desirable a heightened regard for the texture of everyday life, foregrounded the importance of the mundane and the repetitive, and enhanced the spatial sensitivity of historical endeavours, especially towards the home. They thereby allowed a clearer critical understanding of woman as audience, of the primacy of representation, and the nuanced nature of agency. Arguably

---

[1]   Amongst many examples, see Suzanne Torre (ed.), *Women in American Architecture: A Historic and Contemporary Perspective*, New York: Whitney Library of Design, 1977; Lynne Walker, *Women Architects, their Work*, London: Sorella Press, 1984; Peter Adams, *Eileen Gray: Architect/Designer*, London: Thames & Hudson, 2000.

[2]   See Griselda Pollock and Rozsika Parker, *Old Mistresses, Women, Art & Ideology*, London: Women's Press, 1981 or Beatriz Colomina (ed.), *Sexuality and Space*, Princeton: Princeton Architectural Press, 1992.

[3]   See, for example, Daphne Spain, *Gendered Spaces*, Chapel Hill: University of North Carolina Press, 1992 and Doreen Massey, *Space, Place and Gender*, Cambridge: Polity, 1994.

the practices of architectural and design historians have played an equally significant if under-recognised part in the kind of study being undertaken here, offering innovative interpretations of the changing vistas and material culture of day-to-day life.[4] Such work has challenged to considerable effect the character, assumptions, and loci of the field of historical studies within which this volume broadly situates itself. Yet these editors would suggest that this work is not unproblematical and it is their aim to use this collection to offer a model of how these paradigm shifts might be developed further.

Interpretations of the relationship between women and built space may be problematised in various ways. A conventional, and still fertile, area of study concerns itself with the identification and reclamation of female counterparts to the canon of 'dead white males'. This ongoing work, while indisputably important, is self-delimiting in that the canon itself remains fixed and the achievement of equivalency will terminate the exercise: there are only so many women politicians, women planners, or women astronauts. In its acceptance of much older definitions of what comprises historical agency, it perpetuates a stock categorisation of meaningful endeavour, within which women will always remain rare and exceptional.

In response to this very problem there has emerged a far more sophisticated approach which grows directly out of the earlier work of biographical retrieval. In using that information to develop new methodologies, it allows better understandings of where women's practice is actually located, and awards that practice its appropriate historical significance. This has resulted in histories which bring into focus such terrains as patronage, criticism, and women's associative capacities. The value of this shift has been in its radical expansion and, perhaps, undermining of the canon. Nevertheless, these studies do tend to retain a preoccupation if not with the exceptional individual, then with the identifiable protagonist.

A counterpoint to this has been a growing engagement with the anonymous and, to some extent, unknowable woman: the factory worker, the shop clerk, the housewife. Liberated from this need to engage with named and knowable personalities, the particular richness of recent scholarship has marked a defined shift towards a problematisation of the *material*. Surroundings, products, mementos, objets d'art are now more clearly in focus than ever before, as well as arrangements, refurbishments, re-presentations and life practices of maintenance and renewal.[5] Today the

---

4   For a helpful survey of such practices see Joan Rothschild and Victoria Rosner, 'Feminisms and Design: A Review Essay', in Joan Rothschild (ed.), *Design and Feminism, Re-visioning Spaces, Places and Everyday Things*, New Brunswick: Rutgers University Press, 1999 and Judith Attfield, 'What does History have to do with it? Feminism and Design History', *Journal of Design History*, 16:1, (2003), 77–87.

5   See Victoria de Grazia and Ellen Furlogh (eds), *The Sex of Things, Gender and Consumption in Historical Perspective*, Berkeley: University of California

place of the home as the most obvious location of women's space-making has captured the attention of historians and gained legitimacy as a focus for analysis to an extent unimaginable only twenty years ago.

The methodologies espoused by the editors and several contributors to this volume, which are grounded in historical disciplines with a particular focus on architecture and design, may be imagined to dominate the collection as a whole. That they do not is as much evidence of frustration with those disciplines' preoccupations, as it is born from a regard for the work of complementary scholarship. If architectural and design historians may be thought to have a peculiar advantage when considering the spaces of the home, and acknowledged to have had it in view for slightly longer than other disciplines, then it nevertheless remains the case that the current infusion of interest from, for example, social, cultural and economic historians, can only be positive. Yet in turn, those disciplines might benefit from the spatial acuity of architectural and design historians.

This cross-fertilisation might help to direct architectural/design history away from some of its less helpful tropes, such as its identification with concerns interior to professional practice. This has resulted in a tendency to write studies which focus on practitioners, buildings and products, continuing and reinforcing an obsession with the designer as hero. Secondly, and more seriously, it too often fails to draw conclusions from the enormous under-representation of female practitioners, preferring instead to claim those few women who do practise as examples of pioneering genius, whereas it might more rewardingly question this absence and use it as a means to re-frame our understanding of how artefacts large and small are produced. It also contributes to an ongoing mythologisation of the design process and a perpetuation of the fiction in which buildings and objects are designed by one person rather than the many anonymous designers, and others, who in reality contribute to this process.

North American feminist scholars have worked concertedly to move beyond this issue of women's absence from professional practice and have developed crucial understandings of the ways in which women, other than as designers, participate in the making of space.[6] Writings which foreground patronage and social reform have given some important signals as to how the paradigm of making space might be shifted, though perhaps this work has not gone as far as these editors would like.

In contrast to those whose academic concerns are primarily with the processes of production of spaces, are those who have pushed an interest in gender and space in a rather different direction. Informed by

---

Press, 1996 and Irene Cieraad (ed.), *At Home, an Anthropology of Domestic Space*, Syracuse: Syracuse University Press, 1999.

6   Here, see the work of Dolores Hayden, *The Grand Domestic Revolution: A History of Feminist Designs for American Neighbourhoods and Cities*, Cambridge, Mass.: MIT Press, 1981 and Alice Friedman, *Women and the Making of the Modern House, A Social and Architectural History*, New York: Harry N. Abrams, 1998.

psychoanalysis, cultural theory and anthropology, they have instead used gender as a lens of analysis through which to produce *readings* of spaces and things, rather than to develop an understanding of the processes through which such spaces might have been made in the first place.[7] Such a concern, though valuable, is less relevant to the concerns being explored here. It does, however, suggest some ways in which we might understand how the making of built space can and should be understood as an ongoing process rather than a discrete and foreclosed act of production.

In editing *Women and the Making of Built Space in England, 1870–1950* we offer a critique of these foregoing approaches, whilst at the same time acknowledging our roots in them. Like them, we start from the premise of a desire to explore and explain women's relationship with their environments. Where we differ is in the way in which we delineate these material circumstances. The editors work here from a particular definition of what we prefer to call 'built space', by which we mean any material or spatial form which may be understood as playing a part in the production, reproduction, or contesting of gender identities. This means, then, that we are not necessarily limiting our discussion to buildings or artefacts but extending it to include texts, speeches, or living practices, *inter alia*. Moving on from this, through the use of the terms 'making space' and 'space-making' our intention is to parallel this extension of what constitutes space to a similar expansion of those who produce it. 'Making' connotes, we suggest, a broader set of protagonists than those who may be inferred from the term 'to design'. Bringing these two ideas together we argue that buildings, environments and things are made from ideas, performances, uses of space, patronage, and criticisms perhaps more than they are made through the production of plans or prototypes. In so doing we bring into consideration by the historian a whole range of actors as potential makers of space, a large number of whom happen to be female, and thus shift attention away from, and we hope bring an end to, the equation of the act of design only with (predominantly male) architects or designers.[8]

In the ten chapters which comprise this collection, the editors have sought deliberately to bring together authors from a wide range of historical disciplines – urban, literary, labour and social as well as architectural and design – in the belief that their concerns, and a meticulous attention to the evidentiary, illuminates an understanding of the making of space in a way that other critical discourses have not. Their recourse to a wide range of primary sources, and the fact that most of the protagonists and

---

7   See Spain, *Gendered Spaces* or Amy Binghan, Lise Sanders and Rebecca Zorach (eds), *Embodied Utopias: Gender, Social Change and the Modern Metropolis*, London: Routledge, 2002.

8   Notwithstanding this, the Gender and Built Space Research Group at the University of Brighton, to which four of the contributors belong, is also interested in extending this study to the way in which men make space, and has already held a symposium, 'Men Making Homes' (Brighton, January 2004) which began this process.

organisations under discussion have not been considered before – and certainly the claim that they should be understood as makers of space – allows us to offer a book which is original in its aims, its subject matter and its approach.

In choosing the relatively long time frame of 1870 to 1950, the editors are concerned to demonstrate the layering and developmental nature of women's increasing occupations of space. In so doing, a number of themes come to prominence. These are the importance throughout this period of the philanthropic, and latterly voluntary, tradition in providing a training ground for middle-class women through which they could effect urban reforms, the significance of working-class women's voices in the transformation of diverse environments particularly from the 1910s onwards, and the role of all women as authors of the discourses of domesticity. Most startling of all is women's capacity to elide the public and the private in the pursuit of their goals. Nevertheless, the chronological organisation of the book does suggest a suspicion on the editors' part that the extent of women's influence over the making of space – and we believe that they *were* influential, highly so – changed throughout this time. We surmise that this influence went from a multifarious and significant one to a more nuanced one by the late 1940s, the decade with which the book closes.

That the focus of the book is on the English context is deliberate. Despite three decades of concern for understanding the relationship between women and space, the majority of studies in this field have been devoted to either North American or continental European women.[9] To date we have little understanding of how 'making space' was conducted in England, especially in the period after the First World War, something these editors hereby hope to remedy.[10]

---

[9] See, for example, the essays in Debra Coleman, Elizabeth Danze and Carol Henderson (eds), *Architecture and Feminism*, Princeton: Princeton Architectural Press, 1996 and Ute Maasberg and Regina Prinz (eds), *Die Neue Kommen! Weibliche Avantgarde in der Architektur der zwanziger Jahre*, Hamburg: Junius Verlag, 2004.

[10] Studies of English women's environments may be periodised to two main 'campaigns'. The early 1980s saw foundations laid in studies such as Matrix's highly important but much underrated *Making Space: Women and the Manmade Environment*, London: Pluto Press, 1984; other significant early texts include Anthea Callen, *Angel in the Studio: Women in the Arts and Crafts Movement 1870–1914*, London: Astragal, 1979; Isabella Anscombe, *A Woman's Touch: Women in Design from 1869 to the Present Day*, London: Virago, 1984 and Judith Attfield and Pat Kirkham (eds), *A View from the Interior, Feminism, Women and Design*, London: the Women's Press, 1989. This work was then followed in the mid-1980s and 1990s by a second wave of work by North American scholars whose concern was less with 'reclamation' and 'revision' than with 'readings'. See Martha Vicinus, *Independent Women: Work and Community for Single Women, 1850–1920*, Chicago: University of Chicago Press, 1985; Judith Walkowitz, *City of Dreadful Delight: Narratives of Sexual*

Its focus may be limited to one country but, in proper historical tradition, *Women and the Making of Built Space* seeks to use the particular to achieve three more general aims. Its proposition of the category of 'built space' will bring a new dimension to debates about gender and space. In many instances, it offers the first in-depth analysis of the women and organisations under discussion. Finally, it re-conceptualises and reinvigorates notions of women's praxis in the shaping of our material environment.

The Chapters

The recent *Cambridge Urban History of Britain* contains the bald assertion that planning in the inter-war period was a 'partnership, with women's groups helping to shape the new estates'.[11] The specific reference is to a study of housing in Manchester but goes some way beyond the claims actually made by its authors who present a more dissonant account of inputs made by women's groups and which were rejected by other powers in the planning process including, interestingly, a wealthy woman philanthropist. Plainly it would be unwise to attribute any homogeneity of views to women activists, to generalise from a restricted number of examples, or to claim too much for their achievements. Rather this book wishes to occupy precisely this contested space, problematising the professed identities of key players, and documenting the inputs, the dead ends, the elliptical and opaque exchanges between activists and officialdom, however constructed. Importantly, it seeks also to expand the categories of the makers of space.

In the opening chapter, 'Gender, Citizenship and the Making of the Modern Environment', Helen Meller illustrates an early way in which some educated women used the biological 'given' of their gender's predisposition to nurturing, as a springboard for more rather than less visible roles in their communities. They also assimilated contemporary political discourses like citizenship as a pretext for such participation and used this position to

---

Danger in Late-Victorian London, Chicago: University of Chicago Press, 1992; Deborah Epstein Nord, *Walking the Victorian Streets, Women, Representation and the City*, New York: Cornell University Press, 1995; Erika Rappaport, *Shopping for Pleasure, Women in the Making of London's West End*, Princeton: Princeton University Press, 2000. Remarkably little work has considered space-making in the inter-war period apart from in architectural/design history; see Marion Roberts, *Living in a Manmade World*, London: Routledge, 1991; Jill Seddon and Suzette Worden (eds), *Women Designing: Redefining Design in Britain between the Wars*, Brighton: University of Brighton Press, 1994; Lynne Walker (ed.), *Drawing on Diversity, Women, Architecture and Practice*, London: RIBA Drawings Collection, 1997.

[11]   Martin Daunton (ed.), *The Cambridge Urban History of Britain* Vol 3, 1840–1950, Cambridge: Cambridge University Press, 2000, 311.

effect reforms of these environments. In charting this activity, Meller's chapter contributes three key observations to the volume. The first, in common with several other chapters, is to draw attention to the importance of the phenomenon of philanthropy. It was this sphere, which mapped private concerns onto the public realm, that from the mid-nineteenth century, created a platform from which a critical mass of women were able to produce social and spatial environments. Occasionally, this was as designers, but much more frequently it was as patrons, theorists and conceptualists of new ways of living. The second is to link this activity with the emergent discipline of town planning and demonstrate women's considerable agency in this process, though Meller indicates a diminution of their influence as the discipline professionalised. The third is to signal a methodological shift in her own subject discipline of urban history. She suggests an elision between urban and women's history in order that the latter enriches the former. The idea that women's history can transform other disciplines is a central tenet of this book, and one Meller's chapter demonstrates effectively.

A different perspective on the philanthropic tradition is offered by Anne Anderson and Elizabeth Darling's chapter, 'The Hill Sisters: Cultural Philanthropy and the Embellishment of Lives in late-Nineteenth-Century England'. On this occasion, the subject is cultural philanthropy or, as Ian Fletcher terms it 'Missionary Aestheticism'.[12] This combined the charitable concern for the improvement of both social and material conditions with the Morrisian one for the beautification of everyday life, thereby creating another context in which middle-class women could exploit a gendered condition – women's 'traditional' role in creating homes – to enter the public realm. Through their case study of the work of Octavia and Miranda Hill, they show how this led to a distinct philosophy of housing and urban renewal which prioritised the modification of patterns of inhabitation, that is ways of living, over transformations of space. This points to another claim made by this book, which is that incremental changes to existing spaces are as significant and important as the creation of wholly new ones. Indeed, it is tempting, though possibly essentialist, to argue that many of the women under discussion here understood far better than their professional male counterparts that brand new environments do not necessarily achieve reform, rather that improvements to what already exists, and what is familiar, can be far more effective. Lastly, the chapter is the first to rupture the monolithic category 'women', by exposing the chasm between the documented actions of well-intentioned middle-class and aristocratic ladies, and the silence and apparent passivity of some of the intended beneficiaries.

---

[12] 'Missionary Aestheticism' is a term coined by Ian Fletcher in his 'Some Aspects of Aestheticism', in O.M. Braek, Jr. (ed.), *Twilight of Dawn: Studies in English literature in Transition*, Tucson: University of Arizona 1987, 24.

If the first two chapters establish one of the book's central precepts, that women used their synonymy with the home in order to bring the beneficial qualities of the private sphere into the public realm, then the two chapters which follow, by Emma Ferry and Trevor Keeble, offer a further complication of this theme. In her chapter, '"A Novelty among Exhibitions": The Loan Exhibition of Women's Industries, Bristol, 1885', Ferry points to a blurring of the distinction between public and private, through her study of a public exhibition concerning women's employment, which was held in an empty villa in a suburb of Bristol. Further, it exposes more tensions in the category 'women'. Although the exhibition was concerned ostensibly with all women's employment, Ferry's analysis of the items on display and the modes of their presentation suggests that these had more to do with the skilled creative and craft work of middle-class women, or the fruits of their enlightened patronage among rural and peasant women. She coins the term 'double display' to denote the multiple resonances of many of the exhibits.

Trevor Keeble's chapter dextrously maps the diverse influences responsible for the shaping of the late-Victorian domestic interior, moving far beyond the conventionally recognised use of advice texts to the infinitely more subtle playing out of social relations, personal narratives, site visits, comparisons and consumer practices. The well-recognised difficulty of dealing with the particular home, as opposed to the idealised space, is in this case overcome by the survival of the copious diaries of one suburban home-maker and the correspondence of a London cognoscenta. Taken together, these sources yield insights into the broader and more vibrant interplay of forms of personal interaction within the milieu of these protagonists. This highly personal way of making space is, arguably, the most common means through which space is produced by both women and men. Yet, for historians of space, it is the most difficult to posit since it is often ephemeral and temporal, hence the prevalence of theoretical discussions, Lefebvre, de Certeau et al. Through his discovery and close reading of his sources, Keeble offers a valuable model of how this process of making might be reconstructed, recorded and interpreted.

Whereas in Keeble's chapter, the actors and the 'beneficiaries' are one and the same, in Ruth Livesey's chapter, 'Women Rent Collectors and the Rewriting of Class and Gender in East London, 1870–1900', these designations revert to their more usual binary positions. Crucially however, in this account the voices of the reformed are for once more readily detectable. Through her case study of women rent collectors at the Katherine Buildings, a block of model flats in London's East End, Livesey's innovation is to draw on their own documentation of their work to build up a picture of the social and spatial practices which these middle-class women sought to encourage their working-class tenants to perform by means of daily visits and other surveillant practices. This provides not simply a fascinating insight into the lived experience of reformed dwellings, but also important evidence of how a complex interplay between surveillance and counter-surveillance was produced by the different ways the middle- and working-class women occupied, and understood that occupation of, space.

The trend established in Livesey's chapter towards the greater audibility of the economically disadvantaged continues in Karen Hunt's. The women in her 'Gendering the Politics of the Working Woman's Home' are at once more ordinary than Livesey's lady managers and more activist than their tenants. These Socialist and Labour women sought to effect a dramatic expansion of the categories of the political to include the space of the home, and the practices of consumption enacted within it. In particular, the concerted attempts by these women to identify what working-class housewives needed from their homes created a body of evidence and signalled the emergence of a new voice in housing debates. Their presence, and influence on the making of space from the first decades of the twentieth century represents an important shift in political and ideological circumstances. While the attempt to engage and organise large numbers of working-class women might have had the dual purpose of according these campaigners a greater presence within the male-dominated world of left-wing activism, it nevertheless offers evidence against the traditional view of working-class housewives as the passive beneficiaries of legislative change, and suggests that those who are too often presumed to have been altered by the making of space might in fact have been themselves its re-makers.

Attention has already been drawn to the way in which middle-class women exploited ideologies of femininity and the growing contemporary concern with social reform to forge not just spaces for voluntary action but increasingly careers for themselves in the public realm. For many such women, as Livesey and Anderson and Darling have shown, working-class people were, to all intents and purposes, an amorphous mass upon whom they enacted reform. By the second quarter of the century the growth in working-class political subjectivity, aided by the expansion of the franchise, meant that for many middle-class women a belief in a 'top-down' mode of reform was less tenable. Informed and fuelled by the discourse of citizenship, the inter-war period was a crucible within which new roles for women were forged. Thus ensued a phase in which more self-consciously 'professional' women listened with greater acuity and strove to respond more sensitively to, if not act in concert with, working-class women.

This new attitude is exemplified in the design of the All-Europe House which is the subject of Elizabeth Darling's chapter, '"The House that is a Woman's Book come true": the All-Europe House and Four Women's Spatial Practices in inter-war England'. The production of this model house was a response to popular interest in the subject of ideal housing and itself represented a critique of the new social housing built under successive government programmes. It drew explicitly on research into inhabitants' experience of living in just such housing and thereby demonstrates another way in which the opinions of working people were filtered into the reform of the dwelling. The chapter also takes forward the discussion of women's varied careers in space-making into the inter-war period and shows how at that time a range of practices came under this banner, though they may not be recognised as such today. It further considers how changes in the broader world of work, especially professionalisation, and the state's growing role in the provision of welfare hitherto distributed under the banner of philanthropy, had an impact on women's ability to make space.

If the activities of the women Darling describes have largely been erased from the canon of space-makers thus far, then the woman who is considered in Jill Seddon's chapter should, at least, have full claim to visibility. As the only trained architect in this volume, her experience possibly suggests that it is really women, not simply untrained women, who are a problem for the architectural profession. In '"Part-time Practice as Before": the Career of Sadie Speight, Architect', Seddon depicts the challenging interplay of multiple roles, the compromises and accommodations reached, in the day-to-day management of a professional and domestic life. Having established Speight's claim to significance, Seddon describes how the practice of writing, one which was shared by many of her peers in this book and which, for them, served to perpetuate their ideas and identities, was not effective in achieving the same goal of self-memorialisation for Speight herself.

Thus far, it may appear that there is an expansive trajectory in the account we are offering of women's role in the making of built space in England. The final pair of chapters begins the work of problematising the periodisation of change and disrupts the sense of a growing momentum. Gillian Scott's chapter, 'Workshops fit for Homeworkers: The Women's Cooperative Guild and Housing Reform in mid-Twentieth-Century Britain' continues the story started by Hunt, and progresses it through to the immediate post-war period. Reprising the theme of organised attempts to represent the voice and experiences of working women, she shows how wartime reconstruction debates finally created a platform from which this could be heard. The Guild involved itself along with other women's organisations in the immense labour of collecting and collating data from working-class women about their housing needs. This was presented to the wartime committee on whose report post-war housing policy was ultimately based and should be clearly understood as being instrumental in the formation of the post-war landscape of reform and the post-war landscape itself.[13]

Regrettably, as Scott concludes, at the very moment of this undoubted success, circumstances were conspiring to undermine the status of the conventionally-framed housewife. Growing individualism and women's entry into the workforce in ever-increasing numbers would lead to a diminution of the wartime social consensus and the effacement of Guild values.

---

[13]   Ministry of Health (GB), Central Housing Advisory Committee, Design of Dwellings Sub-Committee, *Design of Dwellings*, London: HMSO, 1944 (better known as *The Dudley Report*).

In the final chapter, 'The Housewives' Committee of the Council of Industrial Design: a Brief Episode of Domestic Reconnoitring', Lesley Whitworth amplifies themes of representation, engagement, and data-gathering amongst and for women, this time through her account of an initiative forged within a state-sponsored reforming body. On this occasion the body's concern is with the achievement of improvements in the standard of design of British manufactured products. Utilising a diverse range of archival material, Whitworth reinserts this long-forgotten body into the canon of women space-makers and, more resonantly, demonstrates the far-sightedness of this regrettably short-lived experiment, the shape of whose activities was detectable in other forums for many years after this particular committee closed for business. In so doing, she suggests that the promise of post-war inclusivity cannot be read uncritically into the immediate post-war years, but rather should be understood as contingent, uneven and elusive.

The built spaces in this book are not straightforwardly urban or domestic. They are social, professional, and – more prosaically – storage spaces. They are discourses and artefacts, spaces of accommodation and spaces of protest. This is not a book about architecture.

Figure 1.1
Residents study the plan for a new town, c.1951
Source: Editors' Collection

Chapter 1

Gender, Citizenship and the Making of the Modern Environment

Helen Meller

Patrick Geddes, one of Britain's foremost prophets of modern town planning, believed that men and women had different roles to play in shaping the modern urban environment. In his most influential early monograph, *The Evolution of Sex* (1889), co-authored with his student J. Arthur Thomson, he outlined a series of biologically determined binary oppositions between the sexes that informed their social roles.[1] At the time, he was under the influence of cell-theory and its explanations for the development of life. There were two main processes. The 'katabolic' was profligate of energy, dissipating resources; the 'anabolic' conserved energy, was constructive and nurtured resources. The first was identified with male characteristics, the latter, with female.[2] When Geddes progressed to a career developing ideas about modern town planning, he translated these characteristics into different roles for men and women. Men were the creators, the actors, who engaged vigorously with the public sphere; women were their best help-mates who attended to the private sphere, the home and, in their communities, brought their nurturing skills to place and people, thus contributing much to bringing men's plans to fruition.

In a biologically determined world, this was as it should be. Women of the day who were campaigning for the vote and a place in public life were misguided. In evolutionary terms and in Geddes' opinion: 'what was decided among the prehistoric Protozoa cannot be annulled by Act of Parliament'.[3] Yet the women's movement, whether suffragist and campaigning peacefully for change, or suffragette and forcing the world to listen, placed a different emphasis on these perceptions. Even women unconcerned by the suffrage campaign were not prepared only to follow. If nurturing was a female skill, perhaps they could be creative in the way they used such skills outside their homes. They did not need to compete with men. Caring for the sick and poor had been a traditional female activity for centuries, and starting from that point new ways could be found of

---

1   P. Geddes & J.A. Thomson, *The Evolution of Sex*, London: Walter Scott, 1889.
2   Ibid, 223.
3   Ibid, 267.

undertaking such activities in the modern city. If the purpose of the male-dominated modern town planning movement was to improve the conditions of life in British cities, this had also been the object of women's charitable work. Men still headed philanthropic concerns, but the great outpouring of female energy into philanthropic activities in nineteenth-century cities bore witness to women's belief that they had at least one public role outside their homes.[4]

Undertaking 'good works', caring for the poor of particular urban localities or whole cities and encouraging support for wholesome influences, especially cultural activities such as music, literature and art, were socially acceptable roles for women. They took to such labours in droves. It offered social status and gave women a public role that could be defined as citizenship.[5] Citizenship became a loaded word, imbued with a meaning covering both concern for the public sphere and altruistic concern for society's well-being. For all, suffragists, suffragettes and women opposed to female enfranchisement, the pursuit of citizenship was a way of proving their worth. In his first pioneering planning report, written in 1904 for the city of Dunfermline, Geddes relied on this female voluntary labour to create a better future. He wrote a whole section entitled 'Life and Citizenship' as the key to social evolution. In it, he planned for activities and institutions that would include men and women associating together to promote a flourishing civic culture: culture being the evolutionary tool vital to the creation of a healthy body politic.[6]

The ideal of 'citizenship' would prove uniquely adaptable. Indeed, when the great 'umbrella' campaigning society for female suffrage changed its name in the wake of the introduction of partial female suffrage in the reform act of 1918, it chose to use the word 'citizenship': instead of being the National Union of Women's Suffrage Societies, it became the National Union of Societies for Equal Citizenship. The name embodied the idea that alongside the rights of women went responsibilities, especially moral responsibilities. Its leader, Eleanor Rathbone, wanted the members to engage in 'hard thought about long term objectives'.[7] What role should women play now that they had a chance to operate in the mainstream of national life? For most women though, the question was academic. Family ties, a lack of higher education for women, and few job opportunities, kept women close to home. This had been true before women were enfranchised

4   F. Prochaska, *Women and Philanthropy in Nineteenth Century England*, Oxford: Clarendon Press, 1980.
5   England's major contribution to European philosophical thought at this time was T.H. Green's ideas on citizenship. See M. Richter, *The Politics of Conscience: T.H. Green and his Age*, London: Weidenfeld and Nicolson, 1969.
6   P. Geddes, *City Development: a study of parks, garden, and culture-institutes. A report to the Carnegie Dunfermline Trust*, Bourneville: St George Press and Edinburgh: Geddes and Co., 1904. 176–222.
7   B. Harrison, *Prudent Revolutionaries: Portraits of British Feminists between the Wars*, Oxford: Clarendon Press, 1987, 103.

and remained so for most of the inter-war period. The scope for women's action remained their immediate neighbourhood and the city to which they belonged. This was how Rathbone herself had started in Liverpool, but only a tiny handful of women were to follow her to Parliament after 1918.

Thus for many over the whole period from the 1870s to the Second World War and even beyond, citizenship was not a theoretical concept but a practical issue of commitment to locality. There were many outlets for such commitment: in philanthropy, local government,[8] socio-religious activities, and the support of women's organisations, the political and non-political, feminist and non-feminist.[9] In these ways, and mostly unrecognised by the campaigners for modern town planning, women made a major contribution to creating new ways of urban living more appropriate to an age of mass urbanisation.[10] Out of a sense of citizenship, women developed new ideas on how to improve the quality of the urban environment for those less fortunate than themselves. Mostly as volunteer workers, they had the freedom to be creative, to develop their own organisations and to experiment with ways of improving the physical environment of the poor. At the same time, they were also active in developing a whole host of cultural activities for leisure and pleasure, for rich and poor.[11] Their contributions in this respect have largely been ignored.

This chapter seeks to recapture something of what they achieved, but within the context of a set of very specific concerns. Why has women's role in responding to the problems of urban living been so forgotten despite the effort in recent years to reassess the role of women in the development of modern social work and the welfare state?[12] During the period between the 1870s and the 1930s, women in many cities had made a considerable difference, whether located in settlements or undertaking voluntary work in a number of societies such as the Kyrle, which had branches in many

---

8   P. Hollis, *Ladies Elect: Women in English Local Government 1865–1914*, Oxford: Clarendon Press, 1987.

9   M.B. Simey, *Charitable Effort in Liverpool*, Liverpool: Liverpool University Press, 1951, chapter 5.

10   This element does not feature in standard histories of planning which tend to define the discipline as concerned with the manipulation of the physical environment and urban design. See, for example, A. Sutcliffe, *Toward the Planned City: Germany, Britain, the US and France 1780–1914*, Oxford: Basil Blackwell, 1981; S.V. Ward, *Planning and Urban Change*, London: Sage, 2nd edition, 2004.

11   H. Meller, *Leisure and the Changing City: a Study of Bristol 1870–1914*, London: Routledge and Kegan Paul, 1976, chapters 5 and 6.

12   G. Bock & P. Thane, *Maternity and Gender Politics: Women and the Rise of European Welfare States 1880s–1950s*, London: Routledge, 1994; S. Koven and S. Michel, ' Womanly duties: maternal politics and the origins of the welfare state in France, Germany and the United States 1880–1920', *American Historical Review* 95, 4, (1990); S. Koven and S. Michel (eds) *Mothers of the New World: Maternalist Politics and the Origins of Welfare States*, New York: Routledge, 1993.

provincial cities, or charitable organisations such as Nottingham's Town and County Social Guild, which was copied in Edinburgh and elsewhere. But by the end of the period there was no longer room for the creativity they displayed. Women were left on the periphery and what they had achieved in the past became submerged as new developments, especially the role of the state in providing public housing, gained importance.[13]

There are several reasons that could be put forward to explain this oversight. The first concerns the nature of town planning itself. It was after all, the 'Cinderella' of social welfare policy, having been incorporated into the 1909 Housing Act in a very modest way. The directive to engage in town planning was still only permissive and extremely limited in scope. It referred only to town extension schemes, which the Germans had been planning for at least 30 years.[14] Town planning, as the manipulation of the physical environment, was seen by city administrators at this time as a matter of public health and bye-law regulations.[15] Even those public-spirited women who hoped to demonstrate their qualities of citizenship through being elected onto town councils in increasing numbers by the end of the nineteenth century, were very rarely appointed to sit on the public health committee.[16] Drains, water supply and environmental nuisances were not seen as the province of women. Yet the quality of the urban environment was not only a matter of bye-laws for roads and housing and the provision of drains. The fact that the majority of the population now lived in cities, a sizeable proportion in large cities, made some late Victorians particularly sensitive to the idea that there was a social and cultural aspect to urbanisation which had to be addressed.

It was in this context that many socially responsive women were to make their contribution to addressing the problems of the modern built environment. Such women, in towns and cities throughout Britain, had themselves been set the challenge of learning how to live in a 'modern' city. With the primary responsibility for the health and welfare of their families, they had set about the task with vigour and had surplus energy with which to help poorer female neighbours do the same.[17] The kind of questions they addressed did not initially have much to do with town planning as then defined. Rather it was people-centred or, in the terms of this volume, concerned with patterns of inhabitation. Issues were practical. How to find accommodation? How to improve on what has been found? How to bring up

---

[13]   J. Burnett, *A Social History of Housing 1815–1985* London: Methuen, 2nd edition 1986.

[14]   H. Meller, *Town, Plans and Society in Modern Britain*, Cambridge: Cambridge University Press, 1997.

[15]   J.B. Cullingworth and V. Nadin, *Town and Country Planning in the UK*, London: Routledge, 13th edition 2002.

[16]   Hollis, *Ladies Elect* 449.

[17]   See the autobiography of Margaret Simey, *The Disinherited Society: a Personal View of Social Responsibility in Liverpool during the Twentieth Century*, Liverpool: Liverpool University Press, 1996.

a family in the city and keep them all healthy? How to cope with economic vicissitudes and the vagaries of the labour market? How and where to go to buy things? How, with the technological revolutions in transport to even cross the road? These may be people-centred questions, but answers to all of them were circumscribed by the quality of the built environment.

The process of learning how to live in a technologically advanced environment was not a gendered one. But the regulation of homes and family life were primarily the concern of women and led some to think about the built environment of the present and its future control. Just what this amounted to will provide the substance of the rest of this chapter. Firstly, there will be a consideration of how ideas about citizenship in the period from the 1870s to the 1930s enabled women to take initiatives in developing a response to modern living, feeling that their service was part of a larger movement for change. Secondly, there will be an examination of the kind of roles envisaged for women in the formative years of modern town planning, which was dominated by architects, engineers and surveyors.[18] For their part, the men who became the new professionals rarely considered questions about the social consequences of their schemes outside the framework of urban design, the provision of facilities, and cost. With the advent of professionalism and training in the practice of town planning, women who sought qualifications to join the new profession usually found themselves in subordinate positions.[19]

Citizenship, Philanthropy and a Gendered Response to Modern Living

From the 1860s many women in towns and cities in Britain devoted themselves to voluntary work.[20] These women were mostly middle-class and often lived in purpose-built suburbs such as Edgbaston in Birmingham, the Park in Nottingham and Broomhill in Sheffield. Some had received secondary or tertiary level education in private academic girls' schools and the university colleges which were springing up beyond Oxford, Cambridge and London. By working in their local communities, what these women wanted to do was to respond to a growing national awareness of the division between rich and poor. In *My Apprenticeship*, Beatrice Webb

---

18   Clara Greed, *Women and Planning: Creating Gendered Realities*, London: Routledge, 1994.

19   Ibid.

20   J. Rendall (ed.), *Equal or Different?: Women's Politics 1800–1914*, Oxford: Basil Blackwell, 1987; J.R. Walkowitz, *City of Dreadful Delight: Narratives of Sexual danger in late-Victorian London*, London: Virago, 1992; P. Joyce, *Democratic Subjects: the Self and the Social in Nineteenth Century England*, Cambridge: Cambridge University Press, 1994; Jane Lewis, *Women and Social Action in Victorian and Edwardian England*, Aldershot: Edward Elgar, 1991.

described the impact on her generation of revelations of the extent of working-class poverty in the 1880s.[21]

Even before that, women had taken new initiatives in caring for the poor in central areas. Improvements in public health and orderliness made it much more possible for them to do so. The cleaning and paving of streets, and the reduction in the incidence of epidemic diseases such as cholera, had made it less dangerous to visit poor areas of cities.[22] In Bristol, for example, in the 1860s and 1870s, women, often Quakers or Nonconformists, frustrated by their inability to communicate easily with the poor, set up regular Mothers' Meetings in an attempt to befriend those they wished to help.[23] From such small beginnings, new-style mission centres and settlements developed, in which teams of volunteers, mostly women, undertook to change the quality of lives and the environment of areas where they worked. The Quakers, the Congregationalists and other sects had missions in different areas of Bristol from the late 1860s, and women ran Sunday School and Mothers' Meetings, as well as organising readings and outings for children.

Soon, what was considered helpful voluntary work expanded even further. A Church of England Mission was set up in St Agnes, a small parish cut out of the larger parish of St Barnabas by the Church Extension Committee. St Agnes was made up of a new area of bye-law terraced housing, which automatically excluded the poorest of the poor, but the tenants were certainly not unfamiliar with poverty. In this newly developed area, they represented an 'embryo' new community in the eyes of the volunteers, calling out for the imprint of 'civilising forces' and new approaches to urban living. The Mission was run out of Clifton College, a boys' public school, and it had developed from activities begun there in 1879. By the mid-1880s there was a new confidence in running such 'civilising' missions to the poor. This was due to the setting up of missions in many cities, especially the University Settlement of Toynbee Hall in London's Whitechapel (1883), which had gained great publicity.[24] As Clifton College's headmaster pinpointed in a sermon of 1886:

> the range of interest is very wide. It is not only in directly religious teaching but in the not less necessary work of preparing the soil for the seed to grow; in work

21   Beatrice Webb, *My Apprenticeship*, Harmondsworth: Pelican, 1938, vol. 2, chapter 5.
22   Though the son of the Bishop of Bath and Wells had died of typhus fever contracted during his work on behalf of the poor in the East End of London in the 1860s.
23   Meller, *Leisure and the Changing City*, chapter 6; J. Hannam, 'An enlarged Sphere of Usefulness: the Bristol Women's Movement, c.1860–1914' in M. Dresser and P. Ollerenshaw (eds), *The Making of Modern Bristol*, Tiverton: Redcliffe Press 1996.
24   M.E. Rose and A. Wood, *Everything went on at the Round House: a 100 years of Manchester University Settlement*, Manchester: Manchester University Press, 1995.

for education, temperance and recreation; in art, in gardening, in home industries and economies, in all that makes home and family life more attractive and safe.[25]

When Broad Plain St Philips Nonconformist Mission appointed a new resident warden, George Hare Leonard, it gained an entirely different kind of missionary; one who sought to make Broad Plain a 'University College' for the people of St Philips.[26] He declared:

> In our work we felt constantly the need of bringing beauty into the lives of those who spent their time in dull or ugly surroundings. Much was done to encourage the growth of flowers in window boxes which we made and gave to our neighbours. We had such success that it might be said that whole streets blossomed like a rose. We often had gifts from friends with suburban gardens, but still the demand was insatiable.[27]

Such activities depended in every instance on the support of women. In Bristol in these formative years, men were usually in charge of the missions and the accounts, but the actual work was often done by women.

In a metropolitan context, female leadership of such projects was exemplified by the Hill sisters, both of whom made key contributions to the debate about modern living,[28] and their friend Henrietta Barnett, wife of Canon Barnett of Toynbee Hall, who campaigned to save Hampstead Heath from development and planned the successful development of Hampstead Garden Suburb.[29] In these instances each was part of the Zeitgeist, since the preservation of areas of open space in and near towns and cities had become a widely supported movement as the campaign for public parks developed and areas of ancient common land, under threat from developers, were saved.[30]

---

[25]   J.M. Wilson, 'The Progress of Christian Church life during the last 25 years', *Sermon at Redland Park Congregational Chapel, Bristol* Bristol: privately published, 1886.

[26]   Hare Leonard later became Professor of History at the University College Bristol.

[27]   D.J. Carter, 'The social and political influences of the Bristol Churches 1830–1914'. Unpublished thesis, University of Bristol, 1971, 191.

[28]   On differing aspects of the Hill sisters' work see the chapters in this volume by Anderson and Darling, and Livesey.

[29]   A. Creedon, 'A benevolent tyrant? The principles and practices of Henrietta Barnett (1851–1936), social reformer and the founder of Hampstead Garden Suburb', *Women's History Review* 11:2, (2002) 231–252.

[30]   See B. Cowell, 'The Commons Protection Society and the Campaign for Berkhamstead Common 1866–70', *Rural History*, 13, (2002), 145–162 and F. Stevens, 'Open Spaces for the people; the aims and achievements of Octavia Hill in nineteenth-century London', unpublished MA Dissertation, University of Leicester, 1993.

The Role of Gender in the Formative Years of Modern Town Planning

Whereas the preservation or enhancement of the quality of the built environment was a basic ambition of male town-planning pioneers, women's approach was completely different. The women under discussion here created a feeling of identity among themselves, the poor and their locality that was a crucial element in the civic experience of urban living. This bifurcation of interest is central to this discussion, for it signals why women were so remarkably absent in the formative years of the modern town-planning movement. Within this male domain, ideas of expertise became inextricably linked with the architectural and surveying skills of designing buildings and drawing up plans.[31] Women's emphasis on the experiential aspect of urban life was at odds with their male counterparts' primarily physical and interventionist approach to planning.

The great propagandists for town planning, such as Ebenezer Howard and Thomas Coglan Horsfall, and the most influential modern architect planners, Raymond Unwin and Patrick Abercrombie, were not much exercised by the absence of women working alongside them. They believed they already knew the needs of those women who would occupy the spaces they designed. Their task was to facilitate the biologically determined role of women as wives and mothers: in other words, to build beautiful homes for families and children. Howard, who was not an architect, did go one step further and included women, almost as an afterthought, in the management of his Garden City. Howard's main concern in realising his project was setting up the Garden City's administrative structure, which was to include a number of departments responsible for particular activities. Writing as if this was normal practice, Howard suggested, 'Members (who may be men or women) are elected by the rate-renters to serve on one or more departments, and the Chairman and Vice-Chairman of each department constitute the Central Council'.[32] As Meryl Aldridge has pointed out, 'the key role assigned to women in Howard's scheme is the more dramatic for being taken for granted'.[33]

Aldridge makes the point that at the particular moment of launching the Garden City idea, active, politically minded women had their minds on other things. Current concerns included a newly energised campaign for the suffrage, and developing social services to meet needs recognised in the

---

[31]   See the all-male cast in G. Cherry (ed.), *Pioneers in British Planning*, London: The Architectural Press, 1981. One or two brave women did manage to become surveyors; see C. Greed, *Surveying Sisters: women in a traditional male profession*, London: Routledge, 1991.

[32]   E. Howard, *Tomorrow: a peaceful path to real reform*, facsimile edition. London: Routledge, 2003, 71.

[33]   M. Aldridge, 'Garden Cities: the disappearing "Woman Question"' in S. Zimmerman (ed.), *Urban Space and Identity in the European City, 1890s to 1930s*, Budapest: Central European University, 1995, 15.

wake of the 1904 'Report of the Interdepartmental Committee on the Physical Deterioration of the Working Classes'.[34] Attempts were made to set up a Women's League in 1903 as the Garden City Co. was launched at Letchworth, but four years later it needed re-launching because support was limited.[35] After the war, the Garden Cities and Town Planning Association was revivified, with a focus on building more new towns to help with the housing shortage. In 1920 the Association took space at the Ideal Home Exhibition to promote these ideas. One of the events was a conference to highlight 'women's perspective in the great housing debate', which led to the re-establishment of a women's section of the Association. Yet three years later that too folded.[36] In the aftermath of total war, women's 'perspective in housing' was reoriented. The Women's Section of the Association decided to concern itself with sanitary reforms in rural areas and the work of women as property managers.[37]

The Advent of Professionalism in Town Planning and Geddesian Opportunities for Women

There was one figure though, who, with his biologically determined views on gender difference, still bridged the gap between the world of women and citizenship and the modern town planning movement. Patrick Geddes' sympathy and understanding for a people-centred approach to place and urban environment was both a blessing and a curse for women who shared these concerns. Geddes was among the founders of the Town Planning Institute in 1914, the only one who was not an architect, engineer or surveyor.[38] By this time he was designating himself a sociologist and his special expertise was 'Civics: as applied sociology'.[39] This he saw both as the intellectual side of town planning and as a

---

34   This was called to establish why so many volunteers for the Boer War were rejected on grounds of being physically unfit, see Anna Davin 'Imperialism and motherhood', *History Workshop Journal*, 5, (1978) 9–65.

35   D. Hardy, *From Garden Cities to New Towns*, London: E. & F.N. Spon, 1991, 83.

36   Ibid, 163; Aldridge, Garden Cities, 18.

37   Women were beginning to make their way as professional housing managers, working in voluntary housing associations which flourished in the 1920s alongside the increase of state intervention in housing. See E. Darling, 'Enriching and enlarging the whole sphere of human activities': the Work of the Voluntary Sector in Housing Reform in Inter-War Britain' in C. Lawrence and A-K. Mayer (eds), *Regenerating England: Science, Medicine and Culture in inter-war Britain*, Amsterdam: Rodopi, 2000, 145–172.

38   G.E. Cherry, *The Evolution of British Town Planning: a History of Town Planning in the UK during the Twentieth Century and of the Royal Town Planning Institute 1914–74*, Leighton Buzzard: L. Hill, 1974.

39   P. Geddes, 'Civics: as Applied Sociology'. Lectures delivered to the British Sociological Society Parts I and II 1904 reprinted with notes in H. Meller (ed.), *The Ideal City*, Leicester: Leicester University Press, 1979.

practical means for studying society. For Geddes, 'civics' and 'citizenship' were intimately linked and concerned both men and women though, of course, appropriate activities to demonstrate any commitment to civics were defined by gender.

All students were sent out to undertake 'surveys' of neighbourhoods, but while men made reports on the quality of housing as an outcome of their survey work,[40] women were encouraged to record anything they thought interesting, with this activity primarily intended to facilitate their interaction with the urban environment and thus learn about social engagement. Geddes was giving form to the kind of empirical approach adopted by philanthropic women, but with his own agenda of betterment for place and people together. The Geddesian Civic Survey required patience, enthusiasm, and a disregard for exactly how all the information gathered would be incorporated into plans for the future. It was ideally suited to engage the interest of young women who had become interested in Geddes' ideas. At summer schools at the Outlook Tower in Edinburgh, the centre he had founded for the development of his ideas in 1892, young women joined young male students from the University of Edinburgh who were working with Geddes on his urban renewal schemes in the city.

Students took lessons in the natural sciences, the better to understand the nature of evolution;[41] they took part in 'Masques of Learning', the better to understand interpretations of the past;[42] and they undertook surveys of the city, or went on survey holidays elsewhere, the better to understand the present.[43] In the late 1880s many young women had originally come to

---

[40] Three men working with Geddes produced published surveys: T.R. Marr made a survey of working class housing when he became Warden of ManchesterUniversity Settlement, 1904; H.V. Lanchester made a survey of Madras for Geddes, see *Town Planning in Madras: a review of conditions and requirements of city improvement and development in the Madras Presidency*, London: Constable, 1918; P. Abercrombie did many surveys, the first published being his Dublin plan. See P. Abercrombie, S. and A. Kelly, *Dublin of the Future: the New Town Plan*, London: Hodder and Stoughton, Liverpool: University of Liverpool Press, 1922.

[41] They came not only to study evolution in the natural sciences but also to find themselves and their place in modern society, guided by Geddes' understanding of *Sex in Evolution*, his 1889 monograph.

[42] A version was eventually published: *The Masque of Ancient Learning and its many meanings: a Pageant of Education from Primitive to Celtic times, devised and interpreted by Patrick Geddes*, Edinburgh: Outlook Tower: Patrick Geddes and Colleagues.

[43] Throughout the 1920s, Geddes' ideas were pursued at LePlay House, the permanent headquarters of the Sociological Society. There Mabel Barker ran summer 'surveys' every year at home and abroad which were like educational tours, combining pleasure and education about the natural and social environment. Such activities were part of the Regional Survey movement discussed by C.C. Fagg, leader of the regional survey section of the South-East Union of Scientific Societies in his 'The History of the Regional Survey Movement' *South-Eastern Naturalist and Antiquary* (1928) 32, 71–94.

Edinburgh to study the natural sciences, particularly since the subject was included in the School Code for grant-earning subjects in Scotland.[44] One of them, Rachel Annand Taylor, subsequently assisted Geddes, then part-time Professor of Botany at the University College of Dundee where, in the wake of his 1904 Dunfermline Report, he was considering landscape and garden design as an additional area of practice. His approach to the teaching of garden design had a specifically gendered aspect, for he saw it as it as an educational tool for the study both of evolution and the world of emotions. As a poetess especially inspired by nature, Annand Taylor's role was to stimulate students' rapport with nature in order to develop their emotional commitment and understanding of the concept of evolution.[45]

Geddes' model for female participation in the built environment owed much to the example of his wife, Anna Morton. They met in the 1880s in Edinburgh, when he was involved in setting up the Edinburgh Social Union along Octavia Hill lines. Morton, daughter of a Liverpool merchant, initially understood his passion for social work in the context of current philanthropic practices. When, after their marriage in 1886, she realised the full extent of his commitment to working for social change in radical new ways, she backed him fully after a short period of anxiety at the start of their partnership.[46] In every way thereafter, Morton was in partnership with him and maintained their activities during his frequent absences from Edinburgh.

Her influence was crucial to the success of the Edinburgh Summer Schools, where she presided over the social occasions, organised outings, and made it respectable for young women to take part in the Masques of Learning. She played an important part in sustaining the Outlook Tower and Geddes' publishing activities, and with her daughter Nora, was at the centre of a circle of women in Edinburgh who supported Geddes' work.[47] She helped to organise the International Summer School in Paris held in conjunction with the 1900 *Exposition Universelle*, that launched Geddes as an international figure.[48] Notwithstanding the significance of this work, the official positions at the Outlook Tower were taken by men.

---

[44]   Meller, *Patrick Geddes*, 92–98.
[45]   She afterwards went to London to work as a University Extension Lecturer and her poetry achieved acclaim in the London literary scene before the war.
[46]   P. Boardman, *Patrick Geddes: Maker of the Future*, Chapel Hill: University of North Carolina Press, 1944, 95–111.
[47]   Nora was to follow one of the new careers for women as a landscape gardener and invested many voluntary hours in the cultivation of Edinburgh's public open spaces. In 1917, at the age of 60, Morton died of dysentery in Darjeeling, where she had gone to help Geddes launch his Summer Schools and propaganda work in India.
[48]   P. Boardman, *The Worlds of Patrick Geddes: Biologist, Town Planner*, London: Routledge and Kegan Paul, 1978; P. Kitchen, *A Most Unsettling Person: an Introduction to the Life and Ideas of Patrick Geddes*, London: Victor Gollancz and Co., 1975.

The gendered nature of Geddes' views on how to work for the future gave women a role, but only as supporters to men. He saw town planning as city development: place and people progressing in an evolutionary way to greater perfection and happiness. In all the varied ways in which Geddes sought to understand social evolution and to promote his message about the future, he stayed firm on one thing. As a social evolutionist, he believed that the Man/Woman dichotomy was at the cutting edge of what was bringing about the future.[49] As a planner, he did not just see the problems of place. He saw an interaction of place and people as the vital combination for instigating change for the better. His technique, the civic survey as applied sociology, was meant to be a never-ending process of investigation, revealing the process of constant change. After his success in Paris in 1900, and his work proselytising to change people's understanding of the process of mass urbanisation, he might have disappeared from public view to some extent, but he had the great good fortune to be taken up by architects and propagandists of the early town planning movement seeking new ways of understanding cities.

He was probably most fortunate to have had an opportunity to work with Raymond Unwin, one of the most important figures in the implementation and practice of town planning in the first two decades of the twentieth century. Unwin's career 'paralleled the evolution of British town planning'.[50] He had worked on three of the most influential model community developments before the First World War: Rowntree's factory settlement at New Earswick and Howard's Letchworth Garden City, both with his partner, Barry Parker; and Henrietta Barnett's Hampstead Garden Suburb. He was even commissioned to plan an area of the showcase settlement of Bournville near Birmingham, which was held up as the model of what the future could be for urban workers. Unwin consolidated his position as a leading architect planner by becoming the organiser of the 1910 First International Town Planning Exhibition at the Royal Institute of British Architects. In this capacity, he needed to find a British equivalent to the American, German and French exhibits, which were at the forefront of current thinking in modern town planning. Since town planning was not yet an established practice in Britain, no suitable material was available.

However, in Edinburgh, there was the Outlook Tower and Geddes' carefully developed interpretations of the social and physical consequences of modern urban development. Unwin invited Geddes to bring his material from the Outlook Tower as the British exhibit. This was so successful that Geddes in turn benefited from the experience by making his exhibit into a peripatetic Cities and Town Planning Exhibition and earning his living by

---

49   He was deeply interested in the work of Freud and the developing science of psychoanalysis. He sent his son to Dr David Eder, Britain's first psychoanalyst, before the First World War. Meller, *Patrick Geddes*, 9.

50   M. Miller, *Raymond Unwin: Garden Cities and Town Planning*, Leicester: Leicester University Press, 1992, 2.

going from town to town with it. Geddes' first commission came as a result of the Edinburgh exhibit, which was seen by Lord Aberdeen, Lord Lieutenant of Ireland (1906–1915) and his wife. In the course of his duties, Aberdeen had become particularly concerned with the problems of Dublin housing since it had the dubious accolade of having the worst slums in Europe.[51] Both Geddes and Unwin were invited to Dublin by the Aberdeens, whose combined efforts were intended to prevent its urban problems spiralling ever more out of control.

This is another instance of the way Geddes was able to elicit support from women. Lady Aberdeen was a philanthropist who saw Geddes' ideas contributing to the causes she held dear, which were to improve the lot of women, especially as wives and mothers. Between 1893 and 1898 she had taken the initiative in setting up new organisations when her husband was Governor General of Canada. She had founded the Victoria Order of Nurses and become concerned with women's health. In Ireland, she founded the Women's National Health Association and, on Geddes' arrival in 1911, used her network of women organisers to set up lecture programmes for him and other promoters of town planning, seen in this context as an excellent path to creating higher levels of public health and the conditions necessary for raising healthy families.[52] As a wife and mother of five children, Lady Aberdeen felt she had the experience to appreciate what Geddes was saying about the interaction of place and people, and the need for male planners to understand and be sensitive to the ways in which women used space while caring for themselves and their families.

Dublin provided Geddes with the kind of context that suited him and he responded with enthusiasm. Inspired by European practice, especially German, he instigated a competition for a new plan for Dublin, which he judged.[53] He gave the prize to Patrick Abercrombie from the Department of Civic Design at the University of Liverpool, although with reservations about the practicality of the plan. This was significant because by the time of the plan's publication in 1922, Abercrombie had become convinced by Geddes' approach to planning and the idea of survey.[54] Thus Geddes' principles infiltrated planners' training through Abercrombie, as he was not only to gain the Chair of Civics in Liverpool, but was also to go on to become the leading planner in Britain in the inter-war period and was invited to plan London's post-war reconstruction.[55] Abercrombie's success was not necessarily good news for women in planning: in the course of his

---

51   J. Prunty, *Dublin Slums 1800–1925: a Study in Urban Geography*, Ballsbridge: Irish Academic Press, 1998.

52   M. Bannon (ed.), *The Emergence of Irish Planning 1880–1920*, Dublin: Turoe Press, 1985.

53   M. Bannon, 'Dublin town planning competition: Ashbee and Chettle's 'New Dublin – A study of Civics', *Planning Perspectives* 14, 2 (1999) 145–163.

54   P. Abercrombie et al. *Dublin of the Future*.

55   P. Abercrombie, *Greater London Plan 1944*, London: HMSO, 1945.

career he would refine his approach to survey in ways that materially altered it from the kind of activity envisaged by Geddes.

Initially following Geddes, Abercrombie put survey at the heart of his programmes for training planners. The way to proceed on a planning commission was first, survey, then diagnosis and then plan.[56] But as survey became a planning tool rather than a biological process of interaction between the person engaged in the survey and the place, so it was transformed into a practical activity. Abercrombie began to distinguish between what he saw as a professional survey, executed by planners/architects, and the amateur survey of the Geddesian kind, undertaken by people with an interest in the environment and the future, but without the responsibility of developing specific plans. In the first, the prime concern was to teach practitioners about the importance of elements within the context of the plan, particularly the geographical structure of the region. Architects needed to be taught about watersheds, geology and rock formations, and other such factors, to extend their architectural expertise from thinking about one building to planning a whole area. In the second, the prime concern was to sustain interest in the idea of planning amongst the general public, to encourage a belief in the need for planning to be ever more widely held. He wrote:

> The study of Civic Improvement should begin at school. No intelligent imaginative scholar, making surveys of his or her own neighbourhood, will be able to resist trying to improve it or to prophesy its future ...Now, this is not to suggest that the technique of town planning is so simple that a child can master it, but it is certain that there is a good deal of town planning which consists in the application of common sense based upon knowledge...as no plan will ever be put into execution that has not the intelligent backing of the citizens at large – it behoves the citizen to be not only an amateur town planner himself, but to be able to appraise and thoroughly understand the schemes prepared by his appointed experts.[57]

By making planning the responsibility of every citizen, though only the task of a professionalised few, Abercrombie removed the sphere of activity accorded women under the Geddesian model.

---

[56] P. Geddes, 'The City Survey: a first step – I', *Garden Cities and Town Planning* 1, 1911, 18.

[57] P. Abercrombie, 'Civic Survey in General Education' *Garden Cities and Town Planning* Vol. 11, 2 1921, 33 quoted from M. Dehaene *A Descriptive Tradition in Urbanism: Patrick Abercrombie and the legacy of the Geddesian survey.* Unpublished PhD Thesis, Katholieke Universiteit Leuven, 2002, 136.

Conclusion: The Second World War and its Aftermath: the Last Chapter of a Gendered Response?

If Abercrombie's approach to town planning can be understood as dominant by the late 1930s, nevertheless there were other architects/planners who questioned the social consequences of planning. Perhaps the most important expression of these was the plan for Middlesbrough, carried out by a team led by Max Lock in the last year of the war and published in 1946.[58]

Lock was the most Geddesian of the post-war planners. He believed in social surveys and instituted the most elaborate attempt ever made to carry out such work for a city plan. What he aimed to do in Middlesbrough was to achieve a method whereby his team could be in close touch with the people for whom they were planning in the most professional way possible. Given the exigencies of war, he looked especially to women to help him with this task. The two women who most influenced the survey work were Jacqueline Tyrwhitt and Ruth Glass. Their work for the Middlesbrough plan can, perhaps, be interpreted as a unique combination of both the last in the tradition of the gendered role of women as helpmates of men and the first of the new kind of professional woman in planning.

Glass and Tyrwhitt were educated professional women, each of whom was to make a lasting impression on the conceptualisation of planning activities both in Britain and abroad. Though she never held a permanent post or had a conventional career, Tyrwhitt's influence was to become global, as she involved herself in the promotion of new ideas about architecture and the environment. She gained a worldwide reputation as a publicist for new ideas on how to create social well-being in urban environments, working with leading world architects and organisations such as the United Nations and UNESCO (the UN Educational, Scientific, and Cultural Organisation). She was also Secretary of CIAM (the *Congrès Internationaux d'Architecture Moderne*) between 1951 and 1964, when it ceased to be. Glass also became an international figure in her own field of urban sociology.[59] Having moved from her post at the London School of Economics to be Director of Urban Studies at University College, London, she also led the Urban Sociology Research Group of the International Sociological Association from 1958 to 1975. Her work was more precisely

---

58   *The County Borough of Middlesbrough Survey and Plan* directed by Max Lock, Yorkshire: Middlesbrough Corporation, 1946. For an account of Lock's activities at Middlesbrough and his subsequent influence see the web page of the Max Lock Centre, University of Westminster at <http://www.wmin.ac.uk/builtenv/maxlock/HISTORY.HTM>. Accessed on 18 April 2006.

59   This was a role she had pioneered in her pre-war investigative work on new housing estates. See for example R. Durant, *Watling: a survey of social life in a new housing estate*, London: P.S. King, 1939.

focused on seeking ways to understand the interaction of place and people in the context of the city.

When Lock employed them, he gave them different tasks to perform. Glass was the resident sociologist analysing the social implications of the material. Tyrwhitt was in charge of collecting it. It is a measure of their enthusiasm and competence that the Middlesbrough plan is considered to be the most brilliant of the post-war period because of the wealth of detail it produced, the work of extensive surveys of all kinds.[60] Tyrwhitt was ready to put in the hard labour this entailed, carrying out door-to-door enquiries and collecting material on every conceivable issue, as she was a passionate believer in Geddes' beliefs about planning. Above all, she thought that planners should always think about place and people together and make sure that what looked good on the drawing board was also related to the needs of people in every aspect of their lives.

This was a message that she drummed into servicemen whom she tutored on wartime correspondence courses in town and country planning.[61] She was determined that new recruits to the planning profession, returning to jobs created by the legislation which brought into being a statutory system of town and country planning, would not be swayed by the demands of the moment. The reconstruction of Britain's bombed cities was a matter of urgency, but she wanted the people who undertook the task to be alert to the social implications of their work. Immediately after the war she lectured in North America on planning in the post-war world. In 1947, perhaps her most influential Geddesian publication was issued, a volume on his work in India which emphasised the social and cultural approach he took to planning.[62] She also produced, in 1949, a heavily edited version of Geddes' major book *Cities in Evolution*, to make it as relevant a publication to the post-Second World War situation as it had been after the First World War.[63] Though female, she was a Geddesian figure, devoted to education and action.

In this post-war moment, it seemed possible that the approach to planning embodied in Glass and Tyrwhitt's work might offer a complement to Abercrombie's. That it would not, says much about the evolution of the post-war planning system and the constraints under which it operated. The challenge of building the New Towns, and reconstructing and modernising old ones, as well as developing the framework of administration to carry out these schemes, took an enormous amount of effort. The idea of carrying out time-consuming surveys was just too expensive even where desirable. This

60   M. Hebbert, 'The daring experiment – social scientists and land use planning in 1940s Britain', *Environment and Planning B*, 10, (1983), 3–17.
61   This was under the auspices of the Association for Planning and Regional Reconstruction, an offshoot of the Architectural Association.
62   J. Tyrwhitt (ed.), *Patrick Geddes in India*, London: Lund Humphries, 1947.
63   P. Geddes, *Cities in Evolution*, new and revised edition edited by the Outlook Tower Association Edinburgh, and the Association for Planning and Regional Reconstruction, London: Williams and Norgate, 1949.

was so even though reconstruction was enacted by a generation of planners, many of whom had been trained by Tyrwhitt or who were influenced by another of Geddes' disciples, Lewis Mumford, who reiterated his theory of civics in the book *The Culture of Cities*, first published in 1938.[64] Later, developments in Glass' discipline of Urban Sociology would also offer a challenge both to the centrality of 'place' and to sociology's relation to the planning process. From the 1960s onwards, a generation of male sociologists would eschew the idea of sociologists as the planner's helpmate and promote their role as urban theorists concerned with extrapolating the more general lessons to be learnt from cities about class, society and power relations.[65]

The confidence that had underpinned the ideas and careers of both Glass and Tyrwhitt had been built on the role women as citizens had played in gaining an understanding of the modern urban environment over the previous century. Geddes' biological determinism of the roles men and women could play in their personal interaction with localities had limited what women could do, whilst at the same time confirming their eligibility for certain defined roles. Geddes had wanted to go beyond data collection towards an educational process that enlightened those who undertook the work and involved them creatively in seeking out ways of making changes for the future. Economic and political changes, the growing refusal of women to be limited by their gender, and the continued growth of central government gradually destroyed the context in which such confidence could continue to thrive.

The ascendancy of Abercrombie's planning methodology and the consequent narrowing of the discipline's boundaries significantly reduced the range of practices which it could encompass. Thus from the 1950s onwards, neither Glass nor Tyrwhitt would be so directly involved in the planning process as they had been at Middlesbrough. The absorption of their careers by academia (Glass),[66] publishing and work for global NGOs

---

64   L. Mumford, *The Culture of Cities*, London: Secker and Warburg, 1938. This was the second in a trilogy on conditions of modern life.

65   This was expressed most clearly in a statement issued by the Research Committee of urban sociologists affiliated to the International Sociological Association in 1970 which stated: 'Urban sociologists have been too frequently turned into handmaidens of those practical professions concerned with making physical changes to the built environment. As a result many urban sociologists have become more concerned with the human relations of the city rather than the sociology of the city: it is as if industrial sociologists have turned themselves into personnel officers', quoted in A.S. Milicevic, 'Radical Intellectuals: what happened to the New Urban Sociology?', *International Journal of Urban and Regional Research* 25, 4, (2001), 761.

66   In her post-war career Glass sought to emphasise the importance of Geddes' notion of place in her discipline and to encourage a new professionalism in urban sociology. She used her knowledge of the housing and planning movements of the inter-war years to critique the use of words such as 'neighbourhood' and 'community' in the context of urban reconstruction and

(Tyrwhitt), is arguably evidence of the curtailment of opportunities elsewhere, but equally of their resourcefulness in re-forming themselves as practitioners.[67]

the advent of a national planning system. She particularly questioned the rhetoric of the 'neighbourhood unit' as used in the New Towns, suggesting that 'the magic idea of the "balanced community" lacked sensitivity to the realities of local conditions and preferences', see A. Beach, 'The Idea of Neighbourhood 1900–50', *History Today* 45 (9) 1995, 8. R. Glass, 'Urban Sociology in Great Britain: a trend report', *Current Sociology* 4, 12 (1955) records her disenchantment about post-war developments from the vantage point of the mid-1950s.

[67] Tyrwhitt became a peripatetic and trans-national figure in the post-war years, spending much time in Japan. In 1954, while organising a UN symposium on Housing and Community Planning in Delhi, she met C.A. Doxiadis with whom she shared a common language about human identities and the environment. When he founded the journal *Ekistics* in 1955 Tyrwhitt became its first editor. She remained connected with the journal until her death in 1983. One of her last major publications was G. Bell and J. Tyrwhitt (eds), *Human Identity in the Urban Environment*, Harmondsworth: Penguin, 1972.

Figure 2.1
Interior of the Red Cross Hall, Southwark. Elijah Hoole, 1889
Source: 'The Builder', 9 November 1889

Chapter 2

The Hill Sisters: Cultural Philanthropy and the Embellishment of Lives in late-Nineteenth-Century England[1]

Anne Anderson and Elizabeth Darling

In 1865 the twenty-seven-year-old Octavia Hill took possession of her first block of housing, three slum houses in Paradise (now Garbutt) Place, Marylebone in central London. By the time of her death in 1912 she, and her 'Fellow Workers' as they were known, were responsible for the management of nearly two thousand dwellings across London,[2] and, in the process, had created for middle-class women the new profession of Housing Manager. Unlike some of the women and organisations who are considered in this volume, Hill is hardly an unknown person whose achievements have gone unrecognised for want of an historical paradigm in which they can be included. She is, in fact, amongst the best documented of that generation which, from the mid-nineteenth century onwards, created new areas of work for women,[3] and she has been accorded due recognition for her significant contribution to that transition 'from charity to social work' which underpinned so much of the social history of the twentieth century.[4]

---

[1]   We would like to acknowledge Joseph McBrinn for the notion of 'the embellishment of lives'. See Joseph McBrinn, '"Decoration should be a common joy": The Kyrle Society and Mural Painting', *The Acorn, Journal of the Octavia Hill Society*, forthcoming.

[2]   Peter Malpass, *The Work of the Century, the Origins and Growth of the Octavia Hill Housing Trust in Notting Hill*, London: Octavia Hill Housing Trust, 1998, 9.

[3]   See, *inter alia*, Enid Moberley Bell, *Octavia Hill*, London: Constable, 1942; Jane Lewis, *Women and Social Action in Victorian and Edwardian England*, Aldershot: Edward Elgar, 1991 and Robert Whelan (ed.), *Octavia Hill's Letters to Fellow Workers*, London: Kyrle Books, 2005.

[4]   Frank Prochaska, *Women and Philanthropy in 19th-Century England*, Oxford: Clarendon Press, 18, 133.

A cursory glance through histories of housing, in contrast, will show that the respect she has been accorded rarely extends to the sphere of space-making. The focus on her and her followers' development of a new profession has meant that the physical impact it had on the landscape has been somewhat overlooked. Indeed, the disregard for the spatial implications of Hill's work typifies the attitude to women's contribution to the history of housing as a whole, which is seen to lie primarily outside the conventionally more highly regarded arena of policy making or the architectural design of housing. John Burnett, in what remains the standard housing history, makes no mention of Hill,[5] whilst the feminist histories which have done so much to remind us of women's centrality to the development of social welfare policy in the twentieth century, also focus solely on her management practices.[6] Only Alison Ravetz has viewed Hill's work in terms of the development of social housing across the twentieth century and pointed to her 'unique contribution to housing reform' and her '...lasting influence on housing practice...'.[7]

Ravetz's use of language is helpful here in understanding how women's role in the history of housing has been overlooked. Historically, and Hill exemplifies this, the way in which women have made space has been indirectly through activities such as patronage or the development of theories of how space might be occupied. The creation of new physical spaces has not been their primary preoccupation and, when it has been, its design has been informed by a concern for the practices which might be enacted within them, rather than an overriding concern for the production of new building types or forms. The fact that the majority of Hill's physical space-making was in reconfigurations of plan within existing buildings and the re-forming of patterns of inhabitation, meant that her work could not be included in architectural histories of housing because it rarely manifested in (new) bricks and mortar. John Tarn, for example, concentrates on the much more noticeable, then as now, work of the Peabody Trust and the Improved Industrial Dwellings Company in his study of philanthropic housing.[8] These bodies are deemed more significant than their contemporary Hill because their philanthropy resulted in tangible additions – and a significant number of them – to the built environment. Hill's occasional forays into new building, such as the cottages in Southwark which will be discussed later in this chapter, may be

---

5   See John Burnett, *A Social History of Housing*, (2nd Edition) London: Routledge, 1986.

6   Marion Brion and Anthea Tinker, *Women in Housing, Access and Influence*, London: The Housing Centre Trust, 1980.

7   Alison Ravetz, *Council Housing and Culture, the History of a Social Experiment*, London: Routledge, 2001, 29. That Ravetz does this is because she is able to view social housing as a process, something made up of ideas, practices, policy and legislation.

8   John Tarn, *Five Percent Philanthropy, an account of Housing in Urban Areas between 1840 and 1914*, Cambridge: Cambridge University Press, 1973.

mentioned in housing histories, but their very rarity is seen to point to a larger truth: that women made little impact on the physical transformation of housing in the nineteenth and twentieth centuries.[9]

This focus on what we might call 'signature buildings' by historians of housing and architecture alike, points to the narrow conceptualisation of space-making which this volume seeks to expand. A consideration of Hill's work in housing, the issues which she thought were important in improving the conditions in which the working classes lived, and her preoccupation with the environment beyond the home, will demonstrate the accuracy of Ravetz's estimation and show how a tradition of thinking about space which focused on its re-forming rather than its complete transformation had a long-term influence on England's built environment,[10] and was never more relevant than today. This chapter will also go some way to contradicting another historiographical preoccupation that has prevented serious consideration of women's work in housing. This hinges around the twin assertion that, for the most part, women tended to work individually and at a local level and made little effort to translate this work to a wider territory; as Prochaska puts it, their work was 'pragmatic rather than theoretical...',[11] and, in Hill's case, did not move beyond piecemeal social reform to a wider analysis of social structure.[12] This perceived failure to talk about their work is an intriguing one, for it implies that the work of women like Hill was essentially private and had little impact on the public sphere, whereas Ravetz's observation, and the evidence shown here, suggests the opposite. It is hard to see how this view of Hill's work can be sustained when women's eligibility to comment on housing was largely based on her precedent.[13] The fact that her work spawned a profession would also seem to overturn this particular prejudice. Whilst it is true that Hill may not have analysed social structure in the same way as Beatrice Webb did, nevertheless she did identify major social ills, not just the housing problem but also the effects of air pollution and the lack of open space within the metropolis, and also wrote extensively on the aims and practices of the system of housing management which she developed to resolve them.[14] It is perhaps because Hill's approach to her subject and discipline, though undoubtedly systematic, was not based on the techniques of the then emerging Social Sciences that many historians have found her work problematic. She is perceived to lack the quantitative and therefore, in the

---

9   Tarn, ibid, does mention Hill's cottages but these are accorded much less space than the work of the great Trusts.

10   This theme is explored in a number of other chapters in this book; see Livesey, Hunt and Darling.

11   Prochaska, *Women and Philanthropy*, 223.

12   Ibid, 133.

13   For example, in 1884 she was invited to give evidence to the Royal Commission on the Housing of the Working Classes.

14   See, *inter alia*, Hill's article, 'Trained Workers for the Poor', *The Nineteenth Century*, 33, (1893), 36–43.

too-often stereotypical world of the sciences, 'masculine' basis which would have allowed her observations to be taken seriously.[15]

This chapter will, then, seek to draw attention to the spatial ramifications of Hill's practice of Housing Management. It begins by considering the context in which Hill came to feel that it was her duty to tackle the problem of the conditions in which many of London's working people lived. It then proceeds to a discussion of the system she developed to address this, and the practices of reconfiguration of plan and inhabitation that were enacted on the housing she acquired from the 1860s onwards. It then considers the intriguing problem of how practices which had been developed to address the use of existing spaces were translated into newly built form when Hill, and those influenced by her, commissioned new housing such as the Red Cross Cottages built in Southwark, south London, in the mid-to-late 1880s. From a consideration of such housing, the discussion will then broaden, as did Hill's vision, to her preoccupation with the city as a whole. In this aspect of her work she joined her less well known but, as this chapter will suggest, equally significant sister Miranda who, in 1876, had founded the Kyrle Society.[16] This shared Hill's desire to enrich existing environments but sought to do so on a city-wide level through the provision of amenities such as new public gardens, community activities and the beautification of existing buildings and other sites with murals and other artwork. The aim here, then, is to propose that as well as playing a significant role in the history of social work, Hill, together with her sister, developed a distinctive and influential theory of both housing and urbanism.

Philanthropy and Housing in the 1860s

Philanthropic intervention in the provision of housing for the urban working classes had its origins in the public health scares of the 1840s. In the belief that slums and 'rookeries' were the source of the epidemics which were the scourge of London in that decade, sanitary reformers were the first to advocate the demolition of bad housing and its replacement with new dwellings planned on healthy lines.[17] In 1844, the charity known as The Society for Improving the Conditions of the Labouring Classes (SICLC),

---

15   Ruth Livesey's chapter in this volume provides a counterpoint to this prejudice through its discussion of Beatrice Webb's work.

16   It is interesting to note that whilst Hill is recognised through her inclusion in the *Dictionary of National Biography*, Miranda does not warrant an entry.

17   It should be noted that it would be some decades before there were even the beginnings of a consensus that the state itself should be involved directly in the provision of social housing. It was under the 1890 Housing Act that for the first time local authorities were given the (discretionary) right to build such housing and then without any financial support form central government. State-subsidised housing would only be introduced in the 1919 Housing Act.

which was founded by Lord Shaftesbury and Thomas Southwood Smith (Hill's grandfather),[18] set the prototype for philanthropic housing when it built its first set of model dwellings in Streatham Street, Bloomsbury.[19] Designed by the architect Henry Roberts, the five-storey blocks were planned around a central courtyard and were very plain in their architecture. In plan, the self-contained flats comprised two bedrooms, a living room with range, scullery and an inside lavatory. This was a quite remarkable provision of space and amenity for this date and dramatically different from anything to which the Society's tenants would otherwise have had access. But it was equally as a model of a particular philosophy and economics of charity that the flats were significant. The SICLC intended to demonstrate to the speculative builders who more commonly erected housing for rent, that it was possible to build accommodation for the poorer in society and still collect a return on investment.[20]

The 1860s inaugurated a second wave of philanthropic housing activity in London. Whilst sanitary reform remained an underlying motive for this, this decade saw the emergence of a greater consciousness of a distinct 'Housing Problem'. This had at its root the tension between a burgeoning working-class population and a diminishing housing stock caused by the large-scale demolition of working-class districts to make way for the construction of new roads, railway lines and termini and other commercial buildings.[21] The nature of working-class employment which, particularly among the poorest was often seasonal and therefore erratic, required people to be close to the sources of work and increased the high level of congestion in the heart of the city. In response, the banker George Peabody in 1862 endowed a trust to address the problems caused by the displacement of workers by railway construction, money which his trustees decided to spend on housing. The Peabody Trust and its contemporary The Improved Industrial Dwellings Company, founded by the Alderman Alfred Waterlow, were soon peppering London with large estates of block dwellings very similar to those built by the SICLC in the 1840s.[22]

---

18 On Hill's grandfather, see R.K. Webb, Smith (Thomas) Southwood, in *Dictionary of National Biography*, Oxford: Oxford University Press, 2004.

19 On model dwellings see Enid Gauldie, *Cruel Habitations: a History of Working Class Housing*, London: Allen & Unwin, 1974 and Tarn, *Five Percent Philanthropy*.

20 Most famously the returns were set at five per cent giving rise to the phenomenon known as 'Five Percent Philanthropy'. Returns seem to have varied from four to seven per cent in practice.

21 John Summerson in his *London Building World of the 1860s*, London: Thames & Hudson, 1973, 7, notes that in the second half of the nineteenth century much of London was a permanent building site.

22 These trusts would also benefit from government legislation. The 1868 Artisans and Labourers Dwellings (Torrens) Act and the 1875 Artisans and Labourers Dwellings (Cross) Act introduced the statutory condemnation of slum properties and allowed the rebuilding of replacement housing on the same site; a process almost invariably carried out by the great philanthropic trusts.

It was against this backdrop that Hill first entered the world of housing reform in the mid-1860s. Her approach to reform was to be very different from the great Trusts, not just in scale but also in philosophy, and was informed by two inter-related developments in philanthropic theory and practice which developed from the 1860s onwards and are particularly associated with the Charity Organisation Society (COS), in whose genesis she played a significant role, and the Settlement Movement.[23] Both groups eschewed the prevailing emphasis on financial aid as a primary means to ameliorate the lot of the poor, believing this encouraged them to become dependent on charity and unlikely to change. Instead they preferred an approach which, as Jane Lewis has put it, 'was as much moral and spiritual as material'.[24]

The COS enacted this philosophy by, in effect, becoming an early form of social work agency to which those seeking aid could apply and, following interviews with a COS worker, be directed towards the appropriate form of support, not always monetary. The emphasis on one-to-one work was seen as a significant way to make reform more effective as it substituted the anonymous donor of charity with a human representative who, it was hoped, would be harder to deceive.[25] The Settlement Movement, whose primary concern was to bridge the gap between the classes caused by the middle- and upper-class flight from living in central and eastern parts of London, sought to remedy this by encouraging the middle classes to donate not money but their abilities and their time. Young graduates were encouraged to live in settlement houses in the East End – Toynbee Hall was the first – and share their brains and skills with the local community.[26] At Toynbee Hall, which was set up by Henrietta and Samuel Barnett, and operated from purpose-built premises off Commercial Street in Whitechapel, east London, the local population could, for example, attend classes in literature – the study of John Ruskin's writing *inter alia* – or learn metal work from the Arts and Crafts designer, C.R. Ashbee. The emphasis which the COS placed on forging personal relationships with its

---

[23] There is not space here to consider the full complexities and histories of this phase of welfare history but for a more complete discussion see Jose Harris, *Private Lives and Public Spirit, a Social History of Britain, 1870–1914*, Oxford: Oxford University Press, 1993, Prochaska, *Women and Philanthropy* and Lewis, *Women and Social Action*. It should be noted that although the Settlement Movement proper did not start until the 1880s, it represents the culmination of sentiments which had been widely held, as Hill's views attest, since the 1860s.

[24] Lewis, *Women and Social Action*, 16.

[25] The COS was originally called the Society for Organizing Charitable Relief and Repressing Mendicity; a nomenclature which reflected the widespread belief that indiscriminate charity giving only encouraged the poor to go from charitable society to charitable society claiming relief.

[26] On Toynbee Hall, see Standish Meacham, *Toynbee Hall and Social Reform, 1890–1914*, London: Yale University Press, 1982.

applicants, combined with the artistic and cultural preoccupations of the Settlement Movement, were significant for women like Hill.

Although Hill was born into a distinguished family, it was one beset with financial problems. Her father's bankruptcy in the 1840s and subsequent separation from the family, meant that like many middle- and working-class girls at mid-century, she was required to earn her own living in order to support both herself, her mother and siblings.[27] The question of what work genteel ladies might do was widely debated and it was generally agreed that it was most appropriate for them to work in areas in which the feminine attributes which had been developed during their upbringing and, for some, education could be exercised.[28] Most commonly this saw ladies become governesses or paid companions or, after the Crimean War, nurses; fields in which their 'innate' ability to care could be exploited. For artistic girls, a career in the decorative arts was also a possibility since many would have been taught embroidery and painting in the schoolroom.[29] This translation of skills learnt in the domestic sphere to the public sphere of paid employment, though it was born from a profound gender stereotyping, had a significant side effect for it allowed a particularly dramatic leap into the public sphere to be taken when it was combined with the new theories of social welfare practice embodied in the COS and Settlement Movement.

Their elision of the personal and artistic with the social brought together three traditionally feminine attributes which acted as a springboard for women's direct engagement with the problems of the urban environment. 'Cultural Philanthropy'[30] or 'Missionary Aestheticism',[31] meant that women could assume the role of educator and civiliser beyond their own households without disrupting established codes of class and social behaviour. Thus we find Hill, who 'had been brought up to be deeply conscientious', when beginning work at the age of 14, employed in a series of 'good works'.[32] These included the management of a group of young toy-makers, which drew its ranks from children who had attended a Ragged School, and the post of secretary to the Working Men's College in Red Lion Square, central London.[33] She also worked as a copyist of paintings for John Ruskin, who was a family friend.[34] The connection with Ruskin was to

---

27   See Gillian Darley, *Octavia Hill*, London: Constable, 1990, chapter 1.

28   On the matter of appropriate careers for ladies, see Carol Dyhouse, *Girls Growing Up in late Victorian and Edwardian England*, London: Routledge, 1981.

29   Emma Ferry's chapter discusses this aspect of nineteenth-century women's work in detail.

30   The term is Prochaska's.

31   'Missionary Aestheticism' is a term coined by Ian Fletcher in his 'Some Aspects of Aestheticism', in O.M Braek, Jr (ed.), *Twilight of Dawn: Studies in English literature in Transition*, Tucson: University of Arizona 1987, 24.

32   Darley, *Octavia Hill*, 35.

33   This had been established by the Christian Socialist F.D. Maurice.

34   Darley, *Octavia Hill*, notes there was much demand for copies of Old Master paintings at this time.

prove invaluable for it enabled Hill, who had learnt of the poor living conditions of the working classes through her employees at the toy-making workshop, to do something about them.

Octavia Hill and Social Housing

It was with Ruskin's financial help that Hill was able to purchase the leasehold of the three houses in Paradise Place in April 1865.[35] A year later he helped her to buy the freehold of five houses in Freshwater Place as well as a further house on the Marylebone Road.[36] At these properties she would develop the approach to housing which made her unique. Hill eschewed the dramatic spatial transformation represented by the demolition and new building executed by the great Trusts. Instead, she sought to work within existing slums and transform patterns of inhabitation, producing model dwelling practices, rather than model dwellings. Reform was, then, enacted at the intersection of spiritual and moral improvements with material changes to environment. As Hill said, 'I always believe in people being improveable; they will not be improveable without a good deal of moral force, as well as improved dwellings'.[37]

What were the physical and spatial results of this philosophy? Fundamentally Hill wished to create decent housing in which a sense of 'home' could be fostered. Crucially, as Ruth Livesey shows in more detail in her chapter, for Hill this was an affect of space not its determinant and thus did not require the new forms of space to which the Trusts adhered. Instead her approach, as at Paradise Place, for example, was to thoroughly clean a slum property and effect minor repairs and install a water supply. Then the real work could begin: on transforming the patterns of inhabitation which were performed within these spaces. Here the aim was to instil a sense of ownership and pride in the tenants' dwelling spaces, a process which began with the process of rent collection. Now collected regularly and weekly by the same lady rent collector, the idea was to establish a mutual relationship between tenant and collector in which each had duties to the other. Prompt payment of rent, and cleanliness of rooms, would be rewarded by further and more tangible improvements to the dwelling.

As a cultural philanthropist, Hill believed that material reform was only effective if it was exercised in parallel with reforms which enhanced the moral and spiritual lives of her tenants. For her, this resulted in a particular concern to bring art and nature into their lives as a further means to transform their behaviour. She was highly critical of the 'dreary whitewash' and 'miserable monotony' of the model buildings built by the great Trusts,

---

35   Throughout her housing career, Hill would benefit from gifts of money or land from wealthy benefactors, many of whom were women.

36   Hill lived in Marylebone.

37   Octavia Hill, *Homes of the London Poor*, London: Macmillian & Co., 1875, 104–105.

and sought to individualise and personalise the public spaces of her houses as much as possible.[38] For, as she noted '...few people seemed to think that the poor, as well as the rich, needed something more than meat and drink to make their lives complete'.[39] At Paradise Place she planted creepers and gave the tenants their own meeting space in a small building at the rear of her own house. At Freshwater Place a playground-cum-drying ground was installed and an organ grinder employed to accompany the children's play.[40]

Such small acts might seem unworthy of comment, and indeed patronising, but they point to Hill's conviction that the way a building was used might well be more important than the way it was designed. Rehabilitation and improvement of existing houses could be just as effective, if not more so, as new building. It presented tenants with a sort of housing with which they were familiar and kept tenants in their own locality. It also meant that her rents were lower than those of the Trusts and she was thus able to house a broader range of working-class tenant than her philanthropic contemporaries whose dwellings were too expensive for all except the skilled worker.[41] Such an approach may not have been as tangible as a new block of Peabody flats, but it had significant, if less dramatic, impacts on space.

Throughout her career, the majority of the housing owned or managed by Hill fitted this pattern of the rehabilitation of existing properties which, after basic maintenance, were improved as the mutual contract between Housing Manager and tenants prospered. On several occasions, however, Hill did become involved in the commissioning of new housing, a shift in practice which raises interesting questions about how someone whose whole approach was characterised by a lack of emphasis on thoroughgoing physical transformation, might translate this philosophy into new buildings.

In 1873, a group of houses that had been acquired for Hill in Barrett's Court (now St Christopher's Place, off Oxford Street, London) was found to be beyond rehabilitation and was demolished. Constrained by the footprint of the original building, Hill had no option but to construct a block of tenements in its place on lines similar to those provided by the Trusts. The inadequacy of this typology of philanthropic housing became apparent when, despite the inclusion of a tenants' club and the watchful presence of a lady rent collector, the block was found to be unpopular and lacking in privacy.[42]

---

38 Octavia Hill, 'Colour, Space and Music for the People', *The Nineteenth Century*, May 1884, 745.

39 (Octavia Hill), 'The Kyrle Society', *The Magazine of Art*, 1880, 210.

40 Darley, *Octavia Hill*, 102.

41 Hill was still able to make a profit on her properties, typically of three per cent. See ibid, 103.

42 Darley, *Octavia Hill*, 136, cites the reports of the Court's housing manager Mrs Maclagan to this effect.

The lessons learnt at Barrett's Court were applied a decade later in a series of projects in London, of which the Red Cross Cottage scheme at Red Cross Street, Southwark will stand as typical.[43] Here we can see how the three main aspects of Hill's approach to housing: the desire to foster a sense of 'home', the incorporation of nature and art into the accommodation, and the instilling of a sense of community amongst the tenants, were translated into built form through the use of particular building types and site layouts. Firstly, as their name suggests, these were cottages. Hill had always been fiercely critical of 'buildings' and, perhaps informed by the want of privacy expressed by her tenants in Barrett's Court, she had built here individual houses. As she would later state, 'a third-rate cottage with a small garden, or even a back-yard, is better for a working man than that best tenement that the London County Council can build'.[44]

Red Cross Cottages (Figure 2.2) were constructed between 1884 and 1889, to the designs of the architect Elijah Hoole. The site was a derelict one, bounded by the burnt-out remains of a paper factory. Here were placed, at a cost of £220 each, a terrace of six cottages, designed in a vernacular style with brick fronts and rough-cast upper storeys with bay windows. Their style, it should be remarked, was not accidental and can be understood as an attempt to differentiate them not just in form, but also in appearance, from the stern utilitarian blocks of the great trusts: the Peabody Trust had a large estate nearby on the Marshalsea Road. Further, their rural style was another aspect of Hill's determination to introduce nature back into the city. Each cottage had two rooms per floor, and a small yard to the rear which contained a wash house and lavatory.[45] The houses were popular. A writer in the London County Council's house journal commented, 'the tenants greatly prefer these cottages to sets of rooms in the blocks adjoining'.[46]

As Hill's practice of incorporating greenery and open space into her other dwellings suggests, any housing scheme was not complete without attention paid to both the private and public sphere. At Red Cross Cottages, the public sphere was particularly well developed and, in addition to the houses, a meeting hall and a communal garden were built. Red Cross Hall (Figure 2.3), also designed by Hoole, was intended to be used for a variety

---

43 The other schemes were White Cross Cottages, Ayre Street, Southwark, Gable Cottages in Little Suffolk Street, Southwark, and Charles Street Cottages, Marylebone; all built between 1885 and 1895. On these see Anon, 'Cottage Homes for Artisans', *London*, 4, (1895), 336–337.

44 Lionel Curtis, *Octavia Hill and Open Spaces*, London: Association of Women House Property Managers, 1930, 9. The parallels between Hill's ideas and those of Elizabeth Denby, discussed in Darling's chapter, are striking in their consensus on this point.

45 See Anon, 'Cottage Homes'. The cost of the cottages seems to have been fairly standard for this date. The article refers to houses built by Birmingham Corporation at similar expense.

46 Ibid, 337.

Figure 2.2
Red Cross Cottages and Garden, Red Cross Street, Southwark.
Elijah Hoole, 1889
Photo source: Anne Anderson

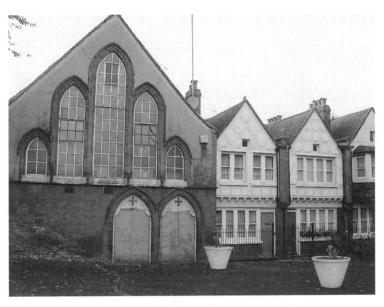

Figure 2.3
Red Cross Hall, Southwark. Elijah Hoole, 1889
Photo source: Anne Anderson

of purposes including, as a writer in *The Builder* noted, 'reading-room, gymnasium and concert-room by turns'.[47] In addition it contained space for a club-room, committee-room and caretaker's room. Adorning the walls of the hall were a series of murals designed by the artist Walter Crane. The subjects were 'taken from deeds of heroism in the daily life of ordinary people, and are not fanciful, but are records of real occurrences' and 'will be treated in a very striking and decorative manner, with great richness and force of colour'.[48] The hope was that the hall's occupants would be ennobled by such edifying subject matter.[49]

To the rear of the hall and cottages were Red Cross Gardens, built on the site of the paper factory. Its timbers were used to construct a shelter at the children's playground on a site which also encompassed '...winding paths, a pond spanned over by a bridge, a fountain, a band-stand...'.[50] Hill described the garden as 'an open-air summer sitting room...where we hope working women will sit and rest and do needlework, and tired men sit and smoke...'.[51] This 'metamorphosed desolate space' was open not just to the inhabitants of the Cottages but, as was the Hall, to all who lived in the local community.[52] It served as a welcome pocket of green in an industrialised area of the city and formed a further startling contrast to the asphalted courtyards of the Peabody dwellings nearby.

The gardens at Red Cross Street were laid out under the aegis of an organisation called the Kyrle Society. The Kyrle was a joint venture between Hill and her older sister Miranda and was an attempt to systematise and enact on a larger scale the small improvements in open space and greenery that Hill had introduced in her housing schemes.

The Kyrle Society

The Kyrle Society, which was founded in 1876 at Miranda Hill's instigation,[53] was named in honour of John Kyrle, celebrated in Pope's

---

47 See Anon, 'Red Cross Hall, Southwark', *The Builder*, 30 (1889), 333.

48 Ibid.

49 The Hall was built on land supplied by the Ecclesiastical Commissioners, the body which oversaw the estates of property owned by the Church of England. In this capacity, it had become responsible for large tracts of slum housing, much of which was in poor condition and which, in the mid-1880s, it approached Hill to manage. Much inspired by her work, the Commissioners would ultimately collaborate with Hill on two major schemes of cottages in south London, for which the Red Cross project was very much a prototype.

50 Mrs Russell Barrington, 'The Red Cross Hall', *English Illustrated Magazine*, 117, (1893), 610.

51 Hill in 1887 cited in Elizabeth Crawford, *Enterprising Women, the Garretts and their Circle*, London: Francis Boutle Publishers, 2002, 221.

52 Mrs Russell Barrington, 'The Red Cross Hall', 610.

53 To avoid confusion, Octavia Hill will be referred to as Hill in this section and her sister by her Christian name.

Epistle to Bathurst 'as one who on limited means provided considerable service to the local poor'.[54] Though founded by Miranda, the Society reflected Hill's belief, as outlined above, in the importance of moral and spiritual changes to the environments of the poor as much as material ones; indeed, many of its aims translated to a broader arena the practices Hill had already introduced in her housing schemes. Thus we find, in 1878, *The Academy* magazine reporting that the Society had been 'set on foot with the view of bringing the refining and cheering influences of natural and artistic beauty into the homes and neighbourhoods of the poor in our large towns'. It gave the Society's aims as:

> 1. To decorate with mural and other paintings, carved brackets, &c., rooms used by the poor for social purposes, such as clubs, school-rooms and mission rooms; 2. To make gifts of pictures and flowers for the homes of the poor; 3. To lay out as gardens any available strips of waste ground, and to encourage the cultivation of plants; 4. To organise choirs of volunteer singers; 5. To co-operate as far as possible with the Commons' Preservation Society in securing open-air spaces in poor neighbourhoods to be laid out as public gardens.[55]

The society took its motto from William Morris who declared, at the first public meeting in 1881, that everybody should try to change society 'To the Utmost of Our Power'.

The Kyrle pursued these aims through the establishment of sub-branches: the Decorative Branch, Music Branch and Literature Branch, each with its own committee. Like Hill's work on her rehabilitated properties these were also attempts to work within the existing fabric of the city; the concern was to enhance not demolish and start again. This could entail, as the Music Branch sought to do through the establishment of choirs or bands, fostering new activities within existing spaces, or making physical additions to such spaces. Perhaps the best example of this practice and philosophy is the Kyrle's Decorative Branch, whose mural painting activities were described as 'not just the embellishment of buildings but the embellishment of lives'.[56] A wall might be beautified with 'heroic story, bright pattern, fanciful fairy tale, sweet groups of flowers; all our skill, all our imagination is ready to be given for these out-of-the-way districts'.[57] Hill, for example, suggested that Kingsley's words, 'Do Noble Deeds', should be painted on a wall near Waterloo Station.[58] One of the earliest schemes of decoration was devised by William Morris for Westminster

---

54 Alexander Pope, 'Moral Essays, III: Of the Uses of Riches' in John Butt (ed.), *The Poems of Alexander Pope*, London: Methuen & Co., 1963, 582.

55 Anon, 'On Art and Archaeology', *The Academy*, 2 March 1878, 197.

56 McBrinn, 'Decoration should be a common joy'. See also Clare A.P. Willsden, *Mural Painting in Britain 1840–1940: Image and Meaning*, London: Clarendon Studies in the History of Art, Oxford University Press, 2000.

57 Hill, *COR*, 1905, 315.

58 David Owen, *English Philanthropy*, Cambridge, Mass: Belknapp Press of the Harvard University Press, 1964, 496.

Hospital, which was proposed by the Dean of Westminster and supervised by Charles Harrison Townsend, who was the secretary of the Decorative Branch.[59] In late 1878 Morris began work on the designs, which were subsequently carried out by volunteers.[60] A Kyrle lady recounted to Hill the pleasure her involvement had given her: 'Do you know, marm, I think it almost a blessed thing to be ill to come here in this lovely place?'. Evidently the sight of this artistic decoration, 'as unexpected as it is lovely', touched the hearts of the poor:

> The thought that so much trouble has been taken to cheer and please them makes them wishful to show, by the future conduct of their lives, that the good lessons they have acquired in the hospital, in which beauty, order, and cleanliness are combined, are not only not lost upon them, but are carried away to their own homes, to be copied as far as means and aptitude will permit.[61]

The Kyrle also spawned a number of provincial groups and it can be seen as the progenitor of England's more than nine hundred civic societies.[62] Groups were set up in Liverpool (1877), Birmingham (1880), Glasgow (1882), Edinburgh (1885), Leicester, Bristol, Cheltenham and Nottingham. Later affiliations include the Beautiful Sheffield League and the Beautiful Warrington Society.[63] These groups were also enthusiastic muralists.[64] The Birmingham Kyrle completed nearly forty schemes of mural decoration in its first decade.[65] In Edinburgh, Patrick Geddes, town planner and Celtic revivalist, also organised commissions for mural painting through the Edinburgh Social Union, and Social and Sanitary Society, which were affiliated with the Kyrle.[66] Anna Morton, his wife, knew

---

[59] Morris was amongst many artists/craftsmen who supported the Kyrle and its mural painting programme. Others included G.F. Watts, Walter Crane and Frederick Leighton, all supporters of the Kyrle, who advocated it as a public art form for moral as well as educative purposes. Townsend was an architect and later designed some of the most significant buildings associated with the Settlement Movement, not least Whitechapel Art Gallery.

[60] The volunteers were middle-class ladies rather than members of the working-class communities at whom the murals were aimed.

[61] (Hill), 'The Kyrle Society', 211.

[62] Vincent Wait, *Bristol Civic Society: The First Sixty Years*, Bristol, 1966, 3.

[63] These groups are listed in the 1910 *Kyrle Society Annual Report*.

[64] Professor Thomas Martin Lindsay, *The Kyrle Societies and their Work*, Glasgow: McLaren & Son, 1883, 6–8.

[65] McBrinn, 'Decoration should be a common joy'.

[66] The Edinburgh Social Union, founded in 1885, was described as 'a scheme for the organisation of all benevolent enterprises! But its special aims are to provide or rather improve existing material surroundings, by decorating halls or school, planting open spaces, providing music and other entertainments for the people'. Letter from James Oliphant to Anna Morton, 6 November 1884, quoted in Helen Meller, *Patrick Geddes: Social evolutionist and city planner*, London: Routledge, 1990, 73. See also Meller's chapter in this volume for a further discussion of Morton and Geddes' work.

the Hill sisters through her charitable work in Liverpool and encouraged him to visit Hill's schemes in London. Through Geddes, the Edinburgh Social Union funded various mural schemes at the Royal Infirmary, the Sick Children's Hospital and the Song School of St Mary's Cathedral.[67]

Another significant area of Kyrle activity was in making gardens for working men and women. Through its patronage, pockets of land which might otherwise have been left neglected or unused were brought into public use. In particular, the Society opened the burial grounds around London churches to public access. Its most public and popular venture was the creation of new public gardens on the site of the former house of the reformer Henry Fawcett which occupied a rare pocket of open space in the densely populated working-class area of Lambeth. The site had been bought for development into housing but the Kyrle launched a campaign to transform it into a pleasure garden. With support from Millicent Fawcett, the potter Henry Doulton, who had worked with Henry Fawcett in Parliament for the preservation of open spaces and whose pottery factory stood nearby, and an 'eclectic selection of bishops and workingmen', the site was saved and Vauxhall Gardens laid out.[68]

The Kyrle would have other impacts on space in England. In the short term, and as a result of Hill's lobbying, the passing of the 1881 Metropolitan Open Spaces Act saw local authorities empowered to receive and maintain gardens transferred to them by trustees. In the longer term, its greatest significance lies in the fact that it gave rise to the National Trust which was founded in 1895. It is now among the largest landowners in England, Wales and Northern Ireland.[69]

Conclusion

This has been a necessarily abbreviated account of one woman's work in housing but the hope is that it has demonstrated Hill's unique approach and suggested how it was far from 'private' in its influence, with a resonance which has continued to the present day. Hill's consistent practice of writing about her work, her engagement with policy making, represented in her lobbying of parliament and its consulting her during the 1884 Royal Commission into the Housing of the Working Classes, would seem to give the lie to the assertion that her work was enacted only at a local level. Likewise, her establishment of the profession of Housing Manager would,

---

[67]   Clare A.P. Willsden, 'Scotland's Mural Renascence', *The Scottish Review*, 29, (1983), 15–22.

[68]   Elizabeth Crawford, *Enterprising Women*, 222. The gardens' designer was Fanny Wilkinson, the first woman to specialise in this discipline in Britain.

[69]   The Trust owns over 248,000 hectares of land, 600 miles of coastline and over 200 properties and gardens. <www.nationaltrust.org.uk/main/nationaltrust>, accessed 22 February, 2005.

as Ravetz observed, be adopted into the twentieth-century programme of council housing.

Hill's approach was, of course, not without problems. Much of her activity seems to modern eyes to be patronising in the extreme. Although she did attempt to respond to workers' desires for housing close to their places of employment, and to foster their desire for a sense of privacy and homeliness, there remains with Hill, as with many other middle-class reformers of this generation, the feeling that for them reform was something done *to* the poor, rather than with or through them.

Nevertheless, there is much in Hill's system that has relevance for the present; both for the practices of history and of housing. For historians, such as those writing in this volume, her work epitomises our assertion that space can be made, or re-made, through alterations to the activities which go on within it, or through minor additions to it, and that these can be as meaningful as new interventions to built space. Further, by expanding the paradigms of history to pay attention to such traditions of space-making, we are reminded of their long-term significance for the shaping of England's environment in the twentieth century.

This is evident in three main aspects. Firstly, Hill's concern to enact reform in housing at the intersection between the social and the material was to be taken up by a generation of housing reformers such as Elizabeth Denby,[70] and through this generation it had some influence over the form of housing provision in the years after 1945. Secondly, and an extension of this observation, Hill's concern for localised solutions to housing, though impossible to enact under the mass programme of social housing undertaken between 1919 and 1979, is now understood to represent a desirable model of practice in the present-day climate in which provision is the responsibility of housing associations rather than central government. Finally, and connected with Hill's emphasis on the local and the existing, there is the undoubted significance of her insistence on the retention of historical diversity within the urban environment. Her policy of rehabilitation and improvement laid the foundations of the conservation movement in the twentieth century and has further resonance today as sustainability becomes a model of reform to guide our futures.

---

[70] See Darling's chapter in this volume.

SECOND EDITION.

𝕷𝖔𝖆𝖓 𝕰𝖝𝖍𝖎𝖇𝖎𝖙𝖎𝖔𝖓 𝖔𝖋 𝖂𝖔𝖒𝖊𝖓'𝖘 𝕴𝖓𝖉𝖚𝖘𝖙𝖗���.

Get leave to work in this world —
't is the best you get at all;

Figure 3.1
Front cover of the catalogue of the Loan Exhibition of Women's Industries
held in Queen's Villa, Queen's Road, Bristol, 26 February–28 April 1885.
Designed by Miss Mary Tothill and engraved by Miss Corbet Harden
Source: Central Library, Bristol

Chapter 3

'A Novelty among Exhibitions': The Loan Exhibition of Women's Industries, Bristol, 1885

Emma Ferry

Bristol may take credit to itself for having devised a novelty among Exhibitions. The present is peculiarly an exhibiting age, but there has not been till now an Exhibition devoted exclusively to women's industries. Bristol has, however, led the way, and the Exhibition just opened is so successful and so interesting that it will be surprising if the example is not rapidly followed in other places.[1]

Reported to be the first of its kind held in England, the Loan Exhibition of Women's Industries (henceforth, The Exhibition) opened at Queen's Villa in the Clifton suburb of Bristol on 26 February 1885.[2] By the time it closed at the end of April, The Exhibition had been visited by more than 18,000 people, and 'had proved to be a success beyond the most sanguine expectations of the promoters'.[3]

Although several of the exhibitors were men, who either owned objects that were exhibited or businesses that were represented, The Exhibition displayed only the work of women.[4] Further, the Catalogue stated explicitly that little effort had been made 'to shew such manufactures as are carried on by the joint labour of men and women, with the aid of machinery'.[5] It also informed visitors:

---

[1]   *Pall Mall Gazette*, 26 February 1885, 4.
[2]   *Clifton Chronicle*, 4 March 1885, 2.
[3]   *Women's Union Journal*, May 1885, 35; *The Bristol Times*, 29 April 1885, 6.
[4]   *Exhibition of Women's Industries*, 1885, [henceforth *Catalogue*] 'Introductory'. Of the 303 exhibitors, 116 were listed as 'Miss' and 91 were listed as 'Mrs' or 'Madame'. Fourteen were female who gave only first and surnames; six were titled women and one exhibitor was the unmarried female doctor Elizabeth Blackwell. Nineteen of the exhibitors were women's organisations and 20 were businesses exhibiting women's work. Twenty-nine were men, for instance, John Ruskin and Albert Fleming both sent samples of linen produced by women at St. Martin's, Langdale. Finally, seven exhibitors (probably women) gave only initials and a surname.
[5]   The machinery that the Committee excluded seems to be that connected with the large-scale factory production of textiles.

51

That all the modern work they will see in this Exhibition is done by women who make a profession of their pursuit, either for art's sake, or for the sake of earning a livelihood. No work is shewn done for recreation or amusement only.[6]

In considering The Exhibition and the space in which it took place, this chapter draws upon the work of Thomas A. Markus, whose study, *Buildings and Power: Freedom and Control in the Origin of Modern Building Types*, analyses the social meanings of buildings.[7] In his discussion of 'Buildings and Knowledge', Markus describes museums, art galleries, exhibitions and lecture theatres and the knowledge that these building types produce. He posits three categories: *visible, ephemeral* and *invisible* and comments:

> Since knowledge is power one should not be surprised by the huge investment in these buildings and their contents by the state, city authorities, Royalty and aristocracy, learned societies, and churches ... And once the working class organised to obtain power it, too, invested capital in knowledge.[8]

Occurring at a time when women were also organising to obtain power, The Exhibition, and the building in which it was held, can be interpreted as a similar investment in knowledge. Extending Markus' model, this chapter suggests that The Exhibition obscured the distinction between private (conventionally gendered female) and public (conventionally gendered male) spaces and briefly transformed Queen's Villa from an empty domestic residence into a building that functioned as a museum and art gallery, exhibition hall and lecture theatre, and thus produced *visible, ephemeral* and *invisible* knowledge.

Based on primary sources that reveal the public response to The Exhibition, this chapter considers the nature of the exhibits and the space in which they were displayed.[9] However, given that the ideological position of The Exhibition's Organising Committee 'shaped the content, classification and explanation' of the exhibits,[10] first it is essential to examine the origins of this event, the class identities of the exhibitors and the exhibited, and the relationship of The Exhibition to the suffrage movement.

---

6   Ibid, 7.
7   T.A. Markus, *Buildings and Power: Freedom and Control in Modern Building Types*, London: Routledge, 1993.
8   Ibid, 169.
9   The Report and Balance Sheet, the Address Book and the Minute Book of the Exhibition Committee, which give details of the planning of the Loan Exhibition of Women's Industries and are in the Helen Blackburn Collection at Girton College, Cambridge.
10 Markus, *Buildings and Power*, 208.

'An Exhibition in many respects novel if not unique, and very interesting and important'[11]

The organisation of The Exhibition was reported extensively in the local press which, in a surge of civic pride, was highly supportive of the event.[12] It was inspired by the success of the Industrial and Fine Art Exhibition held at Bristol's Drill Hall the previous autumn.[13] The profits from this earlier exhibition had been donated to University College, Bristol, 'whose doors were open to the education and technical training of both sexes'.[14] Similarly, the primary objective of the Committee formed to organise The Exhibition was to encourage 'opportunities afforded women for scientific study and technical training',[15] and its members:

> lost no time in putting themselves into communication with the Women's Employment Society in London, the Female School of Art, the School of Wood Carving and the various employers of female labour throughout the country.[16]

These organisations, and others involved with the training and employment of women, submitted exhibits to advertise their activities, to demonstrate the benefits of technical education, and 'to make access to those paths of appropriate work more plain and obvious'.[17] An advertisement heralding The Exhibition in the *Clifton Chronicle* described the range of work to be displayed:

> The principal feature will be Specimens of such works as illustrate the progress made by Women in industries demanding special technical and artistic training. Industrial Occupations, Painting, Wood Engraving, Wood Carving, Articles of Domestic Furniture, Lace, Needlework, Ancient and Modern, Telegraphy, &c., will be shewn.[18]

The industries of women may have formed a unifying theme for the Exhibition, but the displays at Queen's Villa also indicated the middle-class identity of its organisers who were demanding 'greater participation in the

---

[11] *Queen,* 7 March 1885, 247.
[12] Meller's chapter in this volume refers to Bristol's energetic philanthropic activity during the same period.
[13] *Western Daily Press,* 26 February 1885, 6. The Industrial and Fine Art Exhibition ran from 2 September until 29 November 1884.
[14] *Bristol Times,* 27 February 1885, 1. Supported financially by the great non-conformist families of Bristol, the University College of Bristol first opened in 1876 and was the first college in the country to admit men and women on an equal footing: 30 men and 69 women registered.
[15] *Western Daily Press,* 29 April 1885.
[16] *Bristol Times,* 27 February 1885, 1.
[17] *Clifton Chronicle,* 22 April 1885, 5.
[18] Ibid, 11 February 1885, 4.

workforce'.[19] This was reinforced by the motto printed across the front cover of the Catalogue, which had been 'fitly chosen'[20] from Elizabeth Barrett Browning's poem *Aurora Leigh* of 1856: '... Get leave to work / In this world: 'tis the best you get at all'.[21]

The review in the *Pall Mall Gazette* commented:

> though the regular trades – such as the textile industries, in which women of the working classes are employed in large numbers – are represented, more prominence is given in the Exhibition to skilled industries where the employés [sic] are not "hands" and are not reckoned by the thousand, but where each worker brings her own individuality to bear on the product of her industry.[22]

While it offered a reduced admission price of sixpence to working-class visitors on Saturdays, which was 'productive of a much larger attendance',[23] the emphasis was upon the types of remunerative work and technical training suitable for middle-class women. Indeed as the *Clifton Chronicle* noted, the exhibitors were '... for the most part, though not all, women of superior education; some of them women of scientific acquirement ... more of them are women of cultivated taste and skill'.[24]

Many of the exhibitors were also involved with philanthropic organisations, and particularly with lace associations,[25] but while the Catalogue carefully recorded the name of each 'exhibitor', 'artist' or 'designer', the working-class women who actually produced these handmade textile items remained unnamed.[26] These exhibits should be understood as what are here termed *double displays*. These were items that demonstrated examples of dying craft traditions practised by peasant women, but which prioritised the philanthropic work undertaken by the upper-middle class women in reviving them, and whose names appeared in the Catalogue as 'exhibitors'.

Double display was *the* feature of The Exhibition, which was itself a larger example of this strategy. Ostensibly exhibiting the more tangible products of 'feminine industry', The Exhibition was also used to demonstrate the managerial skills possessed by its female organisers. Indeed, with the exception of a male President and Chairman, the Committee that organised The Exhibition was composed entirely of women. This was remarked upon in many reports. Writing in terms that suggested

---

[19] P. Bartley, *The Changing Role of Women 1815–1914*, London: Hodder & Stoughton, 1996, 69.

[20] *Englishwoman's Review*, 14 March 1885, 98.

[21] E. Barrett Browning, 1857, Book III, ll. 161–162.

[22] *Pall Mall Gazette*, 26 February 1885, 4.

[23] *Clifton Chronicle*, 18 March 1885, 5.

[24] Ibid, 22 April 1885, 5.

[25] A. Callen, *Angel in the Studio: Women in the Arts and Crafts Movement 1870–1914*, London: Astragal, 1979, 4–8.

[26] This was also the case in the exhibits of factory-made ceramics displayed by manufacturers.

the display of gendered behaviour, as well as feminine objects, a reviewer, who signed herself 'A Woman, but not an Exhibitor', commented:

> Exhibitions in general present on the opening day a sea of shavings and paper wrappings, interspersed with packing cases and empty or half-empty stands; the Bristol exhibition was a curious contrast to this state of things; the opening day found it in trim and dainty order; the laces, embroideries, pictures and other products of feminine industry were in their places, suggesting the thought that order and punctuality are among the virtues of persons who, as Mr E. A. Leatham says "are not even men".[27]

The gendered nature of The Exhibition may have partially obscured the social position of the exhibitors, but the political intentions of its organisers were unambiguous; the proceeds of The Exhibition were donated to the 'National Society for the Promotion of the Franchise of Women'.[28] This clear connection with the women's suffrage movement was also commented upon in all the newspaper reports.

The *Bristol Times* noted that the idea for The Exhibition 'originated with Miss Helen Blackburn and Mr Alan Greenwell'.[29] A committed suffragist, the Reverend Greenwell was Chairman of The Exhibition Committee, while Helen Blackburn was its Honourable Secretary, as well as Secretary of the West of England Suffrage Society and the National Society for Women's Suffrage (1874–1895).[30] Editor of the *Englishwoman's Review* from 1881 until 1890, she later wrote *Women's Suffrage* (1902), which remains an important text of 'the struggle'. Rather modestly, this publication made no mention of the Bristol Exhibition. However, in 1918, a publication titled *How the Suffrage Movement began in Bristol Fifty Years Ago* noted its propagandising success:

> Among Miss Blackburn's indefatigable activities in Bristol was a bit of indirect Suffrage work – a Loan Exhibition of Women's Industries, which attracted many helpers who had not before been interested in Women's Suffrage, and made a very good object lesson for the general public.[31]

The date of The Exhibition is particularly significant for it occurred at a time when the suffrage movement was in 'a temporary decline', following

---

[27] *Pall Mall Gazette*, 26 February 1885, 4. E.A. Leatham was an author and MP for Huddersfield and brother-in-law of John Bright.

[28] *Bristol Times*, 27 February 1885, 1. The reporter (or J.D. Weston) meant the National Society for Women's Suffrage.

[29] Ibid. Greenwell and his wife joined the Bristol & Clifton Suffrage Society in 1872, see S.J. Tanner, *How the Suffrage Movement began in Bristol Fifty Years Ago*, Bristol: The Carlyle Press, 1918, 9.

[30] Helen Blackburn (1842–1903) *Dictionary of National Biography 1901–1911*, 168–169 and O. Banks, *The Biographical Dictionary of British Feminists*, Volume 1: 1800–1930, Harvester Press, 1985.

[31] Tanner, *How the Suffrage Movement began*, 13.

the rejection of Woodall's amendment to the 1884 Reform Bill by the largest majority returned against such a proposal in the movement's history up to that point.[32] The amendment would have enfranchised about 100,000 property-owning women, and the implication behind its rejection, which was greatly resented by upper- and middle-class women, was that 'masculinity was valued more than class position'.[33] Thus, as an event that prioritised the feminine, The Exhibition must be considered in the context of contemporary gender politics in which many members of the Committee played active roles. Indeed as the *Clifton Chronicle* noted:

> To prove women's capacity for exercising the franchise, probably no better plan could have been devised than to make manifest their intelligence in scientific and artistic pursuits, than by collecting in one building women's finest productions.[34]

The Transformation of Space

Unlike the purpose-built Women's Pavilions and Palaces erected at contemporary international exhibitions,[35] The Exhibition was housed in a 'commodious *residence* opposite the Queen's Hotel'[36] [author's italics] that contained 'besides the entrance hall, three or four rooms on the ground floor, with the same number above'.[37] A sense of the physical space inside Queen's Villa can be gained from the Catalogue and from reviews of The Exhibition published in the local, national and suffrage press. The *Clifton Chronicle* printed several whimsical articles written by the female 'Ghost of the Queen's Villa', which gave the reader detailed reviews and well informed assessments of several exhibits. This was an interesting literary device reflective of the contemporary popularity of psychical science and spiritualism, to which the ghost also referred.[38] Other less fanciful reports described the route taken by visitors, the best example being the guided tour published by the *Englishwoman's Review*.[39]

On arrival, the visitors passed through the Entrance Porch and Vestibule, decorated with 'flags of all nations', into the Hall, where there

---

32 B. Harrison, *Separate Spheres – The Opposition to Women's Suffrage in Britain*, Croom Helm, 1978, 44.

33 H. L. Smith, *The British Women's Suffrage Campaign, 1866–1828*, London: Longman, 1998, 9.

34 *Clifton Chronicle*, 25 February 1885, 5.

35 See P. Greenhalgh, *Ephemeral Vistas: The Expositions Universelles, Great Exhibitions and World's Fairs, 1851–1939*, Manchester: Manchester University Press, 1988, 174–197.

36 *Western Daily Press*, 26 February 1885, 6.

37 *Englishwoman's Review*, 14 March 1885, 97.

38 *Clifton Chronicle*, 11 March 1885, 5. D. Cherry, *Beyond the Frame: Feminism and Visual Culture, Britain 1850–1900*, London: Routledge, 2000, 206–211.

39 *Englishwoman's Review*, 14 March 1885, 97–105.

were displays of woodcarving, ceramics and pictures by Emily Ford.[40] To the right of the Hall, a large reception room, designated Room I, displayed oil paintings and 'art pottery' and was where lectures and music recitals were held. A second reception room (II) displayed watercolours, ceramic plaques and the majority of the textile exhibits including lace, crochet and embroidery. The Tea Room was downstairs and was 'crowded' with portraits of eminent women.[41]

As visitors climbed the stairs they saw diagrams of marine architecture exhibited by the Leven Shipyard, designs for landscape gardening by Fanny Wilkinson,[42] and fans decorated by students at the Female School of Art. Upstairs in Room III was the Dress Section, and in Room IV were displays of drawings, historical relics, peasant textile-crafts and ethnographic objects. On the Landing there were floral displays, agricultural produce, and a demonstration of telegraphy 'worked on the spot, by a pupil from the Red Maid's School'.[43] Room V was devoted to house decoration by R. and A. Garrett,[44] while Room VI exhibited the work of the Bristol Associated Decorators,[45] examples of Nottingham lace, specimens of law-copying,[46] and the architectural and technical tracings sent by the Ladies' Tracing Office. Finally, in Room VII, the visitor viewed examples of Bedfordshire straw work, Birmingham metalwork, wallpaper designs, the inventions of Eliza Turck,[47] and work by the Chromolithographic Studio.

While these exhibits, according to the *Queen*, were 'arranged with care and judgement, and as a whole, constitute a splendid array of women's work', the same article commented on the lack of space for the number of

---

40   See Cherry, *Beyond the Frame*.

41   *Englishwoman's Review*, 14 March 1885, 100.

42   See E. Crawford, *Enterprising Women: The Garretts and their Circle*, London: Francis Boutle 2002, chapter 5 'The Land', 218–239. For a further reference to Wilkinson see chapter 2 in this volume.

43   *Catalogue*, 54. The Red Maids' School is the oldest surviving girls' school in the country. Founded in 1634 by John Whitson, Mayor and MP of Bristol, the original Red Maids' Hospital provided a secure home and training for the orphaned or destitute daughters of freemen or burgesses of the City of Bristol. The School is now an independent school for girls but its archive is held at Bristol Record Office.

44   See E. Ferry, '"Decorators May be Compared to Doctors": An analysis of Rhoda and Agnes Garrett's Suggestion for House decoration in Painting, Woodwork and Furniture', in *Journal of Design History*, Vol. 16, No. 1, (2003), 15–33.

45   *Catalogue*, p. 55, The Bristol Associated Decorators 'was formed in November 1883, with the view of aiding young artists, especially School of Art Students, who it is hoped may find a remunerative profession in House Decoration'.

46   Sent by Mrs Sunter of the Law Copying Office for the Employment of Women at 2 Portugal Street, Lincoln's Inn, London.

47   These inventions were 'Florentine Tapestry Medium for painting in oil colours on unprepared paper, textile fabrics and other Surfaces' and 'Mirrorine for painting on looking-glass, terra cotta &c'. Priced at a shilling per bottle, these products were advertised at the back of the Catalogue.

visitors.[48] The *Englishwoman's Review* also described the rooms as 'crowded' with people and with objects, and the *Pall Mall Gazette* commented that 'every nook and corner of the moderate sized house in which the Exhibition is held is full'.[49] Unintentionally, this overcrowding perhaps suggested that women's work was so extensive that it could no longer be contained in a domestic space.

In a parody of domestic functions and private activities, including cooking, eating, dressing, childcare and 'At Home' entertainments, The Exhibition transformed Queen's Villa into a public space which allowed the production *and* the consumption of knowledge. Indeed, quoting Tennyson, the front cover of the Catalogue stated that 'Knowledge is now no more a fountain sealed'.[50]

Reiterating the dictum that 'Knowledge is power', Markus has commented that 'all museums have political meaning'.[51] Functioning as a museum and thus producing *visible* knowledge, some of the displays in Queen's Villa celebrated the achievements of women over time and from other cultures; the latter reflecting the popularity of ethnographic displays which mapped race directly onto the space and form of Queen's Villa.[52] While the display of certain relics was suggestive of women's role as *custodians* of history,[53] the primary purpose of most exhibits was to illustrate the history of women at work.[54] Examples of antique needlework were important forms of evidence. As the report in the *Queen* noted: 'We were conscious of feeling akin to reverence when we laid hands on some of these old quilts. What a "history of our own times" they could tell!'[55] However, the same reviewer, suggesting how the purpose of work for women was conceived in this context, commented: 'But in all this old work there is the same tale which saddens one in thinking of it – the same tale of monotonous and rather uninteresting life – of work done only to keep the hands from lying idle'.[56]

---

[48]   *Queen*, 7 March 1885, 247.
[49]   *Pall Mall Gazette*, 26 February 1885, 4.
[50]   Alfred, Lord Tennyson, *The Princess*, 1847, Book II, l. 76.
[51]   Markus, *Buildings and Power*, 194. '*Nam et ipsa scienta potestas est*' is attributed to Francis Bacon (1561–1626).
[52]   Part of Room IV displayed 'Indian work, ... and native productions from Madagascar, North America (Indian), Hindustan, Burma, Fiji, Algeria, and Iceland'. The hand-crafted ethnographic objects on display, all of which were exhibited by white middle-class women, included a 'Rush Basket, Head-band and Necklace made by Kaffir women'; Native American bead work and costumes made by the Apache, Cree, and Chippewa tribes; Fijian drinking vessels; and, embroidery executed by Hindu women. These exhibits further complicate the primary issue of *which* women were exhibiting.
[53]   *Catalogue*, 48 described a highly popular exhibit of the relics of King Charles I.
[54]   *Clifton Chronicle*, 25 February 1885, 5.
[55]   *Queen*, 21 March 1885, 302.
[56]   Ibid.

In place of honour was the spinning wheel; spinning being an occupation with symbolic associations for spinsters and one of the 'lost trades', which had 'since the introduction of machinery passed from their hands entirely'.[57] Many of the speeches reported during The Exhibition lamented the demise of spinning and weaving as traditional forms of remunerative employment for women that had taken place in the home:

> Not many years ago every little home had its centre of industry. The spinning jenny, the mule, and the weaving machine enabled girls to produce at their respective homes many little things to support their families in decency, and gave employment to all concerned.[58]

It is significant that the majority of the exhibits shown at Queen's Villa were domestic industries produced in the home, either by working-class women outworkers or middle-class artists and craftswomen. Indeed, as Anthea Callen has noted:

> The crafts most commonly practised by women echoed both traditional and more recent patterns of sexual labour divisions. Embroidery, lacemaking, china painting, jewellery, bookbinding, illustrating and even woodcarving were all activities which could be pursued within the home, often without the need for a special workshop or studio.[59]

The knowledge produced by the organisers of The Exhibition might also be said to have been made in a domestic setting.

Displays within The Exhibition portrayed women not only as makers *in* history but also as makers *of* history. Exhibited downstairs in the Tea Room, and intended as a record of female achievement, was a collection of portraits of more than 90 eminent women who had 'left their mark on the world'.[60] This display was identified in all the newspaper reports as 'the

---

57 *Catalogue*, 'Introductory'.
58 *Clifton Chronicle*, 4 March, 1885, 2.
59 A. Callen, 'Sexual Division of Labour in the Arts and Crafts Movement' in J. Attfield & P. Kirkham (eds), *A View from the Interior: Women & Design*, London: The Women's Press, 1989; 1995 edition, 159.
60 *Catalogue*, 'Introductory'. This collection formed the basis of a bigger collection of eminent British Women, which was later sent to the Chicago Exhibition of 1893. The Royal Commission of the Chicago Exhibition gave Helen Blackburn a grant of £100 to add to this collection. She collected 190 portraits that were arranged in 12 groups: Medieval, Tudor, Civil War, Early 18th Century, pioneers in philanthropy and the advancement of women, pioneers in education, royal ladies, history, science, general literature, poets, fiction, painting, music and drama. The *Western Daily Press*, 28 January 1895 noted that when the Loan Collection was returned from Chicago, Helen Blackburn presented this valuable collection to University College, Bristol to be placed in the Women Student's Room. See L. B. Voss Snook, 'The Woman's Reading Room', *The Magnet* Vol. 2. No. 5, 21 June 1900, 161–162. Sadly, this collection now seems to have been dispersed.

keynote of the Exhibition'.[61] Deborah Cherry has commented that collections of female portraits 'created a visual genealogy of authoritative and powerful women which countered illustrated profiles of masculine high achievers and public figures'.[62] Literally making an exhibition of themselves, many of the contemporary portraits were sent to Queen's Villa by the sitters. This tactic of *self-display* enabled women such as Frances Cobbe Power, Bessie Rayner Parkes, Mme Bodichon, and Dr Elizabeth Blackwell to endorse The Exhibition, to appear in the Catalogue as 'exhibitors' and to attend the event by proxy. Not all the portraits were of women who necessarily supported the suffrage movement; however, all were in favour of extending technical education and opportunities for work.

Functioning as a contemporary trade exhibition and producing *ephemeral* knowledge too, the exhibits at Queen's Villa celebrated current examples of women's work and indicated what might be achieved in the future, given access to technical education. Many of the objects at Queen's Villa were displayed to demonstrate the contribution women could make to British trade, which no doubt had particular significance given the economic depression of the 1880s and the falling value of British exports.[63] Indeed, J.D. Weston, former Mayor of Bristol and President of The Exhibition, commented at the opening ceremony that: 'there appeared no reason to him why many articles should not be produced by their own women rather than they should be imported from France and other countries'.[64]

Inevitably, the Arts, a field of employment that was '...an extension of traditional female accomplishments',[65] were better represented than either science or heavy industry. Nonetheless, the wide range of objects displayed still corresponded to the six broad Divisions that had been used to classify objects displayed at the Great Exhibition of 1851. Thus, there were RAW MATERIALS such as the agricultural produce 'clearly demonstrating that women can be practical farmers'.[66] There were items that fell into some classes of the second Division MACHINERY, including the 'Griswold Knitting Machine', and other exhibits produced by women who had benefited from scientific study and technical training. These included the 'Marks Patent Line Divider, for dividing any line into any number of equal parts',[67] exhibited by a former student at Girton, and the medal-winning invention of Mrs Knevett, titled 'Apparatus to prevent children from being burnt or

---

61   *Pall Mall Gazette*, 26 February 1885, 4.
62   D. Cherry, *Beyond the Frame*, 195.
63   P. Gregg, *A Social and Economic History of Britain 1760–1980*, 8th edition, Harrap, 1982, 368–369. In 1885 British exports were valued at £213 million and imports stood at £371 million.
64   *Clifton Chronicle*, 4 March 1885, 2.
65   Callen, Sexual Division of Labour, 153.
66   *Englishwoman's Review*, 14 March 1885, 98–99.
67   *Catalogue*, 58.

scalded in the absence of their parents'.[68] However, the most impressive display in this category was exhibited by Messrs Denny Brothers of the Leven Shipyard at Dumbarton, and included 'tracings, drawings, and calculations and diagrams of displacement, and stability calculations, used in marine architecture, all the work of women employed by the firm'.[69]

Census figures show that in 1881 the textile industry employed 745,000 women.[70] At Queen's Villa there were exhibits belonging to all ten of the classes categorised in 1851 for the Great Exhibition within the Division MANUFACTURES: TEXTILE FABRICS. In fact, textile products formed the largest category of exhibits, but to avoid displaying machine-made items, almost all were handmade. The tradition of textile work as a female occupation had been emphasised by the displays of historic needlework and spinning, but the majority of the textile exhibits were contemporary pieces submitted by local, regional, national and international exhibitors. There were embroideries worked by the nuns at Manilla Hall, Clifton and exhibits by the Clifton Ladies Work Society. Messrs Morley of Nottingham sent examples of lace and hosiery,[71] and there was an exhibit from the Leek Embroidery Association.[72] Morris & Co. sent embroideries, a portière, and three Hammersmith rugs, handmade by women, which received much praise and attention from reviewers. William Morris also visited The Exhibition and addressed the visitors.[73] However, it seems possible that his comments in support of the family wage and 'the evil resulting from married women engaging in bread-winning work', would have been less popular with his audience. [74] More than thirty per cent of the exhibitors were married women, as were the anonymous working class or 'peasant' women, who made a vital contribution to the family income through their work.[75]

---

68   Ibid, 61.

69   *Englishwoman's Review*, 14 March 1885, 101. The Catalogue gave detailed explanatory notes on the eight technical diagrams exhibited, 36–38.

70   Categories A.V. John, (ed.) *Unequal opportunities: Women's Employment in England 1800–1918*, Oxford: Blackwell, 1986, 'Introduction', Appendix B, 37.

71   The *Catalogue* included a four-page insert entitled 'The Work of Women in the Nottingham Lace Trade'.

72   Founded in 1879 by Elizabeth Wardle, wife of Thomas Wardle, the President of the Silk Association of Great Britain and Ireland. See K. Parkes, 'The Leek Embroidery Society', *Studio*, 1, (1893), 136–40.

73   N. Salmon, *The William Morris Chronology*, Thoemmes Press, 1996, 145. Morris had delivered a lecture on 'Art and Labour' at a meeting sponsored by the Bristol Branch of the Socialist League at the Bristol Museum and Library on 3 March. His 'address' at the Exhibition is not mentioned in the Morris chronology.

74   *Clifton Chronicle*, 22 April 1885, 5

75   A significant number of the newspaper reports written in response to the Exhibition contained references to women as 'bread-winners'. See *Pall Mall Gazette*, 26 February 1885, 4; *Englishwoman's Review*, 14 March 1885, 105; and *Clifton Chronicle*, 1 April 1885, 5.

Many of the textile exhibits came from Ireland, including one that represented an important instance of double display at Queen's Villa.[76] Exhibited by Mrs Ernest Hart, examples of hosiery knitted by famine-stricken Donegal peasants were given a lengthy Catalogue entry. However, rather than describing the work, this explained how members of The Exhibition Committee contributed to this philanthropic effort, supplying the Donegal peasant women with yarn and arranging the sale of the hosiery.[77]

Philanthropic organisations that aimed to revive craft traditions in Scandinavia also sent double displays to Bristol. Swedish embroidery was exhibited by Mrs C. H. Derby, one of the original directors of the 'Handarbetes Vänner' (Friends of Manual Arts at Stockholm); and a Mrs Magnusson, who had exhibited at the International Health Exhibition the previous year, displayed examples of spinning, knitting, and embroidery from Iceland.[78]

Another branch of the textile industry that employed 667,000 women, which had also formed an important exhibit at the Health Exhibition, was displayed upstairs in Room III as an 'Exhibition of Dress'.[79] Despite the displays of national and folk costume and examples of dress from India, Romania, Bavaria, and Egypt, this section had its own agenda:

> The Committee of the Dress Section being limited to space, have only been able to show examples of different types of Modern Dress, that a just comparison may be made between the Rational or Reformed Dress, the Artistic, and the fashionable Present-Day Costume.[80]

Formed in 1881 by Viscountess Harberton and Mrs E. M. King, the Rational Dress Society was well represented at Bristol.[81] Lady Harberton, President of the Society, and 'one of the supporters of the movement for women's enfranchisement',[82] was also among the exhibitors, contributing her own famous design, 'the 'Harberton Walking Costume' with an

---

76 The Irish exhibits also included work by the Royal Irish School of Art Needlework; examples of point lace from Youghal; 'peasant' knitting from Valencia Island, Co. Kerry; and, Irish crochet from the Mountmellick Industrial Association. Helen Blackburn was born in County Kerry.

77 *Catalogue*, 50. Mrs Hart was the founder of the Donegal Industrial Fund, a charity formed in response to a famine in Donegal in the 1880s. See Callen, *Angel in the Studio*, 116.

78 See S.M. Newton, *Health, Art & Reason – Dress Reformers of the Nineteenth Century*, London: John Murray, 1974, chapter 6. The International Health Exhibition was held in Kensington in 1884. Mrs Magnusson also gave lectures at Queen's Villa.

79 John, *Unequal Opportunities*, 37.

80 *Catalogue*, 40.

81 Newton, *Health, Art and Reason*, 108.

82 Ibid, 103.

adaptation of the Eastern Trouser'.[83] Among the exhibits of dress was a 'Model Baby, dressed hygienically' in a set of clothes that had been 'awarded the bronze medal in 1883, given by the National Health Society'.[84] Devised and executed by Miss Loader of Thame, Oxfordshire, to exhibit an improved system of infants' clothing, this wax baby drew more comments than the garments. The *Western Daily Press* referred to this exhibit as 'a delicate hint of women's work in domestic departments',[85] while the *Pall Mall Gazette* commented that 'Very appropriately in this room is a life-size wax model of a baby, the chief of women's industries!'[86]

Given that 49,000 women were employed in the metal manufacture industry and a further 27,000 were also employed in the pottery and glass industries, it was appropriate that The Exhibition also displayed examples of the processes and products, which would have been categorised as MANUFACTURES: METALLIC, VITREOUS AND CERAMIC.[87] The examples of metalwork sent from Birmingham included 'specimens of chains and nails in their various stages', exhibited by Eliza Tinsley & Company. [88]

The work of female ceramicists and glass workers formed a particularly important category in the Exhibition. These displays ranged from the painted glass mirrors of Mrs Hodgson and Mrs Backhouse, and the glass jug 'designed and engraved by young women trained by the Society for Promoting the Employment of Women',[89] to the exhibits sent by larger manufacturers of pottery and porcelain. The work sent by the Bristol firm of Messrs S.J. Kepple & Co. featured in many of the local newspaper reports.[90] One display demonstrated 'that a first rate dinner service can be made by women at the remarkable low price of 4d per plate printed, 6d painted'.[91] Unwittingly, this small price differential also demonstrated the exploitation of female pottery painters. Following a well established precedent at Exhibitions, a second display by Kepple & Co. was designed to show the process of manufacture from raw material to finished product, indicating how women were involved in each stage.[92] This local manufacturer also sent 'upwards of £300 worth of specimens' of 'Art Pottery' which was exhibited in Room I alongside displays from other

---

[83] *Catalogue*, 43.

[84] Ibid, 46

[85] *Western Daily Press*, 26 February 1885, 6.

[86] *Pall Mall Gazette*, 26 February 1885, 4.

[87] John, *Unequal Opportunities*, 37. The figures given for female pottery and glass workers included women employed in the brick and cement industries.

[88] *Catalogue*, 60.

[89] Ibid, 58.

[90] Messrs S.J. Kepple & Co. were based at 3 Clare Street, Bristol.

[91] *Catalogue*, 10.

[92] Markus, *Buildings and Power*, 219–220. The idea of exhibiting processes as well as products dates to the 16th century. At the Exhibition, Messrs. Price of the Bristol Stoneware Potteries, also displayed unfired 'Etruscan vases' decorated with flowers moulded by women, to demonstrate the process of manufacture.

factories employing large numbers of women.[93] These included examples from Doulton's of Lambeth by Hannah and Florence Barlow, Edith Lupton, Edith Rogers, Eliza Simmance and Linnie Watt.[94] These were shown alongside ceramics from Worcester where 'the tinting, gilding, burnishing and all the decoration is women's work',[95] and Crown Derby where 'the painted and raised gold is done by them also'.[96] Significantly, prioritising artistic over technical skill, the Catalogue named the 'designers' of these exhibits from Doulton's while the work from other factories were simply 'women's work'.

Numerous exhibits fell into the fifth Division of MISCELLANEOUS, from the interior decor shown by Agnes Garrett to ephemera such as the hedgehog quill embroidery 'invented and designed by Miss Lucy Griffith'.[97] Finally, The Exhibition included a large number of items classified as FINE ART, including paintings, watercolours and sculpture.[98] There were extensive displays organised by Miss Edith Mendham, with three of the rooms, the landing, and passage used as exhibition space. Among the important loan exhibits were works by Emily Osborn(e), Hilda and Clara Montalba, Mrs Helen Allingham, Mrs Louise Jopling, Mrs Alma Tadema, Madame Bodichon, Mrs Butler, Miss Francesca Alexander and Mrs E.M. Ward. As was the case with the eminent women whose portraits were displayed in the Tea Room, not all of these artists had links with the suffrage movement. They were united, however, in the cause of the Exhibition.[99] The prominence given to the displays of art once more indicated the Committee's middle-class agenda. It is significant that one of four women depicted on the front cover of the Catalogue which illustrated the theme of work was an artist.

Markus has stated that the 'usual way of producing knowledge is to teach' and the 'characteristic teaching space is the lecture theatre'.[100] This was a function that Queen's Villa also fulfilled. Thus, throughout The Exhibition music recitals, cookery demonstrations and a range of international women speakers contributing to the lecture programme imparted *invisible* knowledge to Exhibition-goers.

In Room I, the principal reception room in Queen's Villa, music recitals were performed every Wednesday afternoon and Saturday evening. The *Clifton Chronicle* reported in detail on the musical programme

---

93 *Queen*, 7 March 1885, 2 47.
94 See Callen, *Angel in the Studio*, 51–94 for further detail.
95 *Catalogue*, 119.
96 *Englishwoman's Review*, 14 March 1885, 99.
97 *Catalogue*, 51.
98 At the Great Exhibition the class 'Fine Arts' included only sculpture, models and plastic art; all other fine arts were excluded.
99 See P. Gerrish Nunn, *Victorian Women Artists*, London: The Women's Press, 1987, 132–145; J. Marsh and P. Gerrish Nunn, *Pre-Raphaelite Women Artists*, London: Thames & Hudson, 1997 and Cherry, *Beyond the Frame*.
100 Markus, *Buildings and Power*, 169.

superintended by Miss Farler, which included a 'Pianoforte Recital of Works by Women Composers' performed twice by Mrs Roeckel.[101] The Exhibition programme also advertised a series of lectures given by female authorities on Tuesday and Saturday afternoons. Reflecting suitable occupations for women, these included 'Icelandic Spinning', 'Rational Dress', 'The Medical Education of Women in India', 'Dress, Economic and Technical', 'The Kindergarten System', 'Printing as a Trade for Women', and 'Wood Carving'. Given the close proximity of Bristol's Deaf and Dumb Institute to Queen's Villa, there was also a lecture on 'The Oral System of Teaching the Deaf and Dumb'.[102] Deemed 'an important element' of the Exhibition, several lectures were reprinted in the *Englishwoman's Review*, thus reaching an even wider audience.[103]

Many reviews commented on the growing importance of domestic science and the popularity of the 'practical' or 'demonstrative' cookery lessons given by Miss May Baker and Miss Arnott, 'holding Diplomas from South Kensington',[104] which took place 'deep down in the basement'.[105] There are interesting parallels between this new science practised in the basement of Queen's Villa and the similarly located chemistry laboratories found in many early museums. Markus has explained that while the positioning of laboratories was intended to counter the danger of fire and explosion and to prevent smells percolating upstairs, 'there were also social reasons – chemistry teaching was to a lower class of student'.[106] This socio-spatial positioning was true also of the cookery lessons given at Queen's Villa, which like the classes at the National School of Cookery were aimed largely at working-class women. However, the basement location of the cookery classes was not entirely successful. The *Clifton Chronicle* noted:

> Miss Baker is receiving a desirable amount of patronage in her demonstrative cookery lessons down-stairs, though it is to be regretted that the fumes from the gas-stove used in cooking, at times imparts an odour in the upper regions devoted to art which is far from savoury.[107]

---

[101] *Englishwoman's Review*, 15 May 1885, 212.

[102] Ibid. 15 April 1885, 163–164.

[103] Ibid.

[104] *Catalogue*, 62. Sir Henry Cole founded the National School of Cookery at South Kensington in 1874, which with its low fees aimed to attract and train working class women and servants. Its first Lady-Superintendent was the writer Lady Barker [Lady Broome] who recorded that when the school opened Henry Cole was unhappy because the 'pupils were by no means the class he wanted to get at. Fine Ladies of every rank, rich women, gay Americans in beautiful clothes, all thronged our kitchen, and the waiting carriages looked as if a smart party were going on within our dingy sheds'. Lady M.A. Broome, *Colonial Memories*, London: Smith, Elder & Co., 1904, chapter 16 'A Cooking Memory', 240–254.

[105] *Western Daily Press*, 26 February 1885, 6.

[106] Markus, *Buildings and Power*, 191.

[107] *Clifton Chronicle*, 11 March 1885, 5.

Conclusion

The Exhibition was ostensibly a celebration of women's work, yet the nature of the work exhibited, notably the examples of philanthropic double display and hagiographic self-display, confirmed the existence of 'at least two labour markets for women in Victorian Britain'.[108] The class identity of the politically motivated organisers was also reflected in the spatial arrangement of the exhibits displayed and the lectures that took place within Queen's Villa.

Having stood empty for twelve years, the original domestic function of Queen's Villa was almost over as the building was soon to be converted into a commercial property; another 'shift in function to a new use' which created 'new social relations with new meanings'.[109] However, if a 'building is a developing story, traces of which are always present',[110] then The Exhibition was a short, but important chapter in the narrative of Queen's Villa, which described its temporary transformation from a private domestic space into a public exhibition of work and knowledge. The functions of the drawing room, the dining room, the kitchen, the nursery and the bedroom had disappeared, but the physical form and space of this building remained unchanged and its original purpose remained psychologically and ideologically significant. Thus the built space of The Exhibition parodied the functions and subverted the meaning of the Villa while the 18,000 visitors found it acceptable to view women's industries in a building whose very name displayed its feminine and domestic origins.

---

[108]   Bartley, *Changing Role of Women*, 67.
[109]   Markus, *Buildings and Power*, 31.
[110]   Ibid, 5.

Figure 4.1
Photographic portrait of Emily Hall, c.1865
Source: Bromley Borough Council

Chapter 4

'Everything Whispers of Wealth and Luxury': Observation, Emulation and Display in the well-to-do late-Victorian Home

Trevor Keeble

In histories of the Victorian era, the domestic interior has played a crucial, if marginal, role. Constituting a private counterpart to a public world of commerce, technology and trade, the domestic sphere has been interpreted as a largely static barometer by which the dynamic activities of the public sphere might be measured. Central to our interpretation of this has been the way that the public/private dualism was inscribed through the conventions of gender and class. How and where these conventions were inscribed included elements that were variously textual, spatial and performative. It is with the intersection of these elements that this chapter, in common with other contributions to this volume, is primarily concerned. It considers manuscript evidence drawn from the diary of Emily Hall and the letters of Maud Messel, in a bid to explore the extent to which late-Victorian domestic space was both a gendered and a fluid social construction. Through close reading of these women's writings it is possible to ascertain the centrality of domestic space to their personal and social identities, and as such the role of personal identity in the process of homemaking. Whilst this chapter does not suggest that these women writers did not have male counterparts, it does propose that because the home, whether accurately or not, was so publicly conceived of as a feminine construction that it is through a female discourse that the social nature of this construction may be revealed.

The chapter begins by considering debates surrounding the separate spheres conception of Victorian domestic culture. It does so in order to suggest that the delineation of public and private spaces needs to be more fully considered alongside interpretations of Victorian middle-class consumption which have been characterised through concepts of taste and display. In particular, this discussion will consider the role of Veblen's concepts of conspicuous consumption and emulation, and the extent to which they compromise the coherence of the separate spheres interpretation. It proposes that although these ideas challenge the more conventional notion of the 'private' domestic sphere, they are useful for accessing broader conceptions of 'identity' as related to domestic taste, consumption and homemaking.

Through a close reading of the primary material, the chapter will then address the corresponding acts of displaying, and surveying, the domestic interior within Victorian middle-class culture. Specifically it explores these activities as a means of accessing the perceived understanding of the relationship of the interior and its occupant within the context of taste and identity, and the role that such broad social interaction played in the processes of Victorian homemaking.

Identity and Taste in the Private Sphere

The characterisation of nineteenth-century domestic space as a 'haven' from the harsh realities of the world has proven a most pervasive thesis; one which has come to underpin our historical understanding not just of domesticity, but of the period as a whole.[1] As one aspect of the separate spheres, it must be noted that domestic space has constituted a dramatically less studied and understood counterpart to the public sphere. Undoubtedly, the single most influential study of domestic culture to be published in recent decades is Leonore Davidoff and Catherine Hall's *Family Fortunes. Men and Women of the English Middle Class 1780–1850*.[2] Principally concerned with the formative interrelation between class and gender, this study recounts the formation of English middle-class culture through the consideration of religion and ideology, economic structure and opportunity, and everyday life. *Family Fortunes* is an explicit manifestation of the separate spheres conceptualisation of Victorian culture. It argues for a two-stage separation, firstly of work from living space, and subsequently domestic production such as 'cooking, eating, washing, sleeping' and other 'backstage functions' from the space of 'polite social intercourse'.[3] What is clear from Davidoff and Hall's study is that in spite of the delineation of middle-class life according to public and private ideals, the home fulfilled a vital social function, as confirmed by their assertion that 'a well ordered, well appointed home went some way to counteract the precariousness of middle-class life'.[4] In recent years the extent of these gendered prescriptions of space, and movement through

---

[1]   For an example of this see, J. Wolff, 'The Culture of Separate Spheres: the Role of Culture in Nineteenth-century Public and Private Life', in J. Wolff and J. Seed (eds), *The Culture of Capital: Art, Power and the Nineteenth-century Middle Class*, Manchester: Manchester University Press, 1988, 117–134.

[2]   L. Davidoff and C. Hall, *Family Fortunes. Men and Women of the English Middle Class 1780–1850*, London: Hutchinson, 1987.

[3]   Ibid, 359.

[4]   Ibid, 397.

space, has been questioned.[5] However, in a bid to demonstrate the public participation of women, and the domestic inhabitation of men, these studies have broadly failed to challenge the fundamental designation of the home as a private sphere.

Whether for or against the separate spheres understanding of nineteenth-century history, it is clear that this particular 'framework' has dominated the academic approach to understanding middle-class culture during the period. The most significant outcome of this has been the neglect of the domestic environment in its own right.[6] Whether historians have accepted the public/private dichotomy and acquiesced in the notion that the private sphere is largely beyond the purview of history, or rejected it in favour of positioning women within the public sphere, the result has been that domestic space has been marginalized and remained largely invisible. In the words of Janet Wolff: 'What is missing [...] is any account of life outside the public realm, of the experience of "the modern" in its private manifestations'.[7]

During the nineteenth century, conventions of 'good taste' were central to the construction and consolidation of class identity. By the beginning of that century the word 'taste' was understood as an 'abstraction of a human faculty to a generalized polite attribute'.[8] The evolutionary development of the term taste as an expression of cultural value and judgement is well beyond the scope of this chapter. However, it is important to note that its deployment within the context of nineteenth-century domestic culture was an act of authority and authorship: to have taste was to have the ability to judge. Throughout the nineteenth century the arena and contexts for the evolution of taste changed, and by the final decades of the century the

---

5   A. Vickery, 'Golden Age to Separate Spheres? A review of the Categories and Chronology of English Women's History.', *The Historical Journal*, 36:2, (1993); M. Nava, 'Modernity's Disavowal. Women, the City and the Department store', in M. Nava and A. O'Shea (eds), *Modern Times. Reflections on a Century of English Modernity*, London: Routledge, 1996; J. Tosh, *A Man's Place. Masculinity and the Middle-Class Home in Victorian England*, New Haven and London: Yale University Press, 1999.

6   A significant exception to this is Katherine Grier, *Culture and Comfort: People, Parlours and Upholstery 1850–1914*, Rochester and New York: The Strong Museum, 1988. Grier sought to complicate the separate spheres conception of the home by demonstrating its role as a social arena. For a recent attempt to draw upon Grier's approach to explain homemaking in the first half of the nineteenth century see Margaret Ponsonby, 'Ideals, Reality and Meaning. Homemaking in England in the First Half of the Nineteenth Century,' *Journal of Design History* (special issue: 'Anxious Homes' edited by Lesley Whitworth), 16:3, (2003), 201–214.

7   Janet Wolff, 'The Invisible Flaneuse: Women and the Literature of Modernity' in Andrew Benjamin (ed.), *The Problems of Modernity. Adorno and Benjamin*, London; Routledge, 1989, 154.

8   Raymond Williams, *Keywords. A Vocabulary of Culture and Society*, London: Fontana Press, 1976, 314.

dominant and most forceful mechanism by which these conventions of taste were established and disseminated was the expanding mass culture of that time.

The rapid growth of print media from mid-century combined with the increasing opportunities for shopping, leisure and entertainment to create an ever more disparate and diverse culture of tastes and conventions. In the context of domestic design and culture this was addressed by myriad treatises on the varied aspects of public and private duty. Among the first of these popular treatises on the transmission of domestic taste was Charles L. Eastlake's *Hints on Household Taste*, published in 1868.[9] This book is particularly significant for the study of later Victorian domestic culture for two reasons. The first is that it was written by an architect for a lay readership. Eastlake was, at the time of its publication, Secretary of the Institute of British Architects, and his book, though certainly not the first treatise upon domestic architecture written by an architect, was the first to seek explicitly to expound professional knowledge and judgement. The second reason for its significance was that it set the parameters for future didactic discussion of the space of the domestic interior. The book proved highly influential and through numerous editions found a readership on both sides of the Atlantic. The most prolific source of later domestic design advice was the widely published *Art at Home* series edited by the Reverend William J. Loftie for Macmillan during the 1870s and 1880s.[10] The proliferation of domestic design advice toward the end of the nineteenth century is testament to the fact that during this period it was commonly believed that there existed standards and conventions of domestic taste. Due to this, taste must be understood as a social phenomenon.

In recent years academic discussion of taste has been dominated by the work of French social anthropologist and sociologist Pierre Bourdieu.[11] Bourdieu's conceptualisation of taste enacted within differing 'fields' of activity has provided an analytical understanding of taste as 'capital' arising from 'habitus'. The suggestion implicit to this is that common experience provides common taste, but that this taste is continually in the process of revision according to changing and expanding experience.[12] A number of historians have drawn upon this thesis as a means of explaining cultural

---

9   C.L. Eastlake, *Hints on Household Taste in Furniture, Upholstery and Other Details*, London: Longmans, Green & Co, 1868.

10 The series comprised 12 volumes by different authors on a variety of domestic and leisure subjects and was published between 1876 and 1883. See Emma Ferry, *Advice, Authorship and the Domestic Interior: an interdisciplinary study of Macmillan's "Art at Home Series", 1876–83*, unpublished PhD Thesis, Kingston University, 2004.

11 Pierre Bourdieu, *Distinction. A Social Critique of the Judgement of Taste*, London: Routledge & Kegan Paul, 1984.

12 For a discussion of these positions in the context of cultural theory see Bridget Fowler, *Pierre Bourdieu and Cultural Theory. Critical Investigations*, London: Sage, 1997, 43–68.

change. In the context of explaining the role of elegance and gentility in eighteenth-century women's culture Amanda Vickery, in her study *The Gentleman's Daughter,* has suggested that the influence of Bourdieu's thinking has made historians reconsider the motivations behind consumption more closely.[13] An example of this is Linda Young's recent study *Middle Class Culture in the Nineteenth Century: America, Australia and Britain.*[14] In an attempt to demonstrate class consensus across geographic division in the first half of the nineteenth century, Young has drawn heavily upon the ideas of Pierre Bourdieu to explain the significance of taste and gentility within middle-class culture. Having noted the interrelationship between economic capital and cultural capital, Young has suggested that the late eighteenth and early nineteenth centuries witnessed 'a surge of advice manuals and self-help guides for the would-be genteel, as well as a proliferation of music, dancing, drawing and elocution masters to tutor aspirants in the genteel arts'.[15] Whilst this explanation of taste clearly situates it within the formal realm of education and self-improvement, it does anticipate a high degree of consensual cultural and social experience. Whilst such consensus may have been possible within the more socially restricted culture of the earlier period, its viability as an explanation of later Victorian culture is highly questionable, especially given that the final decades of the nineteenth century have been characterised as a period when class boundaries became increasingly less defined. Young makes clear the value of Bourdieu's conception of taste:

> The important insight given by the theory of habitus is to remove taste from the common-sense perception of being either a product of personal idiosyncrasy or purely a function of wealth; on the contrary, taste is as systematically defined as any of the conventions of social coherence.[16]

Whilst in general this position is a satisfactory explanation of the social determination of taste, there are two significant and problematic issues with it as a historical mechanism. The first is that it tends towards a monolithic characterisation of class culture and structure which, as Young has attempted to show, extends far beyond the immediate locale of everyday life to constitute a global state. The second is that even if this definition of taste – as a corollary of social coherence rather than personal expression – is a viable explanation of historical change, it is certainly not

---

13   Amanda Vickery, *The Gentleman's Daughter. Women's Lives in Georgian England,* London: Yale University Press, 1998, 163.

14   Linda Young, *Middle Class Culture in the Nineteenth Century: America, Australia and Britain,* London: Palgrave, 2002. Another study which relies heavily on Bourdieu's work to provide a 'cultural' characterisation of Victorian domestic and social life is Elizabeth Langland, *Nobody's Angels: Middle Class Women and Domestic Ideology in Victorian Culture,* Ithaca and London: Cornell University Press, 1995, 1–23.

15   Young, *Middle Class Culture,* 21.

16   Ibid.

one which would have been recognised or acknowledged within mainstream middle-class culture in the nineteenth century. Indeed, an emphasis upon taste as a cohesive factor contradicts the Victorian sensibility of taste as the expression of personality.

The social function of taste and consumption was clearly identified in this period by the American sociologist Thorstein Veblen. Veblen's account, *The Theory of the Leisure Class*, originally published in 1899, made explicit the role consumption played in the construction and consolidation of identity.[17] The central mechanisms of this process were identified by Veblen as 'pecuniary emulation' and 'conspicuous consumption'. The explanation of consumption practices as a means of 'other-directed' status striving has become somewhat orthodox in the study of consumption.[18] Veblen's assertion that during the final decades of the nineteenth century the emergent leisure classes of American society spent their money in order to emulate the practices, and tastes, of those whom they perceived to be their social superiors, has provided a model for understanding consumption explicitly in terms of 'status'.[19] The emphasis upon the 'conspicuous' nature of consumption practices highlights the degree to which academic understanding of consumption has often been reduced to a visible or spectacular act of display.[20] During recent years, Veblen's work has continued to influence the study of fashion and dress because its largely reductive proposition that clothing could be interpreted and understood only as appearance has facilitated a critical position for academic enquiry.[21] As a mobile and personalised commodity, the garment, or clothing, may be

---

[17]   Thorstein Veblen, *The Theory of the Leisure Class*, New York & London; Dover, 1994 (originally published in 1899).

[18]   For a comparison of the work of Bourdieu and Veblen in this area, see Daniel Miller, *Material Culture and Mass Consumption*, Oxford: Basil Blackwell, 1987, 149.

[19]   For a critique of this widely held position see Gilles Lipovetsky, *The Empire of Fashion. Dressing Modern Democracy* (translated by Catherine Porter), Princeton: Princeton University Press, 1994, 43–45. Lipovetsky has argued against what he viewed as the sociological reductivism of Veblen's characterisation in order to restate the 'aesthetic' importance of specific fashions. Glennie and Thrift have rejected the emphasis upon emulation and 'diffusionist' explanations within consumption studies because these have commonly emphasised a 'common state' on the part of consumers, and 'unidirectional' character in the transmission of ideas. P.D. Glennie and N.J. Thrift, 'Modernity, urbanism and modern consumption.', *Environment and Planning D: Society and Space*, 10, (1992), 432.

[20]   David B. Clarke has examined the debt that Jean Baudrillard and other twentieth-century writers upon consumption owe to the work of Veblen with respect to this issue. D.B. Clarke *The Consumer Society and the Postmodern City*, London; Routledge, 2003, 48–58.

[21]   This point is clearly evident in his original text which devotes an entire chapter to the consideration of 'Dress as an expression of pecuniary emulation.' Veblen, *Theory of the Leisure Class*, chapter 7.

easily interpreted as a conspicuous outward expression of its wearer's identity, but the same cannot be said of furniture and furnishing. Mobility and visibility, concepts central to recent interpretations of Victorian fashion and urban modernity,[22] are concepts largely denied to the study and interpretation of Victorian domestic furnishing, still defined as it is by the culture of separate spheres. For Bourdieu, and Veblen before him, identity was socially constructed, and yet the designation of the domestic realm as a 'private' space beyond the vision of others, renders the understanding of identity as socially conditioned and achieved through display, somewhat complicated. It is precisely this complication, which this chapter now aims to investigate.

Taste, Judgement and Display

In 1869 Emily (1819–1901) and Ellen Hall (1822–1911) decided to make an addition to their home in the village of West Wickham, Kent, and commissioned the highly regarded architect Richard Norman Shaw to design this (Figure 4.1). The unmarried sisters had inherited the family home, 'Ravenswood', on the death of their father in 1853, and lived there together until their own deaths. The processes of design and building proved extremely vexing for both the sisters and Shaw, who fell out repeatedly during this period over the costs, quality and design of the work.[23]

In spite of very clear misgivings about the work of the architect, it was not long before his addition to their house began to attract welcome attention and it seems that this attention somewhat mitigated the anxieties of recent months:

> Mr Steuart walked home with me & manifested so great a desire to see the new room, that in spite of all the scaffolding being about I took him up – he expressed himself greatly delighted with it = [sic] specially with the ceiling & on seeing the outside laughingly declared that "we shall never be able to endure the old part with its box like squareness – he foresaw we shall soon be altering it."[...] "You are like the gentleman who in an evil hour received a present of a pair of embroidered slippers – it obliged him to refurbish his whole house!"[24]

22 Elizabeth Wilson, *The Sphinx in the City. Urban Life, the Control of Disorder and Women*, Berkeley: University of California Press, 1991; Christopher Breward, *Fashioning London. Clothing and the Modern Metropolis*, Oxford: Berg, 2004.

23 For a discussion of the design and building of the new room see Trevor Keeble, 'Creating "The New Room": The Hall Sisters of West Wickham and Richard Norman Shaw', in Brenda Martin and Penny Sparke (eds), *Women's Places: Architecture and Design 1860–1960*, London: Routledge, 2003, 23–46.

24 Hall MS Diary, 29 January 1871, 294–295. When citing Hall's diaries (hereafter Diary) this chapter will refer to the date of entry and page number. Because there is no systematic order regarding volumes and years this will avoid

Mr Steuart's prophesy was certainly acknowledged in part some weeks later when Hall confided to her diary that 'indeed it is plain that we shall have someday of necessity to alter the outside- the new & the old will else drive us out of our wits. The West bedroom <u>box</u> is unendurable beside the picturesque wing which Mr Shaw has given us'.[25]

Through her record of her visitors' responses to the new room, Hall reconciled herself to it. She began to see it through their eyes, and this significantly altered her opinion of it, and led her to make quite pointed evaluations of her visitors' comments. Having received a letter from her friend the artist Collingwood Smith she noted:

> I cannot but be pleased that Collingwood Smith is complimentary about the new room "I have been trying to describe (he writes) your beautiful room to Mrs Smith: when done & furnished it will be a bijou: one of the most quaint and elegant things I have seen" – from an artist this is acceptable praise.[26]

His comments were certainly found to be more worthy than those of Hall's neighbour Mrs Steuart, whose praise of the room was dismissed as 'not worth much' due to her having 'no taste' and because she 'knows nothing about building – leaving all to her husband'.[27] This evaluation of her neighbours' tastes clearly coloured Emily's judgements of them:

> Mrs C [Collett] admired our room greatly & well she may after the hideous fashion in which they have done up their own library. I fancy from the pictures he puts up on his walls, that Mr. C has as much taste as his decorator, furniture or frame maker! He is a most ignorant – or at least narrow minded man =& has had to do with money all his life which is of itself very imperious unless like the Harrisons its influence is counter acted by the study of higher tastes at all times.[28]

Not all of the commentary upon the new room was so effusive in its praise. Of one visitor's comments Hall noted:

> He criticized the room, with good sense, tho' I don't agree with him. He utterly disapproves of the west window & small panes of glass, saying that windows being intended to be looked out from ought to take advantage of all the improvements art & science makes + not to return to anything of past times (unless it is superior) simply because it is harmonious in style or because the character of the new building requires it for consistency. Have it inconsistent. The lattice work, he does not object to, because the windows are so small &

confusion. Throughout her diary writing Hall established conventions of grammar and punctuation, particularly using the characters -, and =. Although these initially appear somewhat idiosyncratic these are remarkably consistent and have been reproduced as faithfully as possible.

[25]   Diary, 23 May 1871, 377.
[26]   Diary, Friday 29 March 1871, 334.
[27]   Diary, Monday 7 August 1871, 448.
[28]   Diary, Friday 18 August 1871, 468.

there is nothing to see & also because the small iron bars do not cut the sight so much as heavy wood work.[29]

Elsewhere Hall was happy to suggest envy and avarice lay at the heart of any criticism of the room, as is apparent in her description of a visit she received from Mr and Mrs Kingston Oliphant whilst Elizabeth and Gertrude Malkin, her cousins, were staying at Ravenswood:

> Like every body they are enchanted with the new room which is unquestionably a most successful venture. Eliz. & G. are the only persons whose praise has been quite luke warm & very so, so. James [Sherrard, Emily & Ellen's brother-in-law] burst out to G. didn't she think it beautiful, she replied very quietly "You know we have heard so much of it" implying that she does not think it beautiful & E [Elizabeth Malkin] immediately opined "you will find it very dark" – it sounds odd – with 5 windows! But it may be true = having several great trees so near. Then she complains of the stairs up to it "they are trying to my old bones!" "Nonsense" cried E [Ellen] laughing "there are not half as many stairs as to your drawing room & you don't find them trying!" So E [Elizabeth] was silent! I wander [sic] what she expected? Men in armour + gold shields beside them? Or carved stone roses & portcullis' like Hen:VIII's chapel – but our dear cousin never can admire anything which does not belong to herself![30]

What is suggested by this entry is that through the long process of the room's construction it had achieved a degree of fame within the Hall sisters' social circle, and judgement of it was clearly felt to imply judgement of the sisters themselves.

The extent to which domestic space was subject to the surveillance of others is also apparent in Maud Messel's letters (Figure 4.2). Written nearly 30 years after Hall's diary, Messel's correspondence with her mother and father, the *Punch* cartoonist Linley Sambourne, demonstrates the extent to which, even at the end of the nineteenth century, the social conventions surrounding judgement and taste were reflective processes which revealed as much about the person making judgement, as they did about those judged.[31]

During one particular visit to Mr and Mrs Jack Scott in Dundee, Messel was driven to write her mother a lengthy and somewhat unflattering description of her host's home. This letter is highly revealing of Messel's self-perceptions, tastes and preferences:

> This house is large and built like most of the Scotch houses of grey stone [...]But of all the terrible & awful furniture I ever saw, none equals this. They are both so dear & so kind that I feel a brute ever to be so bold enough, even up my sleeve to disagree with all the little tender kindness'[sic], which are put out

---

29 Diary, Monday 18 June 1871, 391.

30 Diary, Thursday 3 August 1871, 441–442.

31 For a discussion of the Linley Sambourne family see Shirley Nicholson, *A Victorian Household*, London: Barrie and Jenkins, 1988 (based on the Diaries of Marion Sambourne).

for us. As I look around my room now, for I am in my bedroom, there is nothing that is not mine, that I can rest my eye on pleasingly. The fire place, bed hanging & curtains are, of course, of very expensive & hideously ugly bluish plush trimmed all round with wool ... to match. The chairs are all in different coloured gaudy stamped velvet. Each with a scarlet cushion in attendance. The pictures I would rather not describe but they look as if they had been taken out of the Christmas number of the illustrated papers. The brass work is ornate & very dirty, except for one or two things which are lackered [sic].The books on the shelf have titles such as "The Bravest of the Brave" and "Clues" two which just catch my eye from this little writing table on which I am now writing to you darling. I have removed <u>four</u> unnecessary pincushions from the dressing table to make room for some of my things & two large glass bottles which were reposing there with no object or aim. I should like to have put them out of sight altogether but instead they have taken up their quarters on a queer sort of table in front of the window where they are the companion of many other things I should take delight in sending off to some other world. (the one below!) A ticking clock keeps me company & rather annoys me for it is so very loud, it ought to go to the nursery where it might be drowned by babies howls. Unfortunately Mr. & Mrs. Jack Scott are childless & therefore there are no dear beings in the house to smash things & it is in great need of the dear beings.[32]

Figure 4.2
Photographic portrait of Maud Sambourne, afterwards Messel, 1896
Source: Royal Borough of Kensington and Chelsea, Linley Sambourne House

---

[32] ST/2/2/328 Linley Sambourne Archive, Kensington Central Library Local Studies Collection. Letter written from Tay Park, Perth Rd, Dundee. Thursday 29 September 1898. All references with an ST prefix are held at this location.

Messel conveyed a very clear sensibility about domestic furnishing and decor, and one which the letter suggests her mother would have shared. In her criticisms of the room, she reluctantly exposed her hosts' lack of taste and refinement. Equating the 'very expensive' with the 'hideously ugly', her comments imposed a moral judgement concerning the expression of wealth through decoration, and this judgement was further conveyed by the comparison of the room's pictures with the ephemeral imagery of a mass media newspaper. Whilst damning the excess of colour, gaudy decoration, lacquer and dirt, Messel also condemned her surroundings for their lack of purpose, object or aim. This double-edged critique masked a more deeply seated criticism of her hosts which she only intimated through reference to their choice of books. Undoubtedly, Messel understood the room from which she wrote to be the expression and manifestation of its owners' tastes, culture and intelligence.

In a subsequent letter she informed her mother, 'I have not yet recovered from my aversion to all the things in this room. They still annoy me when I wake up & all day long when I am in it, until bedtime [...] The jugs are swans which hold only a little & are ridiculous to look at. They annoy me every time I go to wash'.[33] Expressing a Ruskinian dislike of such 'falsity',[34] and having been raised in a notably aesthetic home, Messel's taste must be considered reasonably well informed and this in turn would account for the severity of her judgement. On arriving at the home of their next hosts, Mr and Mrs Manisty of Selkirk, she was able to write more positively of her surroundings:

> We have come to stay in the dearest of little Scotch farm houses, whitewashed & over grown with creepers. It is surrounded by a sweet old garden & there are a number of very noisy cocks in the yard at the side [...] It is so delicious & homely here & the furniture is mostly old & in excellent taste.[35]

In contrast to the evident wealth of their previous surroundings, the more humble farmhouse and its aged and vernacular style appealed to a rather romantic and wistful aspect of Messel's taste.

Observation, Identity and the Process of Home-making

Whilst it is clear that both Hall and Messel participated in and understood the conventions of taste and judgement in the Victorian home, both women's writings betray the extent to which these conventions informed and underpinned their own attempts at homemaking as a means of

---

33   ST/2/2/330 2 October 1898.
34   J. Ruskin, *The Seven Lamps of Architecture*, London; George Allen and Unwin, 1925, 30–33 (originally published in 1849).
35   ST/2/2/333 Monday 10 October 1898, Lewenshope, Yarrow, Selkirk (E.F. Manisty).

projecting status and personal identity. Sensitivity toward the conspicuousness of wealth through furnishing and decoration is present in many of the judgements made by Hall. Constrained by the genteel poverty of spinsterhood, she revealed an ambiguous understanding of the correlation between taste and money as she reflected upon the sometimes detrimental effects of money. Discussing a Mr and Mrs Hoffman she noted:

> He has been extravagant ever since he began life at Oxford: since his marriage he has continually been hiring houses, furnishing them beautifully & then in a few weeks parting with them – she can't be in a house a fortnight without putting pretty things into the drawing room & antimacassars with pink satin bows at the corners.[36]

This transitory over-consumption was found, in spite of the beauty of the houses, to transgress common notions of domestic taste. On a number of occasions Hall speculated on the money her various hosts must have been making in order to be able to afford the things she saw.[37] On one occasion she acknowledged the social cleavage such objects might articulate:

> she is a great beauty and he is said to be the Christy of Bond St. the Hatter but he is reasonably refined in manner, & has cultivated tastes = so that we should be less fortunately well off he showed us a pair of old china vases, which he had the good luck to buy at a small dealers in Kingston for £15 which Wareham, the London dealer promises £40 for, if he wished to sell them.....People can do these things when they make £.......s a day in trade![38]

Although Hall prided herself on her thrift and honesty, noting how 'Lady R [Roden] laughs at me immensely because I always tell folks that plated things are not silver'[39] her inability to afford items was articulated in clearly emotional terms: 'Went to an auction of old furniture, Gries de Flandre which made my eyes water that I could not buy any'.[40] Writing of a visit paid by her neighbour Mrs Hamilton, Hall noted:

> Mrs. H. went into the drawing room to see all the alterations & laughed at our extravagances about the new furniture – I did not say as I might have done – "we buy at auctions & so get it all for half the price that you would give the regular upholsterers"![41]

---

[36]   Diary, Saturday 11 February 1871, 306.
[37]   Diary, Wednesday 5 April 1871 341. Commenting on dinner with the Lawrence Harrisons, Hall speculated 'He is filling his house with pretty things – china, silver & so on, & his wife showed us with great pride her Parisian mugs & old lace – He must be making Pots full! of money'.
[38]   Diary, Wednesday 22 June 1870, 120.
[39]   Diary, Monday 3 July 1871, 410.
[40]   Diary, Wednesday 17 May 1871, 372.
[41]   Diary, Monday 18 June 1871, 392.

Of course another motivating factor for the surveillance of other people's homes was to find inspiration for one's own. Both Hall and Messel reveal such a purpose in their writing. Hall's diary conveyed a reflexivity to her surveillance of others which suggests, although privately, that she was willing to follow a lead:

> Called on Mrs Hamilton.... She showed us the alterations inside =which are very nice indeed & make the home now quite charming – They have put Howard's patent parquet down for several of their sitting room floors: an arrangement which does away with the necessity of carpeting so much. It is a comparatively new invention & so much cheaper than the usual way of parqueting = so I shall try if we also can have it.[42]

This mode of judgement was more apparent in the writing of Messel. Whilst on holiday near Portofino in northern Italy, Messel described for her mother the little local cottage shared by two Englishmen, a Mr Ryle and Mr Hood. Her commentary on their home and their lives within it depicts something of an exotic fantasy. However, her descriptions attest to her detailed interest:

> Their little house is too sweet & must be the sort of place one reads about in a fairy tale. The walls are whitewashed and the furniture is simple & very clean & most of the chairs & sofas are covered with white dimity. Bowls of roses adorned every nook & there were a few books about. The floors are tiled in red & the little kitchen in stone. Two easy chairs awaited their masters outside the home & two hammocks a little higher up in the trees. It might have been the Bears' cottage without the little bear! After a thorough examination & mental inventory of the interior of the cottage we climbed up to a wee stone square with seats all around under a fir tree from which we could see all round the bay & a long way beyond.[43]

Clearly, through her examination of the interior Messel revealed herself to be looking out for styles and arrangements which she might herself adapt or employ within her own home. On another occasion she described for her mother a visit she and her husband Leonard had made to Stonor Park in Henley on Thames. The description emphasised the tasteful luxury of this domestic space and Messel's comparison with her own home:

> The linen is magnificent in all the rooms & imagine darling we sleep beneath £40 sheets! My dressing table cover is made of the finest embroidered linen

---

[42] Diary, Saturday 4 February 1871, 301. There is some ambiguity about Hall's willingness to admit inspiration for fear of lacking originality as is suggested by comments regarding one visitor, a Mr. Smith, who suggested that the newly panelled hall is 'after the style & fashion (with a difference!) of a part of Old Knole – called the gallery, but which is never shown to strangers, save by special order'. Diary, Wednesday 22 March 1871, 331.

[43] ST/2/2/657 5 May 1905, Grand Hotel Splendide, Gare Santa Margherita Ligure, Italy.

edged with lovely fresh crochet! & the towels are all embroidered & everything whispers of wealth and luxury. There are lots of things which I can learn, as

there always are in all houses & little practical things one can copy. Otherwise our own house is run as well or almost as well & the old rooms are much prettier.[44]

The search for inspiration was not, however, confined to private homes. In early 1905 Messel wrote to her mother describing a visit to Hampton Court. Her letter made the reasons for her visit explicit:

I took several notes and made some rough sketches in [my] copy book for the new house. I want to copy some of the beautiful old fireplaces in the palace as they are so simple & yet so suitable to our rooms. I also made some notes about the doors & windows which will be useful to have by one.[45]

Visiting Hampton Court, Messel was looking for stylistic influences for her new house in Lancaster Gate:

The latter part of the palace was built in William and Mary's reign & it is that that we want to copy & being quite in keeping with the outside of Lancaster Gate. Pillars, lobbies & high ceilings were all *en royen* then, so it is an easy framework to build our plan upon.[...] We are going to panel our room entirely with old oak (Tudor) & as Lennie will have his room made into a billiard room mine will not be allowed the name of "boudoir" as he will share it with me, but it will be called the "Oak room" or the "Tudor room". The windows there are going to be copied from old leaded casements & will have yellow curtains. The wall between the two rooms has been knocked down & it will be one room. There will be nice windows like this with little low window seats. These nice windows look to the back so that it does not make any difference to the outside appearance of the house.[46]

The understanding of the Victorian domestic interior as a wholly private environment is also challenged by evidence of the participation of others in the decoration and furnishing of it. Hall wrote on a number of occasions of visitors arriving with gifts of lace and other small items with which she decorated her home.[47] Of a dinner party she recalled how:

Mr. Mant presented me with a little parcel after dinner with a half heard speech about my predilection for old china =& could I accept it – which covered me with blushes as if I were 16! It proved to be a beautiful little salad bowl of Old Dresden in medallions with a delicate yellow ground = a charming little dish, it was most kind & pretty of him & pleased me immensely.[48]

---

44   ST/2/2/859 25 February 1908, Stonor Park, Henley-on-Thames.
45   ST/2/2/650 Sunday 26th March 1905, 27 Gloucester Terrace.
46   ST/2/2/650 Sunday 26 March 1905, 27 Gloucester Terrace.
47   Diary, Friday 30 June 1871, 406.
48   Diary, Thursday 22 June 1871, 400.

Due to the evident pride she took in the decoration and furnishing of her home, the gift of a piece of old Dresden china was a socially intimate act. It reflects the extent to which she was identified as someone for whom this gift would be significant, and importantly as someone who would know what to do with it. On another occasion her writing reveals objects employed in very different circumstances. Whilst describing a visit paid to them by Lady Roden and her daughter Flora, Hall wrote that Roden:

> peeped into the closet in the hall & espying all our small collection of china there begged to be allowed to arrange it in the marqueterie cabinet; at which Flora screamed out in delight that she would help = so some dusters were brought & they set to work & "my lady" made a pair of very dirty hands & speedily relinquished the arrangement to Flora & contented herself with being that young lady's slave & only preparing the cups & jars for her to arrange! which she has done very prettily = a great improvement upon the empty shelves.[49]

This active engagement of others in the display of the home challenges any notion of a static and presented environment that has characterised the home as a separate sphere. It seems that as much as Hall invested herself into her home, she also allowed others to do so.

The home was undoubtedly a significant aspect of both Hall and Messel's personal identities and both women took an immense pride in these spaces. At times Hall was quite candid about her vanity and the personal effects of praise. In May 1871 she and her sister Ellen invited Frederick and Robert Harrison to dinner, and much attention was paid to the new room and the sisters' refurbished hall:

> The two Harrisons being alone at Eden Park we asked them to dine here –& duly exhibited our new toys, as I call them the "library" & the hall – with each of which they are delighted & of which indeed we only ourselves begin to see the beauty = the carpenters have only left the Hall on Saturday tho' it is our own & mostly by our own wits adorned. I must say it is <u>delightful</u> & so pretty –........ The oak is lovely & between us we have managed a mantelpiece which is quite neat & suits well enough with the rest: it has been a sort of dream with me, to have panelled rooms & pretty ceilings & now I have both! & my vanity is flattered besides by knowing that a prettier Hall than ours is not to be seen in the neighbourhood![50]

An entry for July of the same year suggests that although she revelled in the praise of her new room and through her diary did not conceal her pride in it, she was aware that such pride and vanity was perhaps unbecoming. Describing a visit from their friend Rose Anne, Hall wrote:

---

49   Diary, Saturday 1 July 1871, 407.
50   Diary, Tuesday 23 May 1871, 377.

We showed off our new play things – I always feel something proud and vain – the test of the eye strongly. Which I am afraid is wicked. When I open the door to show it for the first time – every body says the same thing & the room is certainly a beautiful one! She was rapturous about it – Even my vanity was satisfied![51]

In a telling sentence Hall made explicit, through her choice of language, the effects of the sisters' spectacular new domestic addition. Commenting on the arrival of their elder sister Laura and her family she noted: 'after luncheon we exhibited the morning room & received as much admiration as we could desire'.[52]

Conclusion

The writings of Hall and Messel illustrate the extent to which the Victorian domestic interior was indeed a social space. This material exposes the ways that social engagement consciously fed the domestic 'design' process of the later Victorian years. In an era which saw the widespread proliferation of consumer culture, the social conventions of visiting provided models of design, behaviour and taste, and these models were understood and interpreted as explicit acts of homemaking. Having noted earlier that the separate spheres conception of the home as a private space was potentially at odds with the proposition that identity is socially constructed, it might be suggested that the late-Victorian domestic interior illustrates the co-existence of both understandings. For whilst this chapter has argued that the interior was subject to social scrutiny and construction, it acknowledges that this was explicitly bound within local social and class structures. Together this matrix of the performative, the textual and the spatial created the late-Victorian domestic interior.

---

[51]   Diary, Monday 31 July 1871, 434.
[52]   Diary, Sunday 10 September 1871, 485.

Figure 5.1
Katherine Buildings, Cartwright Street, East London.
Source: Reproduced by kind permission of Cambridge University Press from J.N. Tarn, 'Five Percent Philanthropy: An Account of Housing in Urban Areas, 1840–1914', Cambridge: Cambridge University Press, 1973

Chapter 5

Women Rent Collectors and the Rewriting of Space, Class and Gender in East London, 1870–1900

Ruth Livesey

> I enjoy the life of the people at the East End – the reality of their efforts and aims, the simplicity of their sorrows and of their joys; I feel I can *realize* it – see the tragic and comic side of it. To some extent, I can grasp the forces which are swaying to and fro, raising and depressing this vast herd of human beings. I feel that my painstaking study of detail will help me towards that knowledge of the whole, towards which I am constantly striving. Anyway, I shall leave steps cut in the rock, from the summit of which man will eventually map out the conquered land of social life.[1]

In May 1888 Beatrice Webb envisaged the East End of London with a new-found sense of detachment and containment.[2] Working as a rent collector at Katherine Buildings in Whitechapel a few years earlier, Webb had been alternately attracted and repelled by her part in what she termed the 'certain weird romance' of philanthropy, 'with neither beginning nor end'.[3] By the time Webb completed this diary entry, however, she had achieved some success with her early publications on social questions and was coming to identify herself as a social investigator, as distinct from the lady philanthropists at work in the East End. In the process of recognising that success, Webb adopted a spatial metaphor which elevated her above the 'constantly decomposing mass' of human beings who drifted in and out of the neighbourhood of the docks and who had provided her first occasion for social investigation in the mid 1880s.[4] Seen from above, that weird romance of endless alternations of tragedy and comedy falls into a pattern

---

[1] Norman and Jeanne Mackenzie (eds), *The Diary of Beatrice Webb vol. 1*, London: Virago, 1982 (MS diary 5 May 1888).

[2] Although the majority of the works studied here predate Beatrice Potter's marriage to Sidney Webb in 1892 I maintain consistency by referring to her by her married name. For a biographical overview of this period of Webb's life see Deborah Nord, *The Apprenticeship of Beatrice Webb*, Amherst: University of Massachusetts Press, 1985.

[3] Mackenzie, *Diary of Beatrice Webb*, 132. Entry dated 8 March 1885.

[4] Ibid.

of generic forces to be grasped and understood by the aerial observer seated in the gods: Webb carves the steps up to where 'man' can map the geography of poverty and turn the crowded streets into perfectly legible space.

This chapter starts with Webb, perversely and precisely, because her commitment to generalising and quantifying social space – to the emergent disciplines of social science and social investigation – was so unusual among the middle-class women rent collectors and philanthropic housing managers whose work forms the subject of this chapter. Whilst Webb's former co-workers at Katherine Buildings expressed freely various forms of dissent from the philosophies of the founder of philanthropic rent collecting schemes, Octavia Hill, all were in agreement with Hill's basic tenet that the success of such schemes lay in detailed work with individual families. Indeed it was Hill's insistence that the work was detailed and relied on 'personal influence' and regular household visits that demarcated rent collecting and philanthropic housing management as 'lady's work' from the 1870s onwards. As we shall see, Hill's rhetoric of place, belonging and community rewrote the London slums as an environment in which the presence of the educated lady on the streets was natural and necessary. Webb's interest in seeing the conquered land of social life laid prone beneath her is a mode of disciplining space with which we are all too familiar thanks to the diffuse influences of Michel Foucault across the academy during the past decade. But women rent collectors in the East End shaped built space in a rather different manner, marking place and belonging out of the minutiae of daily social – and material – exchanges at the level of the street, the staircase and the corridor in a mode that exposes the limitations of disciplinary surveillance.

In offering a critique of the limitations of Foucault's work for an understanding of the practice of space, Michel de Certeau starts with an account of the scopic fantasy of seeing the city mapped out from above. Uncanny as the resemblance is to Webb's vision of the East End, Certeau's essay now comes with its own weird air of tragedy, as he ascends to see Manhattan from the 107th floor of the World Trade Center:

> For a moment, the eye arrests the turbulence of this sea swell of verticals; the vast mass freezes under our gaze ... To what erotics of knowledge can the ecstasy of reading such a cosmos be connected? Delighting in it violently as I do, I speculate as to the origin of the pleasure of seeing such a world wrought by hubris 'as a whole', the pleasure of looking down upon, of totalising this vastest of human texts.[5]

Certeau concludes that the desire to fix the ocean of the crowd on a map in this manner and make it an entirely readable text can only end in fiction. For in order to fulfil such a fantasy the observer must 'remove himself [sic]

---

5   Michel de Certeau, 'Walking in the City' repr. in Graham Ward (ed.), *The Certeau Reader*, Oxford: Blackwell, 2000, 101.

from the obscure interlacing of everyday behaviour and make himself a stranger to it'.[6] On the contrary, Certeau asserts that it is down below, in the streets, that the spaces of the city are written by the wanderings of its common pedestrian practitioners. Spatial usage, he concludes, creates the determining conditions of social life and finds diverse, resilient methods of evading discipline and surveillance.[7]

Octavia Hill and a Place Called Home

Certeau's late twentieth-century terminology of 'pedestrian utterings' might at first seem far removed from the daily practices of women rent collectors in the East End in the 1880s. Yet drawing on the records of Katherine Buildings, the case study which forms the latter half of this chapter, reveals an endless process of marking place within urban space through daily practice at street level. The process emerged from a continuous struggle between lady rent collectors and their working-class tenants concerning the definition, use and ownership of staircases, club-rooms and dwellings. Although Hill's numerous writings on the subject of housing management never envisaged the sort of contests with tenants faced by the rent collectors of Katherine Buildings, she too insisted that place and space were shaped by more than the physical environment and an all-seeing eye. Hill's first venture in rent collecting in Marylebone in 1865 was sponsored by her friend John Ruskin, to whom she promised a five per cent annual profit in addition to the altruistic benefit of seeing an improvement in the appearance and moral tone of the alley and its inhabitants.[8] By 1874, Hill and the host of lady volunteers trained by her were responsible for fifteen different housing schemes throughout London, mostly old, run down streets and courts but with a few newer properties dotted throughout the capital.[9] Hill's philanthropic scheme was a simple one on the face of it: the

---

6   Ibid, 102.
7   Ibid, 105.
8   On philanthropic housing schemes during this period see Eugenie Ladner Birch and Deborah S. Gardener, 'The Seven-Percent Solution: A Review of Philanthropic Housing, 1870–1910' *Journal of Urban History*, 7, (1981), 403–436; John Nelson Tarn, *Five Percent Philanthropy: An Account of Housing in Urban Areas, 1840–1914*, Cambridge: Cambridge University Press, 1973; for Octavia Hill's role in the development of such schemes see Jane Lewis, *Women and Social Action in Victorian and Edwardian England*, Aldershot: Edward Elgar,1991, 34–53; Julia Parker, *Women and Welfare: Ten Victorian Women in Public Social Service* London: Macmillan, 1989 153–164; Caroline Morrell, 'Octavia Hill and Women's Networks in Housing Management' in *Gender, Health and Welfare* Ann Digby and John Stewart (eds), London: Routledge, 1996, 90–118.
9   For a discussion of other aspects of Hill's work see the chapter in the volume by Anderson and Darling; for a consideration of the broader context for this work see Meller's.

perfunctory efforts of the landlord's 'ordinary clerk' were to be replaced by the regular attentions of a 'sympathetic ... lady' volunteer. The weekly round of rent collection was to be transformed into an altruistic gesture and the waged working-class male collector displaced by a handful of ladies, interested only in the tenants and not in personal remuneration.[10]

Hill figured such property management as a proper feminine duty, representing it as an extended version of middle-class women's domestic responsibilities. Like so many middle-class women social activists of the period, Hill's rhetoric of maternalism demarcated a specific female realm of citizenship, as is evident in her argument that 'Ladies must do' rent collecting 'for it is household work'.[11] In demonstrating the ethical benefits of her scheme to her donors, Hill's writings in the 1870s and 1880s represent her as an authoritative mother, disciplining the characters of her unruly infantilised tenants.[12] It was only once slum tenants had learned to 'love' their lady rent collector and feel shame at the prospect of disappointing her with unkempt interiors and drunkenness, Hill asserted, that there was any point in improving the accommodation itself.[13] Whitewash and new window panes were the reward for stirring signs of character growth: only then, when character had been re-inscribed through the new maternal example, would such work have any lasting effect; otherwise the buildings would sink back into disrepair reflecting the inadequate characters of those within.[14] The philosopher Bernard Bosanquet, who worked with Hill in the establishment of the London Charity Organisation Society (COS), spelled out the deeply embedded Idealism of such an approach to social reform when, having accepted that economic and material conditions had 'some' influence on the operation of individual will, he went on to assert that 'circumstance is modifiable by

---

[10] See Eileen Janes Yeo *The Contest for Social Science*, London: Rivers Oram, 1996, 223 for a discussion of a widespread pattern by which middle-class women volunteers replaced waged male workers in such fields of social intervention in the later nineteenth century.

[11] Octavia Hill, *Letter to My Fellow Workers*, London: Houseboy Brigade, 1883; on maternalism and female citizenship see Seth Koven and Sonya Michel (eds), *Mothers of a New World: Maternalist Politics and the Origin of Welfare States*, London: Routledge, 1993.

[12] See for example Octavia Hill, 'Report of an Attempt to Raise a Few of the London Poor without Gifts', London: G Meyer, [n.d. pamphlet].

[13] Octavia Hill, 'Blank Court: Or, Landlords and Tenants', *Macmillan's Magazine* 24 (1871) 456–465 (460).

[14] Octavia Hill, 'The Work of Volunteers in the Organization of Charity', *Macmillan's Magazine* 26 (1872) 441–449 (445); on the significance of 'character' in late nineteenth-century social thought see Stefan Collini, *Public Moralists: Political Thought and Intellectual Life in Britain, 1850–1930*, Oxford: Clarendon Press, 1991, 109–120; Ruth Livesey, 'Reading for Character: Women Social Reformers and Narratives of the Urban Poor in Late Victorian and Edwardian London', *Journal of Victorian Culture* 9:1, (2004), 43–67.

character and character alone'.[15] 'Material conditions', Bosanquet concluded, 'are necessary to existence; but they are themselves dependent to an enormous extent on the energy of the mind which they surround'.[16] From the mid 1870s onwards it was middle-class women who were imagined as the agents of the character transformation necessary in such Idealist analyses of poverty, stimulating individual will into greater efforts through their personal example.[17] They were to be the idea of regeneration embodied: character, will and moral improvement made flesh. Small wonder, then, that Beatrice Webb felt 'rather depressed by the bigness' of the work when she took up rent collecting in Whitechapel in 1885.[18] 'When I look at those long balconies and think of all the queer characters – occupants and would-be occupants and realize that the characters of the community will depend on our personal power', she confessed, 'I feel rather dizzy'.[19]

The predominant Idealism of the social thought disseminated by Hill and the COS in the late-nineteenth century meant that middle-class women rent collectors were defined as makers of place. The material conditions of the built environment were granted such limited powers of determinism that it was the practice of management itself that was imagined to re-structure the lived space of the slums. Drawing explicitly on Ruskin's ideals of separate, gendered spheres, Hill argued that the rent collectors should rule like 'Queens ... each in her own domain', taking complete control 'as they would of their own house, garden or field'.[20] With this rhetorical stroke, Hill transformed the unmapped, unknowable slum spaces of the city into a rural idyll of feminised nostalgia. 'The old word "landlord"', Hill wrote in 1871, 'is a proud one to many an English gentleman, who holds dominion over the neat cottage', but in the city,

> Where are the owners, or lords or ladies, of most courts like that in which I stood with my two fellow workers? Who holds dominion there? Who heads the

---

[15]   Bernard Bosanquet, *Aspects of the Social Question*, London: Macmillan, 1895, vi.
[16]   Ibid, 111–112.
[17]   On the social influence of philosophical Idealism during this period see Melvin Richter, *The Politics of Conscience: T.H. Green and his Age*, London: Weidenfield and Nicholson, 1964 and also A. Vincent and R. Plant, *Philosophy, Politics and Citizenship*, Oxford: Blackwells, 1984.
[18]   For an account of Webb's work in Whitechapel see Nord, *The Apprenticeship of Beatrice Webb*; Rosemary O'Day, 'How Families Lived Then: Katherine Buildings, East Smithfield, 1885–1890' in Ruth Finnegan and Michael Drake, eds, *Studying Family and Community History* Vol. I, Cambridge: Cambridge University Press, 1994, 129–165.
[19]   Mackenzie, *The Diaries of Beatrice Webb*, 133. Entry dated 13 March 1885.
[20]   Octavia Hill, *The Importance of Raising the Poor Without Almsgiving*, repr. from Transactions of the Social Science Association, 1869. See John Ruskin, 'Of Queens' Gardens' in *Sesame and Lilies: Two Lectures*, London: Smith and Elder, 1864.

tenants there? If any among the nobly born, or better educated, own them, do they bear the mark of their hands?... There are in those courts as loyal English hearts as ever loved or reverenced the squire in the village, only they have been so forgotten.[21]

Gareth Stedman Jones and Deborah Weiner have both indicated the reach of this desire to restructure the slums by introducing a new urban squirearchy to the East End, given visible form in Jacobean-revival manor houses like Toynbee Hall and numerous other settlement enterprises of the 1870s and early 1880s.[22] The particular significance of Hill's scheme in this wider picture of philanthropy in 'outcast London' stems from the deeply embedded association of femininity with these nostalgic investments in place and belonging.

The suggestion here is that whilst social surveys and slum clearances of the 1880s and 1890s functioned with a model of spatiality – bodies and buildings frozen by an abstracting glance from above in the process of becoming – both Hill's work and the Idealist phase of the Settlement Movement were rooted in place and being. Feminist geographers such as Gillian Rose and Doreen Massey have done much to draw attention to the gendered connotations of such distinctions between place and space. 'Particular ways of thinking about space and place', Massey suggests, 'are tied up with ... particular social constructions of gender relations'.[23] Whilst the space of modernity, Massey argues, following Henri Lefebvre, becomes an abstract product of the masculine gaze, place retains (problematically) feminised connotations of being and belonging.[24] Rose concludes that 'desired but lost, place seems to stand for nothing other than the inaccessible plenitude of ... the (lost) Mother'.[25] Such underlying psychic investments in the geography of urban poverty naturalised the presence of middle-class women rent collectors on the streets of London for the alms-giving public: not public women but new land*ladies* who promised to replace that lost or neglectful mother. Out of the apparently chaotic space of the slums, Hill's rent collecting schemes seemed to offer a means of marking down the boundaries of place, reinstating social hierarchies, bringing men in from the pubs, women from the doorsteps, children from

---

21   Octavia Hill, 'Blank Court; Or, Landlords and Tenants' *Macmillan's Magazine* 24 (1871) 456–465 (456).

22   Gareth Stedman Jones, *Outcast London: A Study in the Relationship between the Classes in Victorian Society*, Oxford: Oxford University Press, 1971; Deborah Weiner, *Architecture and Social Reform in Late-Victorian London*, Manchester: Manchester University Press, 1994; for a reading of this desire as transgressive eroticisation see Seth Koven, *Slumming: Sexual and Social Politics in Victorian London*, Princeton: Princeton University Press, 2004.

23   Doreen Massey, *Space, Place and Gender*, Cambridge: Polity, 1994, 2.

24   Ibid, 182–183.

25   Gillian Rose, *Feminism and Geography: The Limits of Geographical Knowledge*, Cambridge: Polity, 1993, 60.

the street, and drawing the lines around a definitive and recognisable place called home.

Hill's own investment in such small places of belonging and community is evident from her initial resistance to wholesale slum clearance and the construction of 'regular ... monotonous' model dwelling blocks.[26] Whilst such blocks might promise better sanitary conditions and ensure that the tenants were 'inspected and disciplined, every inhabitant registered and known' by the relevant authorities, Hill argued that existing slum courts and 'cottage property' enabled the collectors to work more effectively with smaller groups of residents.[27]

> For after all the 'home', the 'life', does not depend on the number of appliances, or even in any deep sense on the sanitary arrangements. I heard a working-man say once, with some coarseness but with much truth, 'Gentlemen think if they put a water-closet to every room they have made a home of it,'... [T]here is more decency in many a tiny little cottage in Southwark, shabby as it may be, – more family life in many a one room let to a family, than in many a populous block.[28]

Hill defined 'home' as something quite autonomous from the built environment: an affect of place, rather than a determinate of space. A place called home, according to Hill, was made out of the ineffable qualities of 'decency' and inward-looking family life, and took shape as a known community against the anonymity of modern urban space. Hill's theories of housing reform thus resisted the production of the putatively abstract, quantifiable, disciplinary, urban spaces for the working classes, which resulted from the slum clearance policies of the 1880s. Instead she read into stinking courts of decaying 'cottages' the nostalgic possibilities of place, of 'gardens or fields' and villages for the landlady to rule over with sweet order.

Women Rent Collectors and the Practice of Space in Katherine Buildings

By the time Hill penned her comments on model dwellings for Charles Booth's *Life and Labour* survey in 1891, however, she had come to accept that the future of the housing of the working classes in the city lay in such new blocks, and that it was 'not very profitable to spend time in considering whether this is a fact to rejoice in or deplore'.[29] Housing trusts such as Guinness and Peabody, along with new philanthropic companies like the

---

26   Octavia Hill, 'The Influence of Model Dwellings on Character' in Charles Booth ed. *Life and Labour of the People of London* Vol. II, London: Williams and Norgate, 1891, 262–270, (264).

27   Ibid, 265.

28   Ibid, 267.

29   Ibid, 262.

East End Dwellings Company (EEDC), reshaped the inner London suburbs during the 1880s and 1890s with long ranges of five or more storey blocks of accommodation for working families. The organisations relied on volunteer rent collectors and, increasingly, salaried 'lady' housing managers to effect the making of place alongside their rebuilding of space.

Katherine Buildings, opened in East Smithfield in January 1885, was one of the first such ventures of the EEDC (Figure 5.1). In Webb's autobiography, Katherine Buildings stands as a physical marker of the shortcomings of pre-municipal housing reform. Webb's bleak evocation of its monotony and meanness – the 'sacrifice of decency' and true benevolence in favour of low rents and sanitary buildings – is of a deadening shell that no one could want to call home.[30] Yet the principles of design and construction at Katherine Buildings were heavily influenced by Hill's comments on the requirements of 'homes for the poor'.[31] There was, Hill argued, simply no point in providing sinks, taps and water-closets for individual flats, as the poorest tenants had no idea how to use such things and broke them: communal facilities on each landing were ample for their needs. Tenants needed to be educated by lady collectors in the correct manner of occupying and respecting place before they were provided with all modern conveniences in their built environments. Whilst a few rooms in Katherine Buildings were converted into self-contained accommodation for the lady rent collectors and others, including Margaret Harkness who came to research the life of the poor for a novel,[32] the rest remained 'uniform, cell like apartments' without even running water.[33]

The remaining records of daily life in Katherine Buildings present a consistent process of subversion of Hill's Idealist theories of the feminised place called home. Both the lady rent collectors of Katherine Buildings and their tenants shared with Hill an understanding of the importance of the local, lived practice of space in the construction of belonging and community. In Hill's writings, however, slum dwellers are never full actors in the making of place. Instead, Hill argued that her tenants were reformed by their attachment to the lady collector, rather than to place itself. 'You know', she told her fellow workers, that the tenants 'are yours; they know it; and as the years go on this sense of attachment will deepen and grow'.[34] Belonging and being at home in a state of contentment, Hill suggested, grew out of an affective tie to one's landlady, rather than to place itself. In the course of the continual contest between tenants and collectors in Katherine Buildings, the housing managers moved away from such Idealism and accepted that the physical environment and material

---

[30]   Webb, *My Apprenticeship,* 226.
[31]   The chair and founding director of the EEDC, Edward Bond (1844–1920) was a former associate of Hill's and, Webb noted in her diary, had been the object of her unrequited affection for some years.
[32]   Harkness was Webb's distant cousin. The future novel was *A City Girl.*
[33]   Webb, *My Apprenticeship,* 225.
[34]   Hill, *Letter to my Fellow Workers,* London: Houseboy Brigade, 1879, 5.

inequalities of the buildings structured and delimited the lived experience of space. It was the daily lived practice of space by the tenants that forced the lady collectors to reassess what made a place home. That such contests were also played out in a highly gendered language of power and authority returns to the conclusion that conceptualisations of space and place are ineluctably connected to our logic of masculinity and femininity.

Hill and her followers emphasised that rent collecting overcame 'the embarrassing sense of intrusion' that accompanied other forms of visiting the poor. Rather than crossing the threshold as an uninvited district visitor, the collector went 'naturally as agent for the landlord into the homes of all the families in her charge'.[35] Both the tenants and the lady collectors could agree that the latter had a natural right to be in the tenants' place of residence. It did not take long after the opening of Katherine Buildings, however, for the women rent collectors to realise that this 'naturalness' worked both ways. Webb recalled that the tenants refused to accept Ella Pycroft, the salaried housing manager, and her fellow workers as benevolent despots with a rightful claim to the building and proprietorial concern over their lives. Instead,

> from the outset the tenants regarded us, not as visitors of a superior social status, still less as investigators, but as part of the normal machinery of their lives, like the school attendance officer or the pawnbroker; indeed, there was a familiarity in their attitude, for they would refer to one or other of us as 'my woman collector', a friendly neighbour being given the status of 'the lady next door'.[36]

Whereas Hill assumed that the tenants would recognise that they belonged to their lady collector and hence to their place, in a reversal of Hill's order the tenants of Katherine Buildings marked their sense of ownership over the rent collectors, designating the property managers as a local service; 'my woman collector'. The tenants refused to bestow the authority of ladyhood, let alone queenship, upon the collectors. The collectors were instead necessary authorities made familiar by frequent meetings and regular visits: impersonal representatives of an administrative system who provided access to charitable aid. It was impossible to maintain that sense of distance, elevation and innate superiority which Hill placed at the centre of her theories of 'personal influence' and moral reform, when the tenants insisted on reading the collectors much more pragmatically, as a familiar intrusion and occasional resource. The tenants might have been what Webb termed 'a rough lot' of casual workers from the docks and markets – a lower class of tenants than those usually accepted by Octavia Hill and the Peabody Trust – but they

---

35   Ellen Chase, *Tenant Friends in Old Deptford*, London: Williams and Norgate, 1929, 9.
36   Webb, *My Apprenticeship*, 224.

appear to have had a well-developed proprietorial attitude towards their rooms and their woman collectors.[37]

In the summer of 1886, Ella Pycroft became only too aware of just how deep this sense of rightful possession ran in the minds of her tenants. Far from functioning as the ideal moral exemplar – a lady and little else – to her tenants, she was shocked to discover through Margaret Harkness and Beatrice Webb that the inhabitants of Katherine Buildings had cast her in a romance.[38] She confessed in reply to Webb that she was not offended 'but much obliged to you for telling me the gossip' among the tenants concerning her relationship with Maurice Paul who ran the boys' club in the building, 'And I would be very glad if Miss Harkness would tell me if she hears any more of it'.[39] It appears that she, at least, viewed Paul as nothing more than a friend at this time and was 'rather glad, for that reason only' that Paul had given up running the boys' club at the buildings, removing himself from the scrutiny of the tenants, who had presumed that Pycroft had gone away to marry him during her holiday in the previous month.

Though claiming not to be in the least surprised by Harkness's information, Pycroft added with a breathless rush of self-consciousness,

> because when the boys' club was going & I was going to the men's club twice a week, Mr Paul & I were always at the Buildings at least twice a week together & of course we went home together, & besides he had got into a habit of coming to my room there & I noticed once or twice that if Mr Paul were at the B[uildings] without my knowing it Mrs Roadknight [the caretaker's wife] used to tell me so the minute she saw me as if it were of the utmost importance that I should know.[40]

It is safe to assume that Pycroft was less obliged to Margaret Harkness's diligent powers of observation when her novel *A City Girl* was published the following year, containing, as it does, a discussion among the tenants concerning the lady rent collector's 'follower', who runs the boys' club in the

---

37   Mackenzie, *The Diary of Beatrice Webb*, 134. For a statistical analysis of the occupations of the tenants of Katherine Buildings see O'Day, 'How Families Lived Then'. Writing to Beatrice Webb in February 1886, Pycroft noted 'I ... got about five minutes talk with Miss Octavia Hill the other day ... they have a much higher class of tenants than ours & the cleanliness made me jealous'. British Library of Political and Economic Science Archives, Passfield 2/1/2/7.

38   See Koven, *Slumming*, 193 for another reading of this romance.

39   BLPES Passfield 2/1/2/7 Ella Pycroft to Beatrice Webb 25 June 1886. Maurice Eden Paul (1865–1944), son of the publisher Kegan Paul, was a resident of Toynbee Hall and training in medicine at this time. He and Pycroft became engaged two years later but this was broken off in 1890. Paul went on to become a well-known translator and member of the International Socialist Movement.

40   Ibid.

scarcely disguised 'Charlotte Buildings'.[41] The *Charity Organisation Review* concluded 'Lady rent collectors may learn [from *A City Girl*] some of the impressions which they create in the minds of their clients' and added, 'We hope that they will not be shocked to find that they are suspected of "followers" in the shape of the gentlemen whom they persuade to start clubs and reading rooms'.[42] Some, it seems, were less shocked than others.

The construction of Katherine Buildings displayed the tenants' lives all too clearly to the onlooker. Exterior staircases and balconies meant every movement of every individual could be seen from the yard below (as seen in Figure 5.1). Taps, sinks and water closets were on the end of each balcony to be shared by all, and led to a continual sociable clustering round these facilities, much to the lady collectors' disgust. No one could pass through the buildings unseen. But despite Octavia Hill's concerns that such new model dwellings as Katherine Buildings were over-disciplined and regulated spaces, this was no Panoptican.[43] Instead the communal facilities made each landing a site of exchange of gossip, money and sexual favours: a space that stubbornly resisted the women collectors' efforts to bring families back within a bounded place called home. In one of her more pessimistic moments, Webb recorded that the 'buildings ... are to my mind an utter failure':

> In spite of Ella Pycroft's heroic efforts, they are not an influence for the good. The free intercourse has here, as elsewhere in this dismal mass, a demoralizing effect ... The meeting-places, there is something grotesquely coarse in this, are the water closets! Boys and girls crowd on these landings – they are the only lighted places in the building – to gamble and flirt. The lady collectors are altogether a superficial thing. [44]

The ideals of the lady collectors were ineffectual against the constraints of the architecture of the buildings. The communal facilities made visible the intimate details of the tenants' lives and created a space of sociability that was antithetical to the collectors' ideals of 'decency'. Such spaces of 'free intercourse' also served to unsettle Pycroft's own sense of place as manager. Whilst Ella Pycroft had the right to look into her tenants' homes and lives in the exercise of her duties, she discovered to her discomfort that they had no scruples about looking back at her just as directly, when she

---

41   John Law [Margaret Harkness], *A City Girl*, London: Vizetelly, 1887, 73: 'She told him stories about the lady collectors, gave him quaint descriptions of their ways and doings and described their "followers" as she called the philanthropic gentlemen who conducted clubs and reading rooms in the buildings. It amused Mr Grant to have an East End opinion on West End manners and customs.'

42   Anon. Review of '*A City Girl*', *Charity Organisation Review*, August 1887, 317.

43   Miran Bozovic (ed.), *Jeremy Bentham: The Panoptican Writings*, London: Verso, 1995; Michel Foucault, *Discipline and Punish: The Birth of the Prison*, Harmondsworth: Penguin, 1977, 195–228.

44   Mackenzie, *The Diary of Beatrice Webb*, 186. Undated entry [winter, 1885].

and her visitors climbed the stairs and were exposed to the tenants' levelling gaze. Hill's nostalgic understanding of place was founded on a belief that being 'at home' in the slums would re-institute a definite hierarchy of class positions, born from innate respect for the landlady. The tenants of Katherine Buildings, on the other hand, insisted that Pycroft's occasional overnight residence positioned her as theirs: she belonged to their place.

Contested Definitions: The Meanings of Home in Katherine Buildings

After nearly a year of working in Katherine Buildings, Beatrice Webb started to keep a detailed record of the inhabitants, frustrated with the lack of information she was able to glean concerning abstract 'general questions of the hour' from fellow housing workers like Emma Cons and Hill herself.[45] Ella Pycroft continued to update the record after Webb gave up her regular work in the buildings as a result of her father's illness in December 1885. As Rosemary O'Day has indicated, the resultant record of the buildings serves as a reminder that the notion of the 'family' cannot be simply reduced to 'the occupants of an architecturally defined space' among these impoverished inhabitants of the East End.[46] Whilst Pycroft and Webb structured their record room by room, O'Day points out that its contents reveal that extended and multi-generational families were scattered in different rooms throughout the buildings or left for periods only to return to co-reside with a different set of relations. Gathered on the landings, socialising outside the rooms that were never adequate to contain their family communities, the tenants attempted to fit Pycroft's movements across the city and between the various rooms she rented in working-class dwellings within a model of transitional habitations that was familiar to them: courtship and marriage.[47] As Pycroft and her fellow collectors entered the homes and life spaces of the tenants by right, so too the tenants in return disestablished Pycroft's sense of separation between her world of home, personal life and belonging and her work in the buildings. Margaret Nevinson, who assisted Pycroft in the buildings and lived in Whitechapel in the 1880s, recalled that philanthropic 'voluntary slum-dwellers' were all eventually driven away to wider spaces by 'the sense of countless multitudes of men, women and children all jammed together in indecent

---

45   Ibid, 168; 136.
46   Rosemary O'Day, *The Family and Family Relationships, 1500–1900*, Basingstoke: Macmillan, 1994, 259.
47   On transitional space and the working-class domestic interior see Martin Hewitt, 'District Visiting and the Construction of Domestic Space' in Inga Bryden (ed.), *Domestic Space: Reading the Nineteenth-Century Interior*, Manchester: Manchester University Press, 1999.

proximity'.[48] To be at home in the slums of Whitechapel was to accept that one belonged to a place without tightly drawn bounds of bourgeois privacy.

The club room attached to Katherine Buildings was one of the most fiercely contested spaces managed by the rent collectors. The EEDC primarily designated the room for the recreation of the men of the buildings as an alternative to the pub. It was thus a place that had to occupy a middle ground between private and public space in a manner that echoed the strain between the paired terms public/house. It was here that Maurice Paul and others from Toynbee Hall ran educational clubs for the male tenants and here also that, as Margaret Nevinson recalled, the men were regularly bored and 'compulsorily uplifted' by 'well meant attempts to elevate' their taste in evening entertainment.[49] One evening in February 1886, Pycroft found herself alone with one female companion at a concert in the club-room at which the men staged 'a regular mutiny'.[50] Whilst she and her friend Miss Black sat at the back of the room, the men took over the stage and started singing 'vulgar' songs interspersed with patter of 'vulgar jokes or worse'. When Pycroft attempted to intervene in aid of raising 'the tone of the people & so on' she was hissed at for her efforts and eventually left the room. The massed numbers of men from the 'low set' of the buildings marked the room as theirs by seizing the stage and imposing their familiar culture back upon Pycroft. Undaunted, she met with the offenders the next day to reassert her control and in her letter to Webb that evening Pycroft recounted the brief homily she had delivered to them on the virtues of high culture. But Pycroft's trump card over the men was the indisputable fact of her property rights: '[I] made them clearly understand that the club room was let to me & I'd have no disputing my authority in it, & we parted with smiles all round'.[51]

When it came to struggles with the tenants over the definition of leisure and pleasure in the club room, the Idealism of urban reform was displaced by a thoroughly material language of property rights and ownership on both sides. In this struggle over what belonged in the club-room, the men seem to have accepted Pycroft's authority in much the same manner as that of any East End pub landlady with the power to bar her regulars. It was not, one imagines, quite the meaning of 'landlady' that Hill had in mind when she urged that the poor needed to accept her authority. Pycroft could be granted such limited authority to determine place and belonging in the club room because it was not (quite) home, but a public house for the men.

Despite the pressure of these conflicts, Pycroft's letters to Webb frequently revel in her attempts to tame and domesticate recalcitrant men. Such 'proud conquests', as Pycroft termed it, where she sustained her authority over a roomful of men in a public gathering, were paired with her

48   Margaret Nevinson, *Life's Fitful Fever: A Volume of Memories*, London: A & C Black, 1926, 102.

49   Ibid, 97.

50   BLPES Passfield 2/1/2/7 Pycroft to Webb, 9 February 1886.

51   Ibid.

sense of success in bringing home the male tenants from their 'wild talk' and 'mischief' amidst the radical speakers and meetings in Victoria Park. When one tenant, Mr Downs, had 'his head ... quite turned' by hearing Charles Bradlaugh speak one week, Pycroft felt the need to visit his rooms to check that he had not run off or taken to drink in his excitement at a new world view.

> But to my joy Downs was quietly sitting on the bed making a flannel shirt to go hopping in, & needlework had soothed him, as they say it does women, it was so funny; so I sat down & taught him & his wife to herringbone, an art they had long wished to learn & there was peace.[52]

Pycroft's letter indicates the cross-grained nature of these negotiations of urban space and conventional gendered authority within it. The ascription of conventional gender attributes in Pycroft's account of this visit is revealing in its very instability. She herself moves freely and authoritatively from external space (in terms of class position and geography) into this feminised place of (other people's) home and belonging, encountering and encouraging the peaceful domestication of this working-class man. There is a double distancing at work here, as Pycroft refuses to identify herself either with those nameless ones who insisted that needlework was an occupation best suited to female mental health or with the 'women' subject to such prescriptions. Whilst asserting her own identity through paid public work and 'masculine ambitions', as Webb termed it, Pycroft continued to associate the domestication of working-class men's lives with their potential moral and social regeneration. She excepted herself from the prescriptions of femininity whilst using such discourses of gender to enforce order in the public and private spaces of Katherine Buildings. Pycroft's daily practice suggests that she too understood place and home as a feminised territory of peaceful belonging, but unlike Hill, she attempted to bring the male tenants home through the material practice of domestic crafts, displacing her own problematic femininity as the source of moral reform.

Given what is, it is suggested, such self-conscious testing and subversion of the conventional associations of gender and urban space, it is not surprising that Pycroft and Webb 'read with amusement' an article in *Macmillan's Magazine* in 1888 that outlined the classification of a 'new species' of asexual urban professional women, know as 'The Glorified Spinster'.[53] Judging it a 'cleverish paper', both women took up the term and applied it to themselves in discussing their own ambivalence about marriage and conventional femininity, reaching out for the freedom that came instead from being identified as 'a good fellow' by men and 'ticketed

---

52   Ibid, 21 August 1886.
53   Webb diary entry 3 September 1888, Mackenzie, 1982, 261; Anon. 'The Glorified Spinster' *Macmillan's Magazine*, 58, (1888) 371–376.

Not in the Marriage Market'.[54] Perhaps what struck these readers most forcibly was the article's argument that such an unsettling of the boundaries of gender was inextricably linked to a new understanding of movement in space and time across the city as they scaled omnibuses and walked the streets in all weather. Such self-declared 'Glorified Spinsters' remapped the city as 'like meteors [they] wander free in interfamiliar space, obeying laws and conventions of their own'.[55] For the women rent collectors of Katherine Buildings, living and working in Whitechapel had already done much to dismantle conventional bourgeois identifications between femininity and domestic place, masculinity and public space.

By 1888 Webb, certainly, had broken free of her connection with Katherine Buildings to ascend those steps in the rock up to the lofty point of 'man's' social observation, even if Pycroft was still at work developing an increasingly materialist understanding of spatial practice in Whitechapel. But Webb's first published venture in social investigation after resigning her post at Katherine Buildings had produced yet another contest with the residents back in 1886. Webb's tellingly titled article, 'A Lady's View of the Unemployed at the East', published in the *Pall Mall Gazette* in February 1886, drew heavily upon the meticulous record that she and Pycroft had compiled from the life histories of the tenants in order to lend scientific authority to her Idealist interpretation of unemployment. In her article Webb argued that the cause of hardship in the East End was the 'parasitic' nature of the 'lowest' class of persons who lived in the Buildings and beyond, around the docks.[56] At this point in her career, Webb's social analysis was still shaped by her individualist mentor Herbert Spencer, and hence she concluded that it was the moral will and character of the East End poor that needed improving. Material conditions of existence and economic cycles had a negligible influence, Webb suggested, in the creation of this class.

In the very act of writing this article, at home in the West End, having resigned her 'business connection' (as Webb termed it in the article) with the tenants, Webb worked with certain assumptions about the bounded nature of the East End. Whitechapel is imagined both within and without the article as an enclosed territory where the inhabitants' fates are largely self-determined and where they have no access to what is written about them from the outside. The suggestion here is that it is an analysis that produced a model of urban space in which the East End was a territory with borders impermeable from the inside, attracting by its centrifugal force 'a

54   Beatrice to Richard Potter, November 1885 in Norman Mackenzie (ed.), *The Letters of Beatrice and Sidney Webb* I, Cambridge: Cambridge University Press, 1978; for Pycroft's self-identification see BLPES Passfield 2/1/2/7 Ella Pycroft to Beatrice Potter 21 September 1888; Anon, 'The Glorified Spinster', 372.

55   Anon, 'The Glorified Spinster', 372.

56   Beatrice Potter, 'A Lady's View of the Unemployed at the East', *Pall Mall Gazette*, 18 February 1886.

constantly decomposing mass of human beings' who sank deeper into its mire.[57] Despite its evident trade and transport links, its production and dispersal, reception and packaging of material objects and labour to and from the Empire and beyond during this period, Webb's Spencerian analysis of unemployment read the East End as a territory constituted by the moral degeneracy of its inhabitants. It was a place made by those who were drawn to live there, whose lives and fates existed in profound isolation from the rest of London.

The tenants themselves challenged the underlying spatial assumption in Webb's article that the East End was a place with internally determined problems upon which travellers could report back to civilisation back in the West End with no prospect of criticism or contribution from its subjects. That challenge once again took the form of insisting on the material determinants of the experience of space and reminding the rent collectors that their model of the contained boundaries of a place called home would simply never enclose the practice of life around the docks. Immediately on its publication, Pycroft and Maurice Paul took Webb's article to the boys' club in Katherine Buildings, where Paul made 'Gilburn [?] read it aloud to the boys, & great were the discussions thereon'.[58] Over the following week, Webb's paper caused a 'commotion' in the buildings and Webb clearly 'doubted our [Pycroft and Paul's] wisdom in showing the paper to the tenants'. One tenant, Joseph Aarons, 'was specially angry at your saying that the Buildings were "designed & adapted" for the lowest class of workmen – partly because he will take "low" to mean "disreputable", & partly because he shares our feelings about the construction of the B[uildings]'.[59] Aarons' outrage at his former collector's use of his and the other tenants' life stories to come to these conclusions led him to write to Webb, forcing her to address his objections and the ethics of her own research methods. The fragment of Aarons' letter that has survived enacts his systematic refusal of both the Idealism of housing regeneration schemes promoted by Octavia Hill – the nostalgic hope for village life in the city – and Webb's own construction of the East End as a space bound in by its indigenous problems.

In his letter Aarons repeatedly and bitterly returned to Webb's description of the Buildings as 'designed and adapted' for the lowest class of tenants, with its implication that material environment was determined by social character. Aarons reminded Webb that both the rent collectors and the tenants had speedily come to agree that the communal sanitary arrangements 'have not a tendency to improve the condition or impart a finer tone of morality to a people they were designed & adapted for'.[60] Detailing the instances of sexual impropriety his children had been exposed

57   Webb, *My Apprenticeship*, 21 cit ms diary March 1885.
58   BLPES Passfield 2/1/2/7 Ella Pycroft to Beatrice Webb 19 February 1886.
59   Ibid, 26 February 1886.
60   BLPES Passfield 2/1/2/8/173 Joseph Aarons to Beatrice Webb 2 September 1886 [misdated?]

to as a result of these material arrangements, Aarons thus objected most strongly to Webb's public professional voice concurring with prevalent individualism and Idealism, given that all the collectors had urged the EEDC to abandon this aspect of design. Aarons developed his argument concerning the material determination of daily spatial practice by detailing minutiae: the few facilities in the wrong place, badly thought through; the absence of other necessary objects, that led to the wrong sorts of growth and development in the Buildings. Stench, dust, demoralisation and disease were all produced, he suggested, by the ill-regulated movement of bodies, possessions and waste within the physical limitations of the buildings. The 'great mismanagement and inexperience' of the directors displayed in the design of the Buildings was evidence of their 'utter disregard and contempt' for the physical and moral wellbeing of the poorer working classes. Aarons concluded with that desire to retain small material goods that so often features as the pathetic (or, in this case, bathetic) element of narratives of the desolate homes of the poor during this period. Rather than ideal moral exemplars or disciplinary scientific philanthropy, he suggested, 'what is most practically necessary here to those who have a desire to live in cleanliness is a cupboard' built in each room. Home for Aarons, like Hill, might be desired as a small place of belonging, but without a built environment of self-contained rooms and fitted cupboards it was simply an impossibility.

Aarons' letter to Webb is an uncompromising reminder to his former rent collector that landlords and landladies, employers and investors – philanthropic or otherwise – were intimately involved in determining the material basis of the existence of those in the East End. Rather than 'mapping out the conquered land of social life', this letter insisted that urban reformers recognise the interdependence of the local and the global. Cupboards, sinks, toilets, dustbins mattered; they too had a part to play in the making of place. Webb might have resigned her post at Katherine Buildings, but the tenants' flexible notion of place denoted that she still belonged to their community. Webb should not be an overseeing eye, a cartographer of poverty, but rather she should acknowledge that she had a reputation embedded in Katherine Buildings, one that Aarons suggested he now needed to 're-establish' for her. And she in return ought to explain her inconsistency in contributing to the creation of the space of the Buildings at one time, and then condemning them as the natural product of the lowest of classes at another.

Conclusion: Imaginative Investments

Webb's characterisation of her former tenants as contained in the bounded space of the East End is all the more surprising given the relatively sophisticated picture of working-class geographical mobility contained in the record she compiled of the inhabitants of Katherine Buildings. As we have seen, the record demonstrates the mismatch between tenancies and families, rented space and place of belonging. By tracking the origins and destinations of the tenants, however, the record also defies Webb's imaginative investment in the East End as an isolated territory from which no-one can return: tenants emigrate, move away for work or settle beyond Whitechapel rather than stay stuck in place. One entry in the record suggests through its very oddity the extent to which immersion and belonging in the East End affected Webb and Pycroft's conceptualisation of their own gender identities and spatial practice. It seems in part a shared joke, which contrasts it with the contents of the rest of this rigorous testament to female professionalism. But read against the other entries and Webb's article distilled from such sources, it reveals much about the double-edged way in which women social activists took and used available narratives of gender and class, of patterns of movement through time and space, to shape their own identities.

> No. 97 taken with No. 98 Nov. 1885 – May 1886
> Ella Pycroft Rent Collector of K. Buildings Beatrice Potter ditto shares the two rooms. Ella Pycroft b. Devonshire, daughter of physician (single woman). Came to London 1883 in search of work.
> B. Potter, daughter of timber merchant, born in Gloucestershire, parents North Country. Came to London for family reasons & with the hope of work (single woman) ...
> In religious opinions they are doubtful & differing. Energetic & punctual in professional duties – not absolutely accurate in accounts.
> B.P. especially deficient. E.P. takes the lead in management. B.P. in observation. Both of them are professionally ambitious.[61]

This entry is an obvious pastiche of the formula the rent collectors applied to the tenants of all the other rooms in the Buildings. It has exactly the same structure, breaking down the inhabitants' lives into positivist facts concerning their occupations, places of origin, reasons for moving out of or into Katherine Buildings, religious backgrounds, income and conduct.[62] In effect, Webb turned her quest for personal observation and statistical enquiry inwards, onto herself and Pycroft. The results of this inversion of the investigative eye are very interesting when read in the context of the entire volume. First, by far the majority of entries in the volume are concerned primarily with male tenants as heads of households or single men: there are comparatively few entries for female principal tenancy holders. Second the statement 'came to London in search of work' was one never used by Pycroft or Webb with reference to female tenants: it is a phrase which appears extensively throughout the book, but applied exclusively to men, save this one instance.

---

61   BLPES Coll. Misc. 43 'Record of the Inhabitants of Katherine Buildings'.
62   The formula is also close to the one deployed by the London COS for which Webb had worked briefly in 1883.

By drawing on the subsistence-driven narratives of working-class men, indeed that very migratory practice that Webb criticised in her first published article, Pycroft and Webb were able to give a familiar form and comprehensible structure to their own life histories and movements from the provinces to the East End.[63] The opportunity for Webb and Pycroft to experience relative spatial mobility across London resulted from a widespread anxiety at the absence of a bounded place called home for men and women of the East End. But in order to explain to themselves their new found freedom outside the demands of family, Webb and Pycroft found themselves resorting to a model of flexible community and shifting pedestrian practice shaped by the material conditions down in the streets: that model of space and place lived out by the tenants of Katherine Buildings. Webb could play with such cross-class identifications in the East End, whilst securing her status up West as a lady expert with a lofty view of the 'parasitic' class in Whitechapel. Temporarily halting their meteoric movements through interfamiliar space, these glorified spinsters took a moment to write their lives as if they really did belong in rooms 97 and 98 of Katherine Buildings. Yet as Pycroft first, and Webb rather later came to realise, they were shaped inescapably by a world in which rooms came with cupboards; spaces structured by inside and outside, home and street, public work and private life, secure possession and the screening off of disorder.

---

63   Potter, 'A Lady's View': 'The great majority of the "unemployed" are those who have been pressed out of the working ranks in provincial towns and country neighbourhoods and who have thoughtlessly drifted to the great centre of odd jobs and indiscriminate charity.'

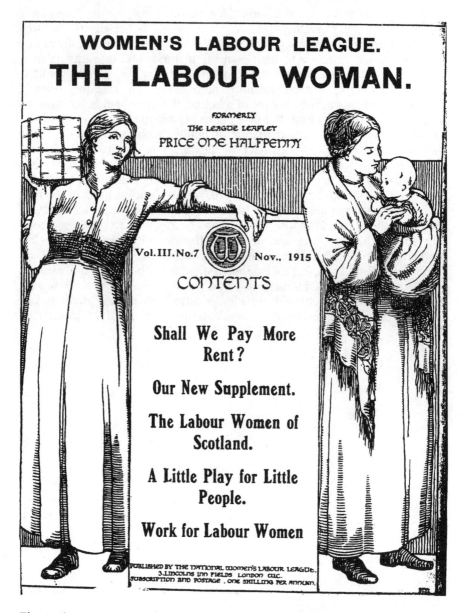

Figure 6.1
Cover of *The Labour Woman* paper, November 1915
Source: By permission of the People's History Museum, Manchester

Chapter 6

Gendering the Politics of the Working Woman's Home

Karen Hunt

This chapter explores an aspect of women's relationship with a particular built space, that of the home. Its focus is the working-class home of the first decades of the twentieth century, wherever this was located physically, whether in houses, tenements, flats or rooms. This domestic space could provide a site for women activists to make a politics which directly connected with unorganised women's everyday experience in a way that the mainstream masculinist political agenda did not.[1] The chapter explores, for one class during a specific period, the political potentialities which underlie women's relationship with domestic built space. To this end, my concern is not only the conditions under which the home as a physical space provided a catalyst to women's political action, but also whether women's arguments for a politics of the home or their actions were gendered.

The subjects here are those politically active women who sought to reach the female occupants of working-class housing with their message of radical change under the banner of socialism. These left-wing activists would variously identify themselves as socialist or Labour women. Socialist women gave their principal allegiance to explicitly socialist parties such as the Independent Labour Party (ILP) and the Social Democratic Federation (SDF).[2] Labour women's focus was the women's groups of the organised working class such as the Women's Labour League (WLL), the women's auxiliary to the Labour Party, and the Standing Joint Committee of Working Women's Organisations (SJC).[3] In the early decades of the twentieth century these women made their politics in a series of spaces both local and national: in meeting rooms, in print and on the streets, in radical and reformist organisations, in mixed-sex political parties and in women's groups. The female activists of the Left, whether leading

---

[1] See K. Hunt, 'Negotiating the boundaries of the domestic: British socialist women and the politics of consumption', *Women's History Review*, 9:2, 2000.

[2] See J. Hannam and K. Hunt, *Socialist Women. Britain, 1880s to 1920s*, London: Routledge, 2002.

[3] C. Collette, *For Labour and for Women: the Women's Labour League, 1906–18*, Manchester, Manchester University Press, 1989. The work of the SJC is considered in the chapters by Scott and Whitworth.

propagandists or local women based in their communities, shared a sense that the women they represented and sought to organise were 'working women'. This term could include women who engaged in paid work, either manual or white-collar, as well as the housewife whose workplace was the home. Such inclusive language meant that the difficult issue of how to attribute a class identity to housewives, or to women teachers, or to female political organisers, was side-stepped. They were all working women whatever their, or their husbands', social origins.

Although male-dominated, the Left had always recognised that they needed to attract such working women to the cause, in their own right but also to sustain the movement as mothers to socialist children and wives to socialist husbands. There was less certainty about the most effective way to reach women. While there were socialist men who were frustrated at what they saw as the conservatism and apathy of women, others were wary of the perceived threat of feminism which seemed to substitute sex war for class war. Central to the problem of how best to reach and to mobilise the unorganised working woman was the Left's understanding of politics.

Socialist politics had traditionally centred on the realm of production: on workers, wages, the workplace and the economy. In contrast, domestic matters had a marginal place within socialist strategy. Yet this might seem to be precisely the arena in which socialist women *could* make woman-focused politics, by renegotiating the boundaries of 'the political'. Socialists generally shared dominant views of what constituted the domain of politics, which was informed by particular understandings of the 'public' and the 'private'. Although the margins of 'the political' expanded within political discourse over the first decades of the twentieth century, everyday domestic concerns such as shopping or housework were rarely regarded as matters which transgressed the arena of politics.

In this context the home was rarely seen as a political space. Indeed when Katherine Bruce Glasier,[4] a leading member of the socialist ILP, published her pamphlet *Socialism and the Home* in 1909 she acknowledged that the more usual cry was the anti-socialist one, 'Socialism against the Home'.[5] Either by appropriating all private property or by the abolition of the family, socialists were represented by their opponents as being fundamentally opposed to all that the home represented in the public mind. Glasier therefore explored an alternative by reconsidering what was meant by the term 'home'. Concluding that others may have palaces and property, but it 'is the workers who have homes', she claimed that 'it is precisely this "home" that Socialism has come to establish for all classes, for all races, and for all time, as the only perfect cradle of the human race'.[6] These homes were not just sentimental creations but were physical spaces. Instead of government squandering money on wars, Glasier demanded that

---

4   See C. Wrigley, 'Glasier, Katherine St John Bruce (1867–1950), *Oxford Dictionary of National Biography*, Oxford: Oxford University Press, 2004.

5   K. B. Glasier, *Socialism and the Home*, London: ILP, 1909, 1.

6   Ibid, 3.

this money should be used 'for the re-housing in garden suburbs of the workers who inhabit the congested, unhealthy ... and rack-rented areas of our industrial towns to-day'.[7]

Other socialists wanted to see the transformation of what went on in the home. For some, housework was a drudgery which might eventually be alleviated by technology and the state, but changes in the organisation of domestic labour would be a consequence of socialism, not a means to it. That socialist men should share in domestic labour and thus challenge the sexual division of labour, was never seriously regarded as desirable by the Left as a whole, either as a political issue or as a practical tactic to encourage female participation in the fight for socialism. Domestic labour was resolutely a woman's issue and a problem for women. Finding a way to address it became closely tangled up with the issue of the domestic workplace, the home, and thus with the issue of housing.

Housing, particularly housing conditions, had long been an issue for socialists. Their demands for better housing were focused through the Workmen's National Housing Council (WNHC), formed in 1898.[8] Although it gained broad-based support across and beyond the socialist and labour movement, it is striking that no women were visibly identified with its work. The approach of the Council was to treat housing as a political issue, campaigning as a conventional pressure group for local authorities to provide adequate accommodation for the working classes. It eschewed more radical tactics such as the use of the rent strike as a weapon in the battle for housing reform.[9] For socialists, slum conditions graphically illustrated the failings of the capitalist system and the need for change. But rent was also an issue. Generally when rent was discussed, it was in terms of the role that rent played as an unearned source of income to the landlord class. In contrast rent, as a part of the ordinary household budget, was rarely aired as a topic for socialist discussion. Nevertheless the WNHC did argue that rent should be related to the tenant's ability to pay and therefore campaigned for local fair rent courts. This call was to be taken up in the rent strikes of the First World War.[10] None of this suggests that housing was seen as a particularly gendered issue by socialist men. Did socialist women see it any differently?

In socialist women's own publications there was a clear desire for 'good homes for all'.[11] Although it was recognised that of all the social problems 'there is none that touches women more keenly than that of housing', practical campaigning for housing reform was not a central feature of

---

7   Ibid, 3–4.

8   See D. Englander, *Landlord and Tenant in Urban Britain 1838–1918*, Oxford: Clarendon Press, 1983; D. Englander (ed.), *The Diary of Fred Knee*, Coventry: Society for the Study of Labour History, 1977.

9   Englander, 'Introduction' to *Diary of Fred Knee*, 19.

10 J. Melling, *Rent Strikes. Peoples' Struggle for Housing in West Scotland 1880–1916*, Edinburgh: Polygon, 1983, 61.

11 J. Dawson, 'Why Women Want Socialism', *Clarion*, 30 April 1909.

socialist women's activities before the First World War.[12] There were occasional discussions within the socialist press of the drudgery of housework and some talk of collective solutions for cooking, cleaning and mending, but there was little focus in this period on the fabric of the home or on its design as a workplace for women.[13] One socialist woman complained in 1914, 'Many working women – model housewives perhaps – would rather spend their time in patching and polishing inside bad houses, than come out for one hour or so to learn how to unite to demand good houses'.[14] The more gendered reading of the home as the workplace of women was to become much more apparent in the years of reconstruction immediately after the First World War and in the discussion of the specific form that the new municipal housing should take.[15] It was during the dislocation of this war that a shift occurred in the way in which the working woman's home was conceived as a site for a practical politics by socialist women. It is to this that the discussion now turns.

Making a Politics of the Home

Although women on the Left had not made housing a priority in their Edwardian campaigns, some thought was given to the relationship between domestic space and women's politics in the immediate pre-war years. Ethel Bentham,[16] later to become one of the first generation of women Labour MPs, argued at the WLL conference in 1913 that the League's purpose was 'to express for the common good the peculiar knowledge and wisdom of women, gained in and through the home, but only to be gained by those who can take other homes than their own into their horizon'.[17] At the following year's annual conference Lisbeth Simm, suffragist and WLL organiser, explored the contradictions surrounding the identification of women with the home.[18] She stressed that the WLL 'heartily approves of the home as one of woman's places', but made it clear that 'When the home is the workshop where woman works alone, her outlook is apt to become narrow'. She therefore argued that 'working women must add politics to the

---

12 *New Age*, 6 October 1904.
13 For example, *Labour Leader*, 5 May 1894.
14 *Labour Woman*, March 1914, 172.
15 See A. Hughes and K. Hunt, 'A culture transformed? Women's lives in Wythenshawe in the 1930s' in A. Davies and S. Fielding (eds), *Workers' Worlds. Cultures and Communities in Manchester and Salford, 1880–1939*, Manchester: Manchester University Press, 1992.
16 See C.V.J. Griffiths, 'Bentham, Ethel (1861–1931)', *Oxford Dictionary of National Biography*.
17 *League Leaflet*, March 1913, 2.
18 C. Collette, 'An Independent Voice. Lisbeth Simm and Women's Labour Representation in the North West, 1906–14', *North West Labour History*, 12, 1987, 79–86.

list of primary duties of home-making... we cannot expect to make good homes unless we see there are good houses'.[19] In order to begin to address how such good houses might be made, the same conference also voiced a radical demand for the time, the employment of women architects to design working people's homes.[20] It also recommended that no municipality should pass any plans without their consideration by 'women of practical experience', by which it meant women like themselves.[21]

If working women were to seek to influence the quality as well as the quantity of houses, then there needed to be some consensus on what women wanted. Indeed, 'housing reform will be a farce if working women are not fully consulted and have not fully considered the question'.[22] So the WLL called a conference specifically for working women to discuss the type of house that would suit them best. The emphasis on providing themselves with the space to consider, without constraint, what was really needed and only then to plan how to achieve it was reflected in the title of the conference report: 'Houses Utopian and How to Get Them'.[23] The focus for the detailed discussion in the first session was the demand for self-contained homes with sufficient water supply, a bathroom, a larder and a scullery, adjacent to open spaces planted with trees. The discussion was determinedly practical, considering matters which they felt male architects overlooked, such as the precise location of a plate-rack in the scullery. As important as this clear and detailed vision was the fact that all the papers in this session were given by a newly recognised type of 'expert': working women who had practical experience in running their own homes. Although there was still room for advice from the Fabian-type of professional expert, such as the reforming town planner Raymond Unwin who spoke in the second session of the conference,[24] working women were now empowering themselves through their claim to their own expertise as housewives. The remainder of this chapter explores a number of ways in which working women sought to develop a politics of the home from 1910 to 1920, and considers the extent to which the experience of the home front during the First World War provided a catalyst for change.

---

19   *Labour Woman*, March 1914, 172.
20   There were very few women architects practising at this time. Three women were members of the Royal Institute of British Architects in 1911, see J. Darke, 'Women architects and feminism' in Matrix, *Making Space. Women and the Man Made Environment*, London; Pluto, 1984, 19. For insights into the challenges facing women seeking employment in this and related professions see chapters by Meller and Darling.
21   *Labour Woman*, March 1914, 176. This was a point that was made again at the Labour Women's Conference in 1920, see *Labour Woman*, May 1920, 80.
22   *League Leaflet*, April 1913, 5.
23   *League Leaflet*, July 1913, 33–37. The conference was organised by the Central Branch of the WLL and held on 30 May 1913 at the Hampstead Garden Suburb Institute.
24   See Andrew Saint, 'Unwin, Sir Raymond (1863–1940)', *Oxford Dictionary of National Biography*.

A Collective Solution?

One of the ways in which the domestic space of the home could be reformed was to remove from it some of the individualised tasks of the housewife. The appeal of such collective solutions, as well as the possibility of their realisation, depended very much on the broader context of the war, particularly the extent to which married women were required in the labour force. The pre-war working women's conference on housing had considered collective solutions to the problems women faced in inadequate housing, such as co-operative cooking and housekeeping. The virtues of existing municipal wash-houses were acknowledged, but it was thought that they would be much more useful with the addition of crêches. Similarly, it was proposed that municipal laundries would be greatly improved if instead of washing the clothes themselves, women could leave the work to properly paid laundry workers. As one delegate observed, 'women used to want to do everything for themselves. Now they are being educated to realise the advantage of co-operation'.[25] Others responded to the issues raised by the conference by stressing that 'it will be a very long time before any kind of communal housekeeping will appeal'.[26] Collective solutions were to remain contentious for working women while they had so little influence on the shaping and delivery of such services.

It was during the peculiar circumstances of the wartime home front that collective solutions began to be seen as possible and even desirable by working women themselves. For example, the question of municipal kitchens gained more prominence. The WLL organised a conference of working women in 1917 to discuss food rationing. The Labour women's organiser, Marion Phillips, proposed that the use of such kitchens should not be compulsory, but where they were set up they should be managed by committees with a large proportion of working women.[27] The experience of the Workers' Suffrage Federation which had set up a People's Restaurant in the East End of London seemed to show that such ventures would be generally welcomed.[28] Indeed, the future Labour cabinet minister Margaret Bondfield felt that municipal kitchens would not only help in the extreme conditions of wartime, but 'would lead to many reforms and comforts in the working woman's life in the future'.[29]

Even under wartime pressures, exporting domestic activities from the home to what were usually municipal spaces remained controversial. Marion Phillips admitted that in her experience the working woman was

---

[25]   *League Leaflet*, July 1913, 35.
[26]   Letter from Kate Turner, *Labour Woman*, August 1913, 55.
[27]   See *Labour Woman*, March 1917, 127. On Phillips see B. Harrison, 'Phillips, Marion (1881–1932), *Oxford Dictionary of National Biography*.
[28]   See E.S. Pankhurst, *The Home Front*, London: Hutchinson, 1932.
[29]   *Labour Woman*, March 1917, 127–128. On Bondfield, see P. Williamson, 'Bondfield, Margaret Grace (1873–1953), *Oxford Dictionary of National Biography*.

not as enthusiastic about co-operative housekeeping as her middle-class sister. She argued that this was not because of working women's conservatism, but rather that these women had other demands, such as more bedrooms and sufficient parlour accommodation to make the social life of the family a real pleasure, none of which had a co-operative solution. Moreover, the middle-class advocate of co-operative housekeeping argued for this 'as *an addition* to the privacy and comfort of ample house room' [author's italics]. Indeed for her, co-operative housekeeping appealed because it would mean that she would not have to engage servants. The situation was very different for the working woman. She needed a 'comfortable cottage' which could then be supplemented by co-operative provision of communal washhouses and kitchens.[30]

Seeking a balance between a desire for privacy and collective provision of amenities continued to be a crucial issue for women campaigning around the politics of domestic space beyond the period of the wartime home front.[31] The issue was, as Phillips put it, that 'the middle class woman should not in her ignorance force upon the woman who knows, a reform which does not suit the actual conditions'.[32] The question of who spoke for the working woman was to remain central to the politics of domestic space.

There is certainly evidence that during the war some working women were discussing how they felt about co-operative or collective solutions to the demands of the daily grind of housework in inadequate homes. In one report of such a discussion, a fine balance was struck between the desire for domestic privacy and collective provision. So shared hot water and heating would be welcomed, as would the provision of childcare in day nurseries; a central laundry also elicited a positive response, but there was no enthusiasm for central cooking or centralised ironing.[33] Yet as the food and fuel shortages bit in the winter of 1918, Labour women renewed their call to extend the provision of National Kitchens, as communal kitchens were now termed, and National Restaurants.[34] Once the nature of such an amenity was explained, it was found that the feared conservatism of working women was overcome. What was less clear was whether collective solutions would only appeal in times of shortage and crisis. Socialist and Labour women were urged to organise to secure representation on local Food Control Committees, for example, while there was a possibility of influencing and even controlling state actions at local and national levels which affected the

30   *Labour Woman*, February 1918, 255–256. See also the comments in A.D. Sanderson Furniss and M. Phillips, *The Working Woman's House*, London: Swarthmore Press, n.d. (1919), 49.

31   See Manchester Women's History Group, 'Ideology in bricks and mortar. Women and housing in Manchester between the wars', *North West Labour History*, 12, 1987, 24–48.

32   *Labour Woman*, February 1918, 256.

33   *Labour Woman*, March 1918, 275.

34   For example, *Labour Woman*, October 1918, 58.

daily lives of working women.[35] It was in this way that a politics which arose from the stresses of working women's daily experience coalesced during the war.

Immediately after the war the deprivations of the home front continued as did the possible appeal of collective solutions. At the 1919 National Conference of Labour Women, women were still divided on their support for National Kitchens. One delegate 'roused much laughter by saying that her husband would rather eat a simple meal that she had cooked than anything which could be obtained at a National Kitchen'.[36] However, others were warm supporters, to the extent that one said that the only way that she could attend the conference 'with an easy mind' was because the National Kitchen provided her family with proper meals in her absence.[37] Yet National Kitchens were generally viewed as a product of the wartime emergency. Such collective solutions were never seen by women on the Left as a total panacea, partly because of their sensitivity over the issue of the home: they accepted that the home was a domestic and private space where women should be relieved of the drudgery of its maintenance, but many feared that anything which could be represented as the abolition of the home would damage their cause. The wartime experience of working women and the debates this prompted amongst Labour women showed that collective and co-operative provision of tasks usually undertaken in the home might supplement the amenities within a working woman's home, but they were no substitute for improving the home itself. The home front had provided a catalyst for women to consider a politics which sprang from the home and which engaged with activities usually seen as beyond political intervention. But was this a politics which would prompt collective action by women, particularly the unorganised working woman?

The Politics of Rent: Domestic Space as the Site of a New Women's Politics

There were a number of ways in which domestic space might become politicised for socialist women, but was it also a possible site for a new form of women's political practice? The issue of rent and the weapon of the rent strike appeared to have this potential, particularly in the period immediately prior to and during the First World War. Rent was certainly a woman's concern even if it was not always recognised as a woman's issue, because it was generally understood that the paying of household rent was part of the wife's responsibility as manager of the household budget, even

---

35   Ibid, 59.
36   *Labour Woman*, July 1919, 78.
37   Ibid.

though tenancies would usually be in the husband's name.[38] In that sense rent was a gendered issue with the day-to-day responsibilities and anxieties, as well as the potential for direct action, falling to women. To what extent did socialist women see the rent strike as a way to politicise domestic space and therefore as a weapon that had peculiar relevance to women?

Rent strikes have tended to be employed by tenants in protest against what are seen as unjustified rent rises and as part of the pursuit of a 'fair rent'. David Englander has traced a series of rent strikes across Britain, particularly in the years immediately preceding the First World War.[39] They were rarely successful because, in his view, 'the cult of home' gripped the working classes.[40] Rent strikes were rarely the preliminary to continuous organisation; rather, they were indicative of the desperation to which the participants were reduced. Some socialists saw the rent strike as a further weapon in the battle against capitalism, but they did not appear to see it as one particularly suited to women. Most rent strikes of the pre-war years seem to have been organised by men, although occasionally the existence of a female crowd (made up of rent strikers and supporters) was commented on. The *Women's Dreadnought* reported of the Leeds rent strike of 1914: 'The women ... are marching about the streets brandishing pokers, rolling pins, and toasting forks, to show that they intend to protect their homes'.[41]

Although rent strikes took place across the country from the beginning of the First World War, the most famous example was the one in Glasgow in 1915, largely because it achieved its demands.[42] These neighbourhood-based strikes throughout the city were characterised by the high level of participation of women. Indeed one of its leaders, Helen Crawfurd, remembered it unequivocally as a 'women's fight'.[43] In wartime 'Red Clydeside', there seems to have been a sexual division of politics with the

---

38   E. Roberts, 'Women and the domestic economy, 1890–1970: the oral evidence' in M. Drake (ed.), *Time, Family & Community. Perspectives on Family and Community History*, Oxford: Blackwell, 1994, 130.

39   Englander, *Landlord and Tenant*, particularly chapter 7. See also Melling, *Rent Strikes*.

40   Englander, *Landlord and Tenant*, 125, see also 124–126.

41   *Women's Dreadnought*, 8 March 1914 quoted in Englander, *Landlord and Tenant*, 158. For the Leeds strike see ibid, 155–161 and Q. Bradley 'The Leeds Rent Strike of 1914',
<http://freespace.virgin.net/labwise.history6/rentrick.htm>, accessed 1 February 2005.

42   Englander, *Landlord and Tenant*, 205–206.

43   H. Crawfurd, unpublished autobiography, quoted in H. Corr, 'Introduction' to Melling, *Rent Strikes*, p.viii. For Crawfurd see H. Corr, 'Crawfurd, Helen (1877–1954), *Oxford Dictionary of National Biography*.

women fighting higher rents – an issue of consumption – while the men fought the Munitions Act – an issue of production.[44]

Women's involvement in the fight for housing reform in Glasgow was channelled through the Glasgow Women's Housing Association (GWHA), which had been formed in 1914 with ILPers such as Agnes Dollan and Helen Crawfurd amongst its leading members.[45] As the activities of the GWHA became more apparent to the readers of the local ILP newspaper *Forward*, so there were calls for the locus of politics to shift from the meeting room to the more domestic space of 'the backcourts – perhaps with a bit of music thrown in'.[46] Although GWHA President, Mrs Mary Laird, addressed ILP meetings on 'Woman and the Home', little of the flavour of any particular 'woman's view' of the rent problem filtered into the paper.[47] The women were congratulated and even encouraged, but it was all from a distance and rarely in the women's own words.[48] At a WLL Conference in Glasgow in November 1915 the rent strikes were claimed to demonstrate the 'immense Womanly potentialities in collective effort' and it was hoped that one result of the agitation would be the election of women members to town councils.[49] Yet there was little sense of why in particular this was a woman's issue. The decision of the GWHA to re-title itself the Glasgow Workers' Housing Association in May 1916 was perhaps indicative of a more general desire to downplay the gendered aspects of the politics of rent.[50]

A few socialist women had already argued for the rent strike as an important political weapon for women, one which could be used to achieve more than a reduction in rents. Late in 1913 Sylvia Pankhurst and other members of the East London Federation of the Women's Social and Political Union (WSPU) began to argue for a new tactic in the fight for women's enfranchisement: 'No Vote No Rent'. Pankhurst argued that this was a way of politicising a key aspect of women's daily domestic experience. It was a weapon which could be used 'at will' provided that it was prepared for with careful organisation.[51] She saw this tactic as women's equivalent of the tax resistance and withdrawing of gold from banks practised by men before the Great Reform Act of 1832, 'for in working class homes, as everyone knows, it is the woman who spends the wages and pays the rent'.

---

44   N. Milton, *John Maclean*, London: Pluto Press, 1973, 91. For further discussion of the gendered politics of the rent strike, see Hannam and Hunt, *Socialist Women*, 149–153.
45   See H. Corr, 'Dollan, Agnes Johnston, Lady Dollan (1887–1966), *Oxford Dictionary of National Biography*.
46   *Forward*, 16 February 1915.
47   *Forward*, 13 March 1915.
48   See, for example, *Forward*, 2 October 1915.
49   *Forward*, 27 November 1915.
50   *Forward*, 20 May 1916.
51   *Daily Herald*, 21 November 1913; B. Winslow, *Sylvia Pankhurst. Sexual politics and political activism*, London: Routledge, 1996, 61–62.

She noted recent examples of the successful employment of the rent strike as a political weapon, citing the Chicago garment workers strike of 1912.[52] The No Rent strike would, Pankhurst promised, 'be absolutely irresistible if women will but trust each other'.[53] Other women were not so convinced. Edith Watson, socialist and militant suffragist, argued:

> To hope for revolutionary direct action on the part of unorganised, neglected (in the sense of not being taught rebellion) wives, sisters and mothers of men who cannot themselves organise decently is to hope for the moon. Rent strikes, consumers' leagues, etc, are only just peeping into daylight and are too weak for much 'direct action' yet.[54]

In terms of Pankhurst's ambitious plan, Watson's prediction proved to be accurate when the 'No Vote No Rent' strike failed to attract supporters in the weeks immediately preceding the outbreak of war, at which point suffrage campaigning was suspended. Later Pankhurst reflected on the reasons for the failure of this new strategy. It was the 'deep-rooted fear amongst the women of "losing the home". ...The risk of it was so terrible as only to be faced in some desperate crisis. I saw that whilst we might continue to propagate the idea, it could only be realized as the result of some crisis'.[55] In trying to envisage a politics which connected with women's everyday experience and to create forms of action which sprang from everyday life, a few socialist women saw the rent strike as a particularly useful weapon for women. But the experience of the immediate pre-war and wartime strikes showed that making a politics within domestic space was too risky for working women most of the time. A convincing case for risking the home for wider political goals had not yet been made to many working women. Only when there was a real danger of eviction, as in the wartime rent strikes, were significant numbers of women willing to organise in this way.

Wartime also meant that more moderate Labour women were more likely to support a tactic which at other times would have been regarded as too radical. Thus the WLL's *Labour Woman* showed its support for the Glasgow action and felt that increases in rent should not be paid, yet did not mention the words 'rent strike'. However, they did acknowledge the gendered nature of the campaign: 'As the men abroad have fought – so have the women fought at home. How many towns will follow Glasgow?'[56] Occasionally there were glimpses that rent might be an issue on which women could be more radical, or at least more prepared to take action, than their men-folk. In 1917, Barking WLL found when canvassing in regard to the Rent Act that there were women who said, 'Oh, yes. I wouldn't pay the

---

52 *Forward*, 24 January 1914.
53 *Daily Herald*, 5 February 1914.
54 *Daily Herald*, 19 February 1914.
55 E.S. Pankhurst, *The Suffragette Movement*, London: Virago, 1977, 528–529.
56 *Labour Woman*, November 1915, 320.

increased rent, but my husband says I had better pay it, otherwise the landlord will have his own back'.[57] Generally the rent strike as a tactic was not much mentioned by mainstream Labour women. Yet the question would not go away. At the 1919 Labour Women's National Conference Mrs Jarratt of Kensington 'advocated a strike policy until the housing problem was solved'.[58]

The success of some of the wartime rent strikes and the key role of women within them did help to change perceptions of rent as both a political issue and a women's issue. But the context of economic and social crisis was clearly crucial, for the war disrupted gender relations and in so doing created the possibility of challenge to traditionally gendered politics. The moment slipped away quickly. After the war the control of most rent strikes seem to have reverted to male-led tenants' leagues.[59] A comparison of the wartime experience of rent strikes with that before and after it, shows that only in crisis did the home became the site of recognised political action. More usually, and less radically, socialist and Labour women saw the working woman's home as a space which could provide a focus to women's demands to be included in the decision making which shaped their communities and neighbourhoods.

The Possibility of Empowerment through a Politics of Domestic Space

One of the effects of the deprivations and pressures of the home front, combined with the winning of the partial enfranchisement of women during the First World War, was to confirm in the minds of many Labour and socialist women that the home was a political space. Thus, according to the WLL:

> The working woman spends most of her time in her home, and yet she has nothing to do with its planning. It is time that this state of things ended. After the war there will be urgent need of a million new houses and as great a need for the re-modelling of those we have. The working woman with a home of her own will be a voter. Let her first effort of citizenship be to improve this home.[60]

---

57 *Labour Woman*, September 1917, 202.
58 *Labour Woman*, July 1919, 77.
59 For example in the Leeds rent strike of 1934, although women could still be found participating at street level as in the East London rent strikes at the end of the 1930s. See 'The birth of the council tenants movement. A study of the 1934 Leeds rent strike', <http://freespace.virgin.net/labwise.history6/1934.html>, accessed 15 October 2004, and H. Srebrnik, 'Class, Ethnicity and Gender Intertwined: Jewish women and the East End Rent strikes, 1935–40', *Women's History Review*, 4:3, 1995, 283–299.
60 *Labour Woman*, March 1918, 271.

Moreover for local activists, debate about the design and construction of sufficient workers' housing was also thought to be the best way 'of gaining the interest and sympathy of the women of their districts'.[61] This exercise in democracy, combined with the importance of the issue to working women's daily lives would, it was hoped, politicise newly-enfranchised women and begin their education as citizens. Labour and socialist women felt that the moment had to be seized.

To this end the WLL consulted with a broad range of women from amongst their membership and beyond, about what they wanted from the new working-class housing which it was hoped would form part of post-war reconstruction. A leaflet, 'The Working Woman's House', set out their ideas and provided plans for an ideal house for a family of five or six, and asked women to consider 'whether it is a woman's ideal house as well'.[62] This chimed with the experience of women not usually touched by political campaigns and had the potential to galvanise them:

> 'the Leaflet is finding its way into places where the people have never imagined the possibility of obtaining a really convenient house, but to whom the new ideas present a vision of what life might be for the woman whose labour was reduced to a minimum, in a house where she would find it possible to make a real home without unnecessary fatigue to herself.[63]

As the secretary of the WLL's Housing Sub-Committee commented:

> It is quite obvious that if women feel really strongly on this subject, as we believe and know that they do feel, they will have to take the matter into their own hands and use their new powers as voters to convince the nation that they are not prepared to accept the conditions of the past.[64]

The WLL had set up an elaborate system of consultation within their own organisation so that their representatives could with confidence claim to voice the views of the working woman on the issue of housing.[65] Yet in many areas it proved difficult to get women included in forums on housing, be they advisory or policy-making. At a national level, the infrequency of the meetings of the Women's Advisory Committee to the Ministry of Health aroused anger and led one of its members to urge women to 'make themselves a nuisance, both locally and nationally'.[66] Many Labour women, however, were sceptical about the value of advisory councils since their membership was unelected and they were only empowered to make recommendations. Mrs Clarke, an elected Labour councillor in Barking,

---

[61]   Ibid.
[62]   *The Working Woman's House*, London: WLL, 1918, 1. This was later expanded into a book, Furniss and Phillips, *The Working Woman's House*.
[63]   *Labour Woman*, June 1918, 19.
[64]   Ibid.
[65]   For example, *Labour Woman*, March 1918, 271–272.
[66]   *Labour Woman*, May 1920, 80.

wondered whether their purpose was simply 'keeping women quiet'.[67] A Labour woman in Middleton argued that the better alternative was to get women onto local councils where they would have 'real power'.[68] However, in 1919 in Oldham, despite the campaigning of local Labour women, not a single woman had been appointed to the committee in charge of the local housing scheme,[69] and by 1921 Labour women felt, that 'Both nationally and locally they have offered the benefit of their advice and experience to the service of the community. But on the whole they have been cold-shouldered'.[70] At this point the possibilities for working women to be empowered through a politics of domestic space seemed to be slipping away, at least through the mechanism of formal politics.

Conclusion

After 1918 with six million women enfranchised and five million added to the local government electorate, there appeared to be new possibilities for women's political participation. [71] The recognition of the home as a political space and one on which women had their own expertise, gave a spur to newly-enfranchised women to engage in the political process, but the culture surrounding the practice of politics together with the understanding of what constituted a political issue remained gendered. Women who tried to take part in local or national government had to navigate this new terrain with care and often in isolation; the limitations of the ways in which women's advice had been co-opted onto local authority committees was also exposed. Whether as voters, local councillors, or even as MPs, it was felt that women needed to be prepared for the responsibilities of citizenship. Labour women put considerable energy into devising a programme to educate for this new role and the home was central to this.[72]

A politics of the home began to rise up Labour women's agenda during the First World War and the concomitant planning of post-war reconstruction. This seemed to have the potential to make an impact on mainstream politics. But did women employ gendered arguments in their pursuit of a politics of the home? Certainly there was a belief that this was a 'woman's issue'. As the WLL noted of its Working Woman's House

---

[67]　*Labour Woman*, March 1920, 36.

[68]　*Labour Woman*, July 1919, 77.

[69]　Ibid.

[70]　*Labour Woman*, March 1921, 35.

[71]　C. Law, 'The old faith living and the old power there: the movement to extend women's suffrage' in M. Joannou and J. Purvis (eds), *The Women's Suffrage Movement. New Feminist Perspectives*, Manchester: Manchester University Press, 1998, 203.

[72]　For example, in a session on 'Citizenship and Home Life' participants would be asked whether domestic spaces would be improved if women were consulted about their planning, *Labour Woman*, June 1918, 14.

campaign: 'It is for the women themselves to press this point and we have every reason to believe that our campaign has given them the opportunity and the stimulus to do so'.[73] In the 1920s, there were still differences over the politics of the home between women and men on the Left. These were less about the consensus that housing could be a 'woman's issue' than its relative place on the political agenda.[74] As housing reform became a more pressing issue in the inter-war years, coupled with feminist and other attempts to revalue the housewife as a worker, so aspects of the housing issue moved from the private to the public arena. Not all women on the Left were keen to claim housing as a women's issue, as they had learnt from experience that such a designation necessarily implied marginality for the issue and its proponents. That of course did not mean that housing, or rent, were not gendered issues, but what was crucial for women activists was how they chose to *represent* these issues within the broader political discourse of the time. The place of domestic space as part of a politics of everyday life became an increasingly important test of the extent to which women on the Left were able to reconfigure the mainstream political agenda in the first decades of the twentieth century.

This chapter has demonstrated that for women on the Left the home could be the site of a woman-focused politics. However, bringing these politics into the mainstream was more difficult than many women anticipated, particularly when the politics contained a challenge to gender relations. When women took those politics out of the home and into the street, as in the rent strikes, they were seen to be at their most challenging, for they were able to mobilise large numbers of previously unorganised working women. But such moments were hard to sustain. The challenge for women on the Left was how to make a politics which connected with the daily lives of unorganised working women, as well as with the mainstream political agenda. The wartime years showed that the working woman's home, and all the issues associated with it, could provide a catalyst for women's political action. The task for the post-war years was to make space on the broader political agenda to develop a gendered politics of the home.

---

73   Ibid, 19–20.
74   See Hughes and Hunt, 'A culture transformed?', 82–83.

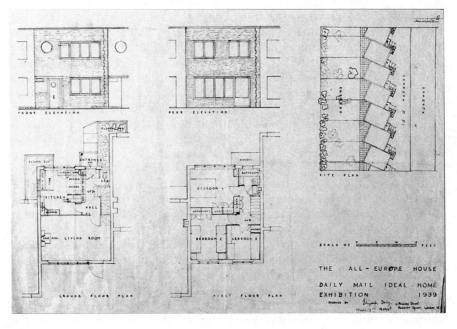

Figure 7.1
The All-Europe House, designed by Elizabeth Denby, 1939
Source: Courtesy of the RIBA Library Drawings Collection

Chapter 7

'The House that is a Woman's Book come True': The All-Europe House and Four Women's Spatial Practices in Inter-war England

Elizabeth Darling

In April 1939, the *Daily Mail* Ideal Home Exhibition (DMIHE) opened at the Earl's Court Exhibition buildings in west London. As was usual for this series of exhibitions, its centrepiece was a 'village' of show houses constructed by the leading speculative house builders of the day. Traditional in style, though packed with 'all mod cons' within, they represented the apogee of an Exhibition whose goal was to introduce its predominantly female lower-middle-class audience to the latest in consumer goods from tin-openers to houses.[1]

Nestled amongst these monuments of consumer spectacle was a rather different house. This was the All-Europe House (AEH): a flat-roofed and brick-built terraced house, noticeably modern in comparison with its neighbours, and specially commissioned by the Exhibition's organisers. Its purpose was not to bewitch potential owner-occupiers with commodified domesticity but, instead, through its design and furnishing to offer visitors an alternative vision of the form state-subsidised social housing could take. Described in the Exhibition catalogue as 'the house that is a woman's book come true', the AEH captured the imagination and admiration of both the lay and specialist press. A *News Chronicle* journalist described it as '...sweet and sane, livable and loveable',[2] whilst an architectural journalist declared it '...the one really worthwhile feature of the exhibition...'.[3] In the longer term the proposal that a small terraced house should be a part of the state's social housing programme was ratified by the wartime *Design of Dwellings* report.[4]

---

1   See Deborah Ryan, *The Ideal Home through the 20th Century*, London: Hazar Publishing Ltd, 1997 for an account of the DMIHE.
2   Jill Adam, 'Humanity House', *News Chronicle*, 14 April 1939, 5.
3   Anon, 'Events and Comments', *Architect and Building News*, 158, (1939), 25.
4   Ministry of Health (GB), Central Housing Advisory Committee, Design of Dwellings Sub-Committee, *Design of Dwellings*, London: HMSO, 1944, 44–45.

The AEH was commissioned from the Housing Consultant Elizabeth Denby by the Exhibition's principal organiser, George Grimaldi.[5] Her brief was to produce '...a working-class three-bedroomed house for the Exhibition, which will embody the best ideas of modern European practice as surveyed in her recently published book on the subject'.[6] Grimaldi then approached the government body, the Council for Art and Industry (CAI), to provide a team to design the interiors of the house. Its Chair, Frank Pick, appointed an all-women sub-committee which comprised Denby, Dorothy Braddell, Cycill Tomrley and Christine Veasey. Their task was to demonstrate 'how good design and economy may be combined' in the furnishing of a working-class home.[7]

As a project conceived and designed by a team of women, the AEH seems almost tailor-made for consideration in this volume, especially if we consider that the DMIHE, though its primary audience was female, only occasionally featured women's work as designers of the houses which were on display.[8] Its suitability as a subject for this collection is further enhanced if we remember the significance of its presence at a popular exhibition and its influence as a prototype for housing provision in Labour's post-war New Jerusalem. A part of this chapter will, then, be concerned to offer an account of a fascinating and hitherto little-known project, and the women who made it. But beyond this, in its focus on a project built in the inter-war decades, this chapter allows an understanding of how middle-class women's careers as space-makers had developed since the much better-documented period before 1918 and shows how they built on the foundations laid by such predecessors as Octavia Hill and Henrietta Barnett. Like the other chapters in this grouping then, it stands as a corrective to the assumption, one based more on a lack of research than

---

The housing manuals which governed the design of post-war social housing drew heavily on the Report's recommendations.

5   The commission was reported in a letter to Frank Pick, Chairman of the Council for Art and Industry (CAI), dated 4 August 1938, CAI papers held in the National Archive, BT/57/22/408/38. The CAI was set up in 1934 under the auspices of the Board of Trade and was part of a renewed campaign to improve standards of design in British industry.

6   Ibid. By this date, European social housing was offered as a benchmark for English provision. For example, Lewis Silkin, "Continental Housing Lessons for Municipalities", *The Town and County Councillor*, 1 (1936), 11.

7   Ibid. See Lesley Whitworth's chapter for further discussion of design in the working-class home.

8   Although women designed interiors and stands for the DMIHE, the only woman-designed house exhibited hitherto, in 1930, 'The House that Jill Built', was as a stunt. It was the result of a *Daily Mail* competition for its married women readers to design a house for themselves. See Ryan, *Ideal Homes*, 64–65.

fact, that women's influence over the making of built space ended some time around 1918.[9]

Further, the discussion points to the possibility that it was in this period that women's influence over the making of space was at its most diverse and influential. The portfolio of skills possessed by the four-woman team which produced the AEH was immense. Denby, under the title Housing Consultant, practised as a designer, writer, broadcaster, campaigner for issues from health reform to the need for clean air, and was also chief buyer for and director of a furniture shop, and a housing manager. Dorothy Braddell was a designer of graphics and interiors, particularly kitchens; she also enjoyed a career as a writer and broadcaster. Cycill Tomrley was an active member of the Design and Industries Association and a writer on design. Christine Veasey was an adviser on furnishing and decoration who also wrote on these subjects. They may be little known today but, in 1939, they were all sufficiently renowned, and their expertise valued enough, that they were invited by a government-sponsored committee to contribute to a major public exhibition.

The suggestion in this chapter will be that the AEH may be best understood as a project which embodied the culmination of the tradition of women as space-makers which had begun in the 1870s. It will also suggest that, at the same time, the AEH was a portent of the ways in which that tradition would subsequently decline in the post-war years. Here, then, by tracing the commissioning of the AEH and the careers of its designers, both before and after its completion, the intention is to demonstrate the contexts in which women's influence as space makers was won, and lost.

Creating the All-Europe House

The AEH was commissioned from Elizabeth Denby as a special feature for the 1939 DMIHE some time before August 1938.[10] Although most commonly associated with the celebration of home ownership, each exhibition usually included displays or features which addressed contemporary social concerns. Throughout the 1930s, the issue of slums and slum clearance had been the subject of much public debate and, by

---

9 Although by no means extensive, there is a comparatively large literature which explores the work of pioneers such as Hill and Barnett, see, for example, Jane Lewis, *Women and Social Action in Victorian and Edwardian England*, Aldershot: Edward Elgar, 1991. Some design histories have looked at women's work as architects/designers in the inter-war period – see Jill Seddon and Suzette Worden, *Women Designing, Redefining Design in Britain between the Wars*, Brighton: University of Brighton Press, 1994 – but there is little work which explores other forms of space-making in this period; something this volume seeks to remedy.

10 No evidence appears in the CAI papers about the precise date; this reference comes from the Pick letter cited in note 2.

1939, the first fruits of a government-sponsored clearance and rebuilding programme could be seen in England's inner cities.[11] It is not surprising, given the domestic preoccupations of the DMIHE, that a display which dealt with what should replace the nation's slums should have appealed to the Exhibition's organisers that year. The form the display should take, however, was tempered by the context in which it would be shown. An exhibition, especially one such as the DMIHE, required 'stunts' or a story on which to hang what might otherwise be seen as a rather worthy display. Denby offered them both.

As Grimaldi had explained to Pick, the idea for the house came from a book by Denby which had recently been published: *Europe Rehoused*. This survey of social housing practice in continental Europe, combined with an evaluation of its relevance to British practice, provided the inspiration for a project whose form would be derived from the best features of European housing design.[12] More than this, however, and giving the house its required 'stunt' value, was that the form of what became the AEH would differ dramatically from current planning orthodoxy. This stipulated that slums could only be replaced by blocks of flats because of the cost of land in inner-city areas. Denby's solution to slum clearance by contrast, was to propose the construction of what she called 'mixed development' schemes, in which land was developed into clusters of terraced housing for families and blocks of flats for single people and elderly couples, alongside extensive amenities such as schools, community centres, laundries and shops.[13] By proposing higher densities than were then common, 25 rather than 12 to the acre, Denby argued it was possible to build such developments on inner-city sites at the same cost as local authority flatted schemes. The combination of the continental inspiration and the departure from planning orthodoxy was, it can be conjectured, irresistible. The further selling point of Denby's gender is summed up in the by-line used in the DMIHE catalogue, 'the house that is a woman's book come true'.[14]

But who was Denby and why were she, and the women who collaborated on the interior, chosen to create the AEH? The fact that they were all sufficiently well known to have been invited to participate in the DMIHE in 1939 has already been noted, as has the fact that their names and work are now unknown to most historians. This shift from contemporary recognition to present-day disregard is an historiographical elision familiar to those architectural historians whose focus operates outside the discipline's traditional territories. A group of women, only one of whom (Braddell) had anything approximating to a professional training in design, though not architectural design, who produced a house for a

---

11 See for example LCC, *London Housing*, London: LCC, 1937.
12 Elizabeth Denby, *Europe Rehoused*, London: George Allen & Unwin, 1938 (April).
13 A plan of this proposal was included in a display to accompany the AEH, see Anon, 'Homes and Ideals', *Architect and Building News*, 158, (1939), 25–26.
14 DMIHE *Catalogue*, 10.

populist exhibition, does not fit the paradigms of a discipline more usually preoccupied with major public buildings, nor the conceptualisation of the architect as a professionally trained individualist hero (not heroine).

The tropes of architectural history may explain the present disregard for the lives and work of this group of space-makers, but they do not explain their employment in the 1930s. The suggestion here, and the logical conclusion given the evidence presented, is that in the inter-war period it was entirely normal that women whose backgrounds and training, as will be shown, varied from the voluntary sector to the Regent Street Polytechnic, should have been deemed capable of creating a work of architecture when today they almost certainly would not. In Braddell, Denby, Tomrley and Veasey then, we are presented with a near complete cross section of the spatial practices which women had developed since the pioneer days of the 1870s, as well as evidence that by this date, although their gender was often remarked upon, their eligibility to engage in space-making, whatever their background, was not. A brief outline of each of these women's careers will demonstrate this.

Women's Spatial Practices in inter-war England

Denby, and the team which built the AEH, had in common middle-class backgrounds, a high level of education and an engagement with social issues. For them, and women like them, who entered the world of work at the close of the Great War, there existed a number of role models on which to draw when they sought employment. The 'pioneering' work of well-known figures such as Josephine Butler, Beatrice Webb, Octavia Hill, Henrietta Barnett and Agnes and Rhoda Garrett had established new careers for women in fields which ranged from interior decorator to social worker.[15] All these 'woman-made' disciplines informed – directly or indirectly – the making of space and had, by 1914, made a considerable impact on much of England's social and built landscape. Institutions such as girls' and mothers' clubs, and spaces which ranged from Hampstead Garden Suburb to countless middle-class homes and the post-1918 'Homes fit for Heroes' campaign, all owed a great deal to these women for both their instigation and form, as earlier chapters in this volume have shown.

Common to many of these disciplines was their origin in organised voluntary work. It would remain a significant employer of, and platform for, women throughout the inter-war period. Tomrley and Denby's careers

---

[15]   See Elizabeth Crawford, *Enterprising Women: The Garretts and their Circle*, London: Francis Boutle Publishers, 2002, and Martha Vicinus, *Independent Women, Work and Community for Single Women, 1850–1920*, Chicago, University of Chicago Press, 1985. The campaigns of working-class women were also significant though there is not the space here to discuss it. See the chapters by Hunt and Scott for a discussion of this aspect of space-making.

exemplify this particular strand of space-making and also demonstrate how changes in the voluntary sector had an impact on their careers.

In the 1930s Cycill Tomrley was known for her work for what has rarely been described as a voluntary organisation but which, in the context of this chapter, is best understood as such: the Design and Industries Association (DIA). This was formed in 1915 to campaign for design reform through the improvement of contact among artists and designers and manufacturers and was run on a voluntary basis by a central committee.[16] To campaign was a central plank of voluntary activity; its purpose to draw attention to issues overlooked by government or other powerful institutions. In the DIA's case its campaigns were directed against the aesthetic and economic indifference of the state and manufacturers towards design rather than purely social issues, though the idea that design had broader implications for society's improvement was shared by many in the DIA. No evidence has survived to explain how Tomrley came to be involved with the DIA but it is known that she studied painting at the Slade School of Art, a training which gave her, perhaps, a predisposition to work in the sphere of design.[17] For the DIA she specialised in addressing the problem of how to furnish the working-class home both economically and, in keeping with DIA philosophy, necessarily with modern taste. Typically this entailed creating model interiors in dwellings on the new estates erected by local authorities under the government's social housing programme.[18]

Tomrley's work in this capacity would have brought her to the attention of the CAI even if that body had not been led by a former president of the DIA. In 1936 she was recruited to participate in its investigation into the 'Working Class Home: its Furnishing and Equipment'.[19] Her inclusion in the team to design the interior of the AEH was a natural extension of this earlier role. As well as this work for the DIA and the CAI, Tomrley pursued a writing career and published the book *Furnishing Your Home* in 1939.[20]

If it is slightly tenuous to consider Tomrley a typical representative of the voluntary sector, the career of Elizabeth Denby fits much more comfortably into this category and she is perhaps best understood as an

---

16 See Raymond Plummer, *Nothing Need be Ugly: the first Seventy Years of the DIA*, London: DIA, 1985.

17 Memo from Tomrley to Gordon Russell, 1959, file C1708 'Comments on Student Behaviour entering Industry' in papers of the Design Council Archive, University of Brighton. I am grateful to Lesley Whitworth for directing me to this rare source on Tomrley's life; she otherwise remains an elusive space-maker.

18 See, for example, 'The Designer and her Problem', *Design for Today*, 1, (1933), 175–184.

19 See the resulting report, CAI, *The Working Class Home, Its Furnishing and Equipment*, London: HMSO, 1937; there was also an exhibition held of approved designs in early summer 1937.

20 Cycill Tomrley, *Furnishing your Home*, London: Allen and Unwin, 1939.

heir to the campaigner Octavia Hill.[21] Having taken a Certificate in Social Science at the London School of Economics, Denby began her work in the voluntary housing sector in 1923 and spent a decade in the slums of north Kensington as the (paid) Organising Secretary of the Kensington Housing Association and Trust (KHT).[22] Her duties were diverse. Whilst much of her time was spent in general administration, her responsibilities also encompassed fund-raising, campaigning for housing reform and liaising with potential tenants. As a result of this she came into contact with similar campaigners and organisations in London and was active in the promotion of collaborative work across the sector to persuade central government to address the slum problem; something which was ultimately successful.[23] This work brought her a first-hand understanding of the problems faced by those in poor housing, as well as a detailed knowledge of the means by which their conditions could be improved.

Denby's career in the 1920s can be seen as a direct continuation of the tradition of women's hands-on engagement with housing issues which were initiated by Hill but, in significant ways, her work in Kensington also embodied changes in the voluntary sphere which would have a major impact on its function as a crucible for the development of women's spatial practices. The most significant of these was the gradual displacement of the voluntary sector by the state as the main provider – and hence policy maker – of social welfare. This was a process which began in the early 1900s and was completed irrevocably after 1945. In the inter-war period, the emergence of a 'mixed economy of welfare' saw the voluntary sector become, in many fields, an agent of the state in the distribution of welfare, a process which meant it followed rather then led policy. For women this had two main ramifications: the gradual erosion of a significant space in which they had enjoyed considerable influence, and the increasing codification and regulation of their work as central government demanded new standards of practice from those whom it employed.[24]

The voluntary housing sector, in the 1920s at least, was relatively unaffected by these changes. The focus of central government social housing policy on re-housing the skilled working classes in cottage estates

---

21 On Denby see Elizabeth Darling, '"The Star in the Profession she created for herself": A Brief Biography of Elizabeth Denby, Housing Consultant,' *Planning Perspectives*, 20:3, (2005)

22 On the KHT, see Andrea Tanner, *Bricks and Mortals, 75 Years of the Kensington Housing Trust*, London: Kensington Housing Trust, 2001.

23 Slum clearance acts were passed in 1930, 1933 and 1935. On these campaigns see Elizabeth Darling, '"To induce humanitarian sentiments in prurient Londoners": the Propaganda Activities of London's Voluntary Housing Associations in the Inter-war Period', *London Journal*, 27, (2002), 42–62.

24 This is a necessarily simplified version of events, for further discussion of this see ibid, and Patricia Garside, 'Central Government, Local Authorities and the Voluntary Housing Sector 1919–1939' in Alan O'Day (ed.), *Government and Institutions in the post-1832 UK*, Lampeter: Edwin Meller Press, 1995.

on the peripheries of towns and cities left the slum problem untouched and its amelioration remained primarily the work of the voluntary sector. Housing associations, like the KHT, did however have to work increasingly with local authorities and many started to employ salaried workers like Denby whose professional qualifications gave them an authority, and arguably skills, which a volunteer might have been thought to have lacked.[25] Thus this sector remained a significant arena for women to amass expertise and influence in built space well into the 1920s.

It was only in the next decade that this began to change. By then it was becoming clear that housing associations would not play a substantial role in the slum clearance programmes then being introduced. Instead local authorities would be given primary responsibility for the new housing which would replace Britain's slums; this despite the major campaign by the voluntary housing sector that it should take that role. This shift in government policy coincided with Denby's increasing desire to become more involved in the design of housing and in 1933 she resigned from the Trust to embark on a new career as an independent practitioner, a role she labelled Housing Consultant.[26]

Denby seems to have been the only person at this date to use the term Housing Consultant to denote the practices she undertook and it is tempting to consider her unique because of this. But the activities of the other women considered in this chapter, and indeed elsewhere in this volume, suggest that in what they did, rather than what they called themselves, there were many at this date who pursued similar careers.[27] The 1930s saw a growing engagement with the problems associated with modernity in Britain – mass urbanisation, mass democracy, the growth of the mass market and so on – and a demand for, and supply of, experts to advise policy makers on how best to address its implications.[28] Denby was one of many whose particular knowledge was relevant to contemporary concerns and who was able to pursue a career in dispensing her expertise. Perhaps what distinguished Denby from her peers was the range of her knowledge. Whilst someone like Tomrley specialised in furnishing in this period, Denby added housing design, housing management and health reform, *inter alia*, to this portfolio.

She was certainly able to sustain a career. Her work as co-designer with the architect Maxwell Fry of two blocks of modernist flats for workers helped make her name. She augmented this profile with a number of

---

25 Under the 1924 Housing Act, housing associations could seek subsidies for building from the Ministry of Health.
26 Denby's desire for a career change is recorded in an undated memoir (c.1960). Her papers are held at the Harry Simpson Memorial Library housed in premises at the University of Westminster.
27 Not least Veasey, who was called an adviser.
28 For a more detailed discussion of this see Elizabeth Darling, *Re-forming Britain: Narratives of Modernity before Reconstruction*, London: Routledge, 2007.

authoritative articles on housing policy and in 1938 her book, *Europe Rehoused*, based on research undertaken with the support of a fellowship from the Leverhulme Trust was published.[29] Denby also devoted much of her energies to the furnishing of the working-class dwelling and collaborated with another London housing association, the Saint Pancras House Improvement Society, on the establishment of a shop, House Furnishing Ltd, which stocked affordable and well-designed goods for the Society's tenants (and others). It was this work which led Denby to be appointed as principal investigator to the same CAI committee which Tomrley had joined in 1936.

In the same year, Denby attracted considerable press attention when she became the first woman to address a sessional meeting of the Royal Institute of British Architects (RIBA). In a speech entitled 'Rehousing from the Slumdwellers' Point of View' she offered a coruscating critique of contemporary housing policy which, as its title suggests, drew on interviews she had conducted with people re-housed on local authority cottage or flatted estates.[30] Of flats, she reported that her interviewees commented on the absence of lifts and a private balcony, the lack of sound insulation, ugly architecture and inefficient and inconveniently placed equipment, as well as the lack of imagination in the use of land around flats. She observed: '[flats] are intensely unpopular among working people, who consider that they provide an environment which is entirely unsuitable for family life'.

Denby also noted that many of the criticisms about flats were equally applicable to the cottage estates built on the fringes of English towns and cities. In addition were problems associated with the expense of living at a distance from work, something exacerbated by the absence of cheap shopping centres or friendly tradesmen who would give credit. She drew this part of her speech to a close with the declaration:

> with all my heart I agree with the working man and woman that the choice for a town dweller between a flat at fifty and a cottage at twelve to the acre is a choice between two impractical and unnecessary extremes.

In the second half of the speech she outlined her proposal for an alternative model of housing for slum dwellers, one which addressed the lived experience of working-class families and acknowledged the fact that their opinion was '...overwhelmingly in favour of some form of development which houses the people nearer to their work and nearer to the

---

[29]   These were R.E. Sassoon House, Peckham, south London, 1934 and Kensal House, north Kensington, west London, 1937. See F.R.S. Yorke and Frederick Gibberd, *The Modern Flat*, London: The Architectural Press, 1937, 102–103 and 98–102 respectively for accounts of the schemes.

[30]   The speech is reproduced as Elizabeth Denby. 'Rehousing from the Slum Dwellers' Point of View', *Journal of the Royal Institute of British Architects*, 44, (1936), 61–80. All quotations are taken from this speech and the subsequent discussion until signalled otherwise.

companionship of the centre of the town'. The result was the first version of the house-type and planning scheme which would be exhibited in 1939.[31] She commented, 'as a woman in touch with working women [this scheme] I feel embodies things which are important to working people and discards things which are unimportant...'.

The speech was not well received. The President of the RIBA summarised the general response with his comment 'I cannot imagine any mere man having the courage to stand up here and tell us that the work of our architects and social reformers is in the wrong direction'. Although the speech pre-dated the DMIHE invitation by two years, it ensured that Denby was a familiar – perhaps notorious – enough name in the worlds of housing and architecture that her appointment by Grimaldi would bring in publicity for the Exhibition.

The two other members of the team which created the AEH did not share the notoriety of Denby. Nevertheless the careers of Christine Veasey and Dorothy Braddell highlight parallel traditions of women's interaction with built space which had been established before the war but which were also undergoing changes at this date.

Of all the women under discussion here, Veasey has proved the most elusive; yet it is possible to extrapolate from the small amount of information known about her the broader implications of her practice. In a pamphlet entitled *Good Furnishing* which she edited for the Times Furnishing Company Ltd, she is described as a furnishing and decorating adviser and it was, perhaps, in this role that she enjoyed a second commission at the 1939 DMIHE as the co-arranger of a display called 'The Story of an English Room'.[32] She also seems to have worked as a journalist, producing articles on contemporary design for art journals such as *The Studio*.[33] For us, her occupation of this role draws attention to the considerable territory which women had occupied as commentators on built space dating back to Mrs Beeton, if not much earlier, a tradition which continued into the inter-war period in two main strands. First there were women who wrote manuals on home management, with particular emphasis on labour-saving, in a period when live-in servants were becoming increasingly hard to find.[34] Secondly, there were the women journalists – itself a distinctly modern career 'type' – who wrote for the new women's magazines about design and the home, a phenomenon which was prompted by the house-building boom of the late 1920s onwards, and the demand for advice from first-time owners on how to furnish and occupy

---

31 As in 1939 she proposed a mixed-development scheme; the main difference was that in 1936 the terraced cottages were to be built at densities of 40 per acre.

32 Christine Veasey (ed.), *Good Furnishing*, London: Times Publishing Co. Ltd, n.d.

33 See Christine Veasey, 'Lighting the Home of To-day', *The Studio*, 108, (1934), 199–202.

34 See, for example, Dorothy Constance Peel, *The Art of Modern Housekeeping*, London: Warne, 1935.

their new houses. Both exploited the synonymy of women with the home to create careers which led to an engagement with the public sphere through the space of the text.

Finally, Dorothy Braddell who, alone amongst her fellow team members, had received a professional training in design.[35] It is known that Braddell attended King's College, London. We may infer from her later specialism in kitchen design that she was a student in its Department of Domestic Science.[36] After King's she studied art and decorative art at the Regent Street Polytechnic and Byam Shaw School of Art. For the period this was the best training in design disciplines available. Her career began in the 1920s when the majority of her work was graphic and exhibition-stand design for advertisers. In the 1930s she became well known for her work in designing labour-saving modern kitchens, a subject on which she also wrote. One such piece appears in a collection edited by Patrick Abercrombie, whose pre-eminence in the field of planning by this date suggests a certain regard for Braddell's work.[37] Like Denby and Tomrley, she also served on the CAI committee which investigated the furnishing of the working-class home and was thus an obvious choice for inclusion on the AEH project.

Braddell's professional training in design is significant for it points towards new areas of spatial practice for women which opened up in the inter-war decades: professions which dealt with built space but which had hitherto been closed to women. Under the 1919 Sex Disqualification (Removal) Act, women were, for the first time, able to undertake training as Chartered Surveyors. In the longer term this would offer an alternative route to the professionalism sought equally by the Society of Women Housing Estate Managers, founded by Octavia Hill's successors.[38] Perhaps more significantly, the profession of Architecture slowly began to become more accessible to women from 1918 onwards, with the number of women training as architects increasing very gradually as the decade wore on. In the early 1930s the RIBA, architects' professional body, established a Women's Committee.

The full implications of the marginalisation of the voluntary sector and the rise of the professions on the one hand, and a bureaucratised welfare state on the other, were yet to be fully felt in the years during which the ideas for the AEH were formed. At that time no-one commented on the fact that the woman who designed the AEH was not the one with the formal training to do so; nor that the practices of the women involved entailed the

---

35   I rely here on Jonathan Woodham, 'Braddell, Dorothy Adelaide' in the *Dictionary of National Biography*, Oxford: Oxford University Press, 2004.

36   No evidence survives, however, to substantiate this.

37   See Dorothy Braddell, 'The Interior, Kitchens, Bathrooms etc', in Patrick Abercrombie (ed.), *The Book of the Modern House*, London: Hodder and Stoughton, 1939. On Abercrombie, see Meller's chapter in this volume.

38   See Marion Brion and Anthea Tinker, *Women and Housing: Access and Influence*, London: Housing Centre Trust, 1980, for more on this rivalry.

shaping of space through textual discourse as much as through the manipulation of materials. Their expertise was more important than the media through which it was exercised.

The All-Europe House

The AEH was on display at the DMIHE between April and May 1939. What did visitors see? Denby had designed a flat-roofed terraced house, constructed in brick and in a modernised Georgian style (Figure 7.1). To the front the house had a small terrace, to the rear, 'just enough private garden for the family to be able to grow flowers, vegetables and sit outdoors in comfort'.[39] Site plans showed how the house was intended to form part of an echelonned terrace which was arranged so that the gardens backed onto a communal garden. The house was built to the same space standards (860 square feet) and cost (approximately £500) as a typical local authority house; it was envisaged that it would be built at densities of 25 per acre.

Denby planned the interior to have a large living room (12 by 18 feet) which spanned the rear of the house, and a kitchen-dining room, planned on labour-saving lines, which overlooked the front garden.[40] Upstairs were two children's bedrooms, a main bedroom, bathroom and WC, and copious cupboards. In such a house, the catalogue declared, 'the housewife...would find herself fresher, spending less money, with more leisure than she had ever had in the past, while her home would form part of a compact and pleasant street in the town'.[41]

The furnishing, planning and equipment of the interiors of the AEH was shared amongst the CAI sub-committee, and a fictional family was invented as their client. This comprised 'a sensible, rather cultured artisan couple with a son and two daughters'.[42] Their income was assumed to be three pounds ten shillings a week, of which ten shillings a week went on rent.[43] For them the AEH was to be rendered '... comfortable, homely and an illustration of the maxim that art is inherent in life, implicit in work, and

---

[39]   DMIHE, *Catalogue*, 93.
[40]   This configuration of plan would be used in the post-war housing built in Harlow. See Judith Attfield, 'Inside Pram Town', in Judith Attfield and Patricia Kirkham (eds), *A View from the Interior*, London: The Women's Press, 1989.
[41]   DMIHE, *Catalogue*, 93.The comment about the street refers to Denby's design for a mixed development scheme, see Anon, 'Homes and Ideals'. For another perspective on sympathetic debates about the beneficial effects of well-designed homes on women's lives see the chapters in this volume by Scott and Whitworth.
[42]   DMIHE Press Release, 'All-Europe House, Continent's Best Ideas in One Dwelling', April 1939, BT/57/22/A408/38.
[43]   Minutes of the DMIHE sub-committee of the CAI, 3 February, 1939, BT/57/22/A408/38.

Figure 7.2
The All-Europe House: the boy's bedroom, designed by Christine Veasey
Source: Courtesy of the RIBA Photographs Collection

Figure 7.3
The All-Europe House: the girls' bedroom, designed by Christine Veasey
Source: Courtesy of the RIBA Photographs Collection

not something difficult to be sought or purchased' by the decoration experts, as the Catalogue described them.[44] Denby designed their living room and hall, Braddell the kitchen, Tomrley the parents' bedroom and Veasey the children's bedrooms.

In response to the brief, the team produced a house whose interiors were notable for their light colours at a time when dark colours for paintwork and floor covering prevailed in working-class housing and whose surfaces were to be easy to clean. A similar emphasis on labour-saving could also be found throughout in the use of lightweight and built-in furniture. Denby's living room, for example, contained a settee and two easy chairs upholstered in navy blue fabric, and two hard chairs, a sideboard and table made from either cherry or elm. The walls were painted in a light oyster colour and the floor was covered with an Axminster carpet whose colour is not recorded. Floorboards were stained with ash-grey paint 'which will not show footmarks', whilst the hall and staircase had haircord carpet runners.[45] In the kitchen, Braddell ensured that it was 'copiously equipped' with washing machine, refrigerator and sink fitted with the innovative Garchey waste-disposal system. Its main furniture was a refectory table with cushioned benches so meals could be taken there too. The room was softened by the use of fabrics: a floor-length dark blue curtain to screen off the eating area from the equipment area, calico trimmed with red piping for the bench upholstery, and batik curtains at the windows.

Upstairs, Tomrley furnished the parents' bedroom with a four-foot divan bed with waxed-oak headboard and a chest of drawers and dressing table in natural oak. The floor was linoleum and covered with two rugs. Reports describe her use of 'cottage wallpaper and coloured bedcover' and the resulting 'general air of cosiness'. The dividing room between this room and that of the couple's two daughters was formed by a wall of cupboards; indeed the house was well-equipped with storage space, a provision which reflected its designers' understanding that this was something overlooked in working-class housing.[46] Veasey's schemes for the children's rooms took a rather gendered, though not entirely stereotypical, approach: the two girls had a colour scheme of rose pink, powder blue and white with palest primrose woodwork, whilst the boy's was navy blue and white with touches of red; as in the parents' room, floors were covered in linoleum with rugs placed on top. Noteworthy in both was Veasey's care to ensure that the children had space to do their homework: it was a commonplace fact at this

---

[44]   DMIHE Press Release, 'All-Europe House...'.

[45]   Descriptions of the interiors are taken from Anon, 'The All-Europe House designed by Elizabeth Denby', *Journal of the Royal Institute of British Architects*, 46, (1939), 813–819; DMIHE, *Catalogue* and minutes of the DMIHE sub-committee of the CAI.

[46]   It also recalls the words of the Katherine Buildings' tenant described in Livesey's chapter in this volume who spoke of the want of even a cupboard in his rooms.

time that many working-class children's education suffered because there was no place for them to study at home. In the girls' room, in addition to a chest of drawers, a dressing table was fitted whose lid, when open held a mirror but which, when closed, formed a flat surface on which the sisters could work. The boy who, the Catalogue tells us, was intended for a career in the Navy, was provided with a proper desk and a chest of drawers.

As already noted, the house and its interiors were well received. With reference to the plan of the house and the accompanying mixed-development scheme, the *New Statesman's* critic summarised the desire of many reporters when he said 'I only hope that Miss Denby's ideas will break down a few of the rigid traditions which make so many Housing Schemes both dull and expensive'.[47] A reporter from *The Times* spoke approvingly of the living room's 'liveable, homely atmosphere', and the parents' room which was 'more old-fashioned, and has a cottage-flowered wallpaper, a striped seersucker bedspread, and green curtains bordered with red, which give the room a very cheerful air'.[48] It was not just the press who thought well of the AEH. In addition to her role as designer, the CAI employed Tomrley to remain on-site and document visitors' responses. She reported on the almost unbroken stream of visitors and the particular attention they paid to the kitchen. Also noteworthy was that 'several of them have remarked how human the house is compared with the others and I have heard exclamations of approval, but none of dislike, except criticisms by the middle-class person that the house is small'.[49]

The success of the AEH, as evidenced by the approbation received from press and consumers alike, is testament to the skills of the women involved in its design. For all of them, the realisation of the house at a major public exhibition must have been a dream come true and an affirmation of the legitimacy and value of the type of spatial practice which they pursued. In the spring of 1939, then, all looked positive for the team which made the AEH, but what were the longer term implications for the spatial practices and ideas it embodied?

Conclusion: After the All-Europe House

At the beginning of this chapter it was suggested that the AEH represented both a peak in women's influence over the making of built space and the beginnings of its decline. Considered firstly in terms of how it represents this peak, the most important observations to be made about the AEH relate to the problem which it sought to resolve: the satisfactory re-housing of former slum dwellers. As already noted, Denby's proposal for housing

---

47   Critic, 'A London Diary', *New Statesman and Nation*, 6 May, 1939, 675.
48   A Correspondent, 'An All-Europe House, a Pocket Ideal Home', *The Times*, 28 April, 1939, 21.
49   Tomrley to Pick, 15 April 1939, minutes of the DMIHE sub-committee of the CAI, BT/57/22/A408/38.

schemes which combined terraced houses with blocks of flats must be viewed as having succeeded in its brief, for the principle of mixed development would achieve official approval in the 1944 *Design of Dwellings* Report, and post-war housing estates such as those built at Alton East and West in Roehampton, west London (1950–1959) stand as testament to its adoption by local authorities.[50] This would suggest that it was correct to argue that throughout the inter-war period, middle-class women in their various guises as consultants, commentators and so forth, remained as active and influential in the re-forming of environments as their pre-Great War counterparts.

If, however, we consider the AEH in terms of those who were involved specifically in its design, then the longer-term view is more complex. To date it has proved difficult to trace what happened to Veasey, but the fortunes of her three co-designers varied considerably after 1945.[51] Cycill Tomrley was amongst the first employees of the ground-breaking Council of Industrial Design (CoID),[52] the heir to the CAI, whilst Denby, having served on several wartime reconstruction committees, completed only one further major project after 1945, an interior at the CoID-sponsored 'Britain Can Make It' (BCMI) exhibition of 1946.[53] Thereafter she worked as a writer. Braddell also contributed to BCMI and continued to practise as a designer until her retirement in the late 1960s.[54]

The differing careers of those who made the AEH have a great deal to tell us about how the conditions for women's spatial practices changed in the post-war world. Whilst before the war Denby and Tomrley had combined designing with other activities, writing, committee work and so on, after the war, with the early exception of Denby's work at BCMI, neither would be involved so directly in the design of spaces again. Their space-making was confined, in Denby's case, to writing, and in Tomrley's to her role in an institution which sought to influence the status and future of design in Britain. That Braddell was the only one who sustained a career as a designer signals the key shift in context in this period: the 'take-over' of space-making by professionally-qualified practitioners.[55]

---

50 See Miles Glendinning and Stefan Muthesius, *Tower Block*, London: Yale University Press, 1994.
51 A series of handbooks on needlework were published by a company called Christine Veasey Publications in the 1950s.
52 She would remain there until her retirement in 1966. Thanks to Lesley Whitworth for this information.
53 BCMI was organised by the Council of Industrial Design and was intended to show how design-led industries could kick-start Britain's post-war economy. See Patrick J Maguire and Jonathan Woodham, *Design and Cultural Politics in Post-war Britain*, London: Leicester University Press, 1992.
54 Woodham, *Dorothy Adelaide Braddell*.
55 Helen Meller's chapter in this volume demonstrates how this shift in circumstances affected women in town planning.

As has already been noted, the growth of professionalisation in areas which women had traditionally dominated was already underway in the inter-war years, though its primary impact was on areas only indirectly connected to space-making, such as social welfare work or housing management. This process was connected to the take-over by the state of areas of welfare provision previously the sole remit of the voluntary sector and saw the state demand specialisation and professionalisation from those it employed. So whilst, to put it rather crudely, a figure such as Octavia Hill had been part social worker, part housing manager and part social theorist, by the 1930s state bureaucracy demanded that a woman had to specialise in one of these disciplines alone; it is, after all, in the nature of a profession to monopolise a specific area of practice. The establishment of the Welfare State from 1945 onwards completed the process of the institutionalisation and bureaucratisation of the areas of welfare provision in which women had previously prevailed. It also cut off the main training ground in which women had developed their skills by the marginalisation of the voluntary sector under the post-war settlement.

Whilst it was possible in the 1930s for women such as Denby or Tomrley to negotiate this changing landscape by moving away from the voluntary sector and assuming the role of independent specialists, it was much more difficult to do this in the post-war era. For women like them, whose practices entailed design in addition to their work as writers, reformers and advisers, the fact that the post-war settlement also placed the design of housing in the hands of architects was a further problem. Their lack of formal training excluded them from participation in a discipline which was now a fully fledged profession. Further, since architecture was almost entirely a male profession, the chances that it could become a platform for women's views equivalent to the pre-war voluntary sector were, at least at this time, limited. The suggestion here is that in order to remain in work as architects, women had to submit to the discourse of the professional architect rather than to that of femininity or sisterhood.[56]

In the post-war era, then, the circumstances which had allowed women to form space through both design *and* discourse and whose qualifications derived from hands-on experience rather than membership of a profession, no longer existed. Given these shifts, was it still possible for them to exert influence? Perhaps yes, though it entailed the surrendering of design practice and the embracing of one single discipline in recognition of the fact that specialisation now signalled expertise. For Tomrley, it must have seemed possible to exert influence through her employment at the CoID. For Denby, it was possible to retain a foothold in debates about the built environment through the space of the text. She contributed, for example, to

---

[56] Jill Seddon's chapter on Sadie Speight allows an understanding of how difficult it was as a woman to negotiate professional life.

the *Architectural Review*'s campaign against post-war planning's preoccupation with new towns.[57]

There is then a rather bitter-sweet conclusion to this chapter. On the one hand, it points to the end of a tradition of women's influence over the making of space which had seen women combine – often in one person – a variety of disciplines to create a distinctive contribution to the re-forming of built space in England, one which continued throughout the inter-war period and had an influence beyond it. On the other hand, it suggests that in the post-war era this diversity of practice was superseded by specialisation of practice and that the places from which women could influence space-making diminished as they were subsumed into the professions and institutions of the Welfare State. But there was one place left which retained its power: the space of the text. So whilst it may be difficult to find figures equivalent to Hill or Barnett after 1945, women's command of discourse which continues to prevail today in the work of writers such as Jane Jacobs and Alice Coleman, means that women still retain an influence over contemporary urban form.[58]

---

[57]   See Elizabeth Denby. 'Oversprawl' in Ian Nairn (ed.), *Counter Attack against Subtopia*, London: Architectural Press, 1957 (originally the *Architectural Review* of December 1956)

[58]   Jane Jacobs, *The Death and Life of Great American Cities*, London: Jonathan Cape, 1962 Alice Coleman, *Utopia on Trial, Vision and Reality in Planned Housing*, London: Hilary Shipman, 1990.

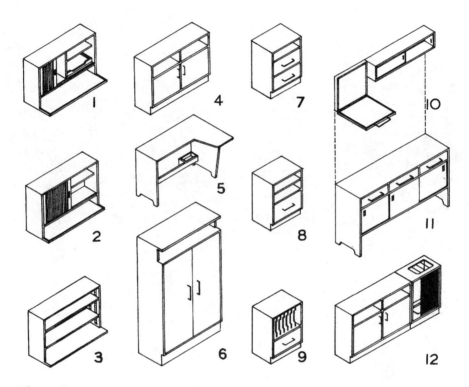

Figure 8.1
'Good Form' Unit Furniture range. W. Rowntree and Sons publicity leaflet, c.1938
Photo source: Jill Seddon

Chapter 8

'Part-Time Practice as Before': The Career of Sadie Speight, Architect

Jill Seddon

Reflecting upon the impact of feminist thought on the academic discipline of Design History over the past twenty years, Judith Attfield makes the point that whilst there has been considerable development in a much wider field of gender, as opposed to women's, studies, some of the most recently published work 'suggests that many of the problems identified in the first wave of "women and design" literature still apply'.[1] In one of those early and seminal 'first wave' texts which have informed much of the work of later art and design historians, *Old Mistresses: Women, Art and Ideology*, Griselda Pollock and Rozsika Parker proposed methods of tackling the 'problems' which still hold such currency. They argued that it was not sufficient merely to unearth forgotten female artists or designers and somehow make room for them in the canon; rather, what was required was the deconstruction of a patriarchal society and its institutions, and an understanding of the ways in which women have been, and are still, marginalised and excluded.[2]

How, then, do the achievements of a professionally qualified, talented, well connected and popular woman get written out of architectural history? According to architectural historian Lynne Walker, it happens in a variety of ways:

> Women's architectural production in the late 1920s and 1930s was very well received and well-illustrated in the building press, but modernist architectural history has either ignored it, as in the case of the 'pioneering' Factory Offices, Derby 1929–31, designed by Norah Aiton and Betty Scott; misattributed their work (Mary Crowley); absorbed their names and reputations into their partners' (Sadie Speight) or depicted it as a representation of the designer's femininity.[3]

1   Judith Attfield, 'What Does History Have To Do With It? Feminism and Design History', *Journal of Design History*, 16:1, (2003), 77.
2   Griselda Pollock and Rozsika Parker, *Old Mistresses: Women, Art and Ideology*, London: Women's Press, 1981.
3   Lynne Walker, "Concrete Proof: Women, Architecture and Modernism", *Feminist Arts News*, 3, (1986), 8.

In focusing on one of the individuals named above, Sadie Speight (Figure 8.2), and in particular her own phrase, 'part-time practice as before',[4] this chapter aims to progress beyond the act of reclamation, important though that is, to an exploration of complex issues of creative partnership and the processes of historiography. In accordance with the methodology of Pollock and Parker, it examines aspects of two institutions as they related to Speight's working life: the British architectural profession, particularly its role in the rise of British modernism, and, more complicatedly, marriage and the impact of personal relationships upon professional partnerships. Thus it proceeds from a brief account of the significant events of Speight's career to an analysis of the ways in which her achievements have been either acknowledged or, more often, ignored, by subsequent historians and critics.

By taking an historiographical approach this chapter also seeks to re-emphasize the usefulness of biography as a means to understanding the practice of design. Within architectural and design history there has been a suspicion of biography as a methodology because its emphasis on the individual appears to perpetuate the approach taken by Nikolaus Pevsner in his *Pioneers of the Modern Movement From William Morris to Walter Gropius*, first published in 1936. In this text he proposed a linear progression from the work of one proto-modernist 'hero' to another, a model which it is particularly important to challenge in the case of Speight. Here, a recording of the specific circumstances of an individual woman's life will help to explain certain negotiations and compromises which took place on a personal level, and position them within the much wider social and cultural context in which the subject lived and worked.

It is also important to consider how a case study of Speight might be sited within other theoretical debates, since her experiences were not unique and are not limited to the practices of architecture and design. Analysis carried out by social scientists can provide a useful model in this respect. During the early 1980s a number of writers sought explanations for the exclusion of women, both as individuals and collectively, from what Mary O'Brien christened 'male-stream scholarship' in these disciplines.[5] Artemis March identified three mechanisms by which this is achieved: 'Exclusion, Pseudo-Inclusion and Alienation'.[6] The second of these, which 'appears to take women into account, but then marginalises them', is the

---

4   Notes compiled by Sadie Speight for Lynne Walker, and in her possession, in connection with the exhibition 'Women Architects: Their Work' held at the Heinz Gallery, Royal Institute of British Architects (RIBA), 1984.

5   Mary O'Brien, *The Politics of Reproduction*, London: Routledge Kegan Paul, 1981 quoted in Beverly Thiele, 'Vanishing Acts in Political and Social Thought, Tricks of the Trade', in L. McDowell and R. Pringle (eds), *Defining Women:Social Institutions and Gender Divisions*, Cambridge: Polity Press, 1992, 26.

6   Artemis March, 'Female invisibility in androcentric sociological theory', *Insurgent Sociologist,* 11:2, 99–107, quoted in Thiele, ibid, 27.

most helpful in an examination of Speight's career. March elaborates, 'Women become defined as a "special case", as anomalies, exceptions to the rule, which can be noted and then forgotten about. What is normative is male...'.[7] These effects may be observed when considering the treatment of women architects and designers who are excluded from 'mainstream' histories, whilst receiving critical attention in exhibitions such as ' Women Architects, Their Work' of 1984 and 'Women Designing: Redefining Design in Britain Between the Wars' of 1994.[8]

Personal and professional partnerships are very complex entities with many characteristics specific to those individuals affected, and difficulties of interpretation can become magnified when people are involved in shared acts of creation. Whitney Chadwick and Isabelle de Courtivron claim that '...given our culture's emphasis on solitary creation, one is always constructed as Significant, and the partner as other'.[9] They outline some of the ways in which both historians and literary scholars have begun to deconstruct this complicated area. These include 'retrieval', 'setting the record straight', and 'examining reciprocal influences'.[10] The category of those retrieved encompasses those who helped to 'create the conditions, the inspiration and the atmosphere for their partner's artistic production', a process named 'mothering the mind' by literary scholars Ruth Perry and Martine Brownley.[11]

Elements of all three methods would seem to be appropriate in the case of Speight. Her inclusion, with others, in the *New Dictionary of National Biography* is one measure of the process of retrieval, although at ten per cent of all entries the number of female entries is lamentable. 'Setting the record straight' can to some extent be achieved by painstaking and accurate research. It must be noted, however, that the only publicly-accessible primary source material which relates directly to Speight's working life is to be found in her husband's papers: there is no Sadie Speight archive.[12] Disentangling 'reciprocal influence' is much more difficult and is unlikely to have a definitive outcome. In the case of Speight and Martin the problem is worsened by conventions of scholarship which privilege architecture over industrial design and insist upon attributing large architectural projects, which have involved whole teams of people, to a single individual.

7   Ibid.
8   Held at the Heinz Gallery, RIBA, Portland Place, London (July–August 1984) and University of Brighton Gallery (March 1994) respectively.
9   Whitney Chadwick and Isabelle de Courtivron, *Significant Others: Creativity and Intimate Partnership*, London, Thames & Hudson, 1993, 8.
10 Ibid, 10.
11 Ruth Perry and Martine Watson Brownley (eds), *Mothering the Mind: Studies of Writers and their Silent Partners*, New York and London: Holmes and Meier, 1984.
12 Sir Leslie Martin papers (uncatalogued), RIBA Archive. I am grateful to Eleanor Gawne, Archivist, for access to these papers.

Sadly there is ample evidence that the processes of elision and exclusion identified in the following case study of Speight, cannot be assigned to history, but have continued through to the present. Architect Denise Scott Brown wrote a polemic entitled 'Room at the Top? Sexism and the Star System in Architecture', in 1975, which she held back from publication until 1989 fearing a hostile reception which might damage her career. It did, however, circulate in *samizdat* form and achieved a sympathetic following. In the article Scott Brown recounts with some bitterness the myriad ways in which her work has been misattributed, undermined and ignored in favour of that of her husband and professional partner, Robert Venturi. She catalogues what she calls 'the petty apartheid' of social occasions when 'architects' are differentiated from 'wives', the ignoring of information sheets issued to journalists and critics which list the appropriate credits for building projects and writings, and the omission of her name altogether. It comes as little surprise when Scott Brown states, 'These experiences have caused me to fight, suffer doubt and confusion, and expend too much energy'.[13] In a postscript to her original piece she points to potential signs of progress such as a rise in female admissions to architectural schools in the United States, and affirmative action programmes, but concludes that, at the end of the 1980s, little had changed. She appears to have reached an accommodation with her situation:

> Over the years, it has slowly dawned on me that the people who cause my painful experiences are ignorant and crude. They are the critics who have not read enough and the clients who do not know why they have come to us. ... the scholars whose work we most respect, the clients whose projects intrigue us, and the patrons whose friendship inspires us, have no problem understanding my role.[14]

Underlying all Scott Brown's negative experiences, however, there is an acknowledgement that a creative partnership is a complex relationship about which it is difficult to make definitive pronouncements. Even she admitted, 'We ourselves cannot tease our contributions apart'.[15]

In addition to the methodological shifts outlined above, one further ingredient is yet required for a measured assessment of the life and work of Speight and that is, as Lynne Walker pointed out twenty years ago, a sustained reassessment of modernism and its legacy. This would entail the abandonment of a history dependent upon a string of pioneering architects

---

13   Denise Scott Brown, 'Sexism and the Star System', in J. Rendell, B. Penner and I. Borden (eds), *Gender, Space, Architecture: An Interdisciplinary Introduction*, London: Routledge, 2000, 259. The text was originally published in Ellen Perry Berkeley (ed.), *Architecture: a Place for Women*, London and Washington: Smithsonian Institution Press, 1989.
14   Ibid, 264.
15   Ibid, 260.

and acknowledged 'great buildings' – Henry-Russell Hitchcock's 'actual monuments',[16] for one which is based on a more fundamental acknowledgement of a relationship between house builder and homemaker, and its significance for women both as clients and users of architecture, and as architects themselves. It would also allow an interpretation of a career that embraced industrial design and writing, as well as architectural practice, to be viewed not as some kind of 'watering down' of potential, but as a significant engagement with the social project of modernism itself.

A Short Biography

Sadie Speight was born into a professional family in Lancashire in 1906; her father was a medical practitioner.[17] Both she and her sister Kathleen, who specialised in modern languages, studied at Manchester University. Sadie Speight graduated with first-class honours from the School of Architecture there in 1929. She was an outstanding student, as indicated by the fact that she became a Prix de Rome finalist and was awarded the Zimmern Travelling Scholarship and, later, the Neale Bursary from the Royal Institute of British Architects (RIBA). These successes funded a period of travel and study abroad. Her field of study at this time was wide-ranging, both in geographical location and historical period. Her research report, compiled in 1934, is devoted to 'Isabelline Architecture in Spain 1474–1504'.[18] In 1930 Speight received the RIBA's Silver Medal and was elected an Associate; in 1932 she held the Faulkner Fellowship at Manchester University, and gained her Master's degree in 1933. Between 1930 and 1934 she also worked as an architectural assistant for the firm of Halliday and Associates in Manchester.

As a well qualified and highly regarded graduate, Speight embarked on a career path shared by many of her male contemporaries in modernist architecture, including that of her future husband, but also inflected by her domestic partnership. In 1935 she married Leslie Martin, who had been a fellow student at Manchester (Figure 8.2).[19] He was by then Head of the School of Architecture at Hull College of Arts and Crafts and employed his wife as a part-time tutor. She worked two hours per week at a rate of eight shillings per hour, which was sixpence per hour less than her fellow part-time tutor and two evening tutors, all male.[20] Concurrently, Speight and

---

16 Henry-Russell Hitchcock and Philip Johnson, *The International Style*, New York, W.W. Norton and Co., 1932, 19.

17 An occupation is not recorded for her mother.

18 Sadie Speight, 'Isabelline Architecture in Spain 1474–1504', 1934. Manuscript presented by the author to the British Architectural Library, RIBA.

19 On their marriage certificate, under the heading 'Rank or Profession', Martin's entry appears as 'Architect' whereas, for Speight, the space is left blank.

20 File MLA 11.7, Max Lock papers, University of Westminster. I am grateful to Elizabeth Darling for this reference.

Figure 8.2
Sadie Speight, c.1975
Source: Courtesy of Sue Martin Mason

Martin also collaborated on the design of a number of private houses, all adhering to the geometric, flat-roofed tenets of modernism, one of which incorporated a studio and was commissioned by the textile designer and painter Alastair Morton, who was to remain a friend and correspondent of Speight.[21] Between 1938 and 1939 the partnership designed a kindergarten at Northwich in Cheshire, thus allying themselves with significant reforms in infant welfare and education that found their material expression in the clean lines and rational planning of modernist architecture.[22]

The period immediately preceding the Second World War was also important for the publication of Speight's and Martin's convictions about the future development of modern architecture and design. Along with the painter Ben Nicholson and sculptors Naum Gabo and Barbara Hepworth, they were founders of 'Circle', a grouping of modernist practitioners whose intention was to carry out 'an international review of painting, sculpture and architecture'.[23] Martin, Nicholson and Gabo edited *Circle, International Survey of Constructive Art*, which was published in 1937, while Speight and Martin published *The Flat Book* in 1939. During the war Speight was a

---

[21]   Morton's house was illustrated in *The Architectural Review*, 86 (1939), 13. It was Morton to whom Speight confided her frustration at working with Nikolaus Pevsner (see note 50).

[22]   See H. Myles-Wright and R. Gardner-Medwin, *The Design of Nursery and Elementary Schools*, London: The Architectural Press, 1938. Speight and Martin's kindergarten was illustrated in *The Architectural Review*, September, 1939.

[23]   Sadie Speight, 'Circle Report No. 1', 1936. Martin papers.

Figure 8.3
Sadie Speight and Leslie Martin
in the 1930s
*Source: Courtesy of
Sue Martin Mason*

member of the Design Research Unit (DRU), founded by a group of architects and designers to help define and coordinate the role of industrial design in Britain's post-war reconstruction.[24] Whilst there she became involved in the design of household appliances.[25] This direct experience of industrial design led to her substantial contributions to 'Design Review', a regular feature in *The Architectural Review* from 1944. She further committed her ideas about modern design to print in a chapter entitled 'Inside the House' which formed part of a collection of essays, mostly by DRU members, published under the title *The Practice of Design* in 1946.

It was during the post-war period that Speight's and Martin's careers began to diverge markedly. With Leonard Manasseh, she designed the Rosie Lee cafeteria for the landmark Festival of Britain in 1951. The cafeteria formed part of the Festival's Live Architecture exhibition, which comprised a new neighbourhood of working-class housing at Lansbury,

[24] 'Notes on the History of the Design Research Unit 1943–1969', Archive of Art and Design (AAD), National Art Library, Victoria & Albert Museum, London, AAD 3–1980–28.

[25] Speight's DRU projects included an electric kettle for Beethoven Electric Equipment, illustrated in DRU, *The Practice of Design*, London: Lund Humphries, 1946, 120.

east London.[26] This element of the Festival was described as '...a brave new world where plans, first formulated at the height of the blitz, are now being translated into bricks and mortar'.[27] Although it did not receive the same publicity as other Festival sites, it was to have a far greater impact on Britain's post-war built environment. In the decades that followed, Speight continued to work on architectural, interior and exhibition design commissions whilst also bringing up a son and daughter, both of whom subsequently were to train as architects.[28]

Martin, meanwhile, was developing a career which led to his recognition as one of Britain's leading architectural practitioners. During the war he was appointed chief architectural assistant to the London, Midland and Scottish Railway, described by Diana Rowntree as '... a creative centre of the hitherto unsung modern movement', and then became deputy to the chief architect of the London County Council (LCC), Robert Matthew, with whom he collaborated closely on the design of the Royal Festival Hall.[29] In 1953 Martin took over as chief architect of the LCC and three years later was appointed to the Chair of the School of Architecture at Cambridge University, where he stayed until his retirement.[30] He was knighted in 1957. Much of Speight's effort during the final phase of her own career, before she became progressively incapacitated by motor neurone disease, was devoted to the documenting of her husband's achievements. She died in 1992.

Attribution, Acknowledgement and Interpretation

Speight's involvement in, and contribution to, the formative stages of British modernism are clear even from the simple listing of the key events of her professional life given above. Her omission from most historical accounts of the movement raises historiographical questions concerning attribution, acknowledgement and interpretation to which there are no straightforward answers.[31] The respective roles of Speight and Martin in the

---

26   H. McG. Dunnett, *Guide to the Exhibition of Architecture, Town-planning and Building Research*, London: HMSO, 1951.
27   'Live Architecture Down at Poplar', *The Sphere*, 2 June, (1951), 381.
28   I am grateful to Sadie Speight's daughter, Sue Martin Mason A.A.Dipl, ARIBA, for answering queries about her mother's work and providing images of her mother and father. Speight's son, Christopher (Kit) Martin was described as director of the Phoenix Trust (UK Historic Building Preservation Trust) in *Who's Who* (2000).
29   Diana Rowntree, 'Obituary', *The Guardian*, 2 August, 2000.
30   See Leslie Martin, *Buildings and Ideas 1933–1983: From the Studio of Leslie Martin and His Associates*, Cambridge: Cambridge University Press, 1983.
31   For further consideration of these issues see Elizabeth Darling, 'Elizabeth Denby or Maxwell Fry? A Matter of Attribution', in Brenda Martin and Penny Sparke (eds), *Women's Places: Architecture and Design 1860–1960*, London: Routledge, 2003.

formation of Circle, and the volume of the same title subsequently published, are indicative of future developments.

At the first meeting of the Circle group in 1936, Speight was elected Secretary and Treasurer. In her minutes, Nicholson, Martin and Gabo are recorded as in attendance, and she and Hepworth are noted '...also present...'.[32] Of the three editors, Martin appears to have been the most involved in commissioning pieces from some of the key figures of international modernism. Between 1936 and 1937 he corresponded with, amongst others, Marcel Breuer, Walter Gropius, Le Corbusier, Maxwell Fry and Lewis Mumford. Speight meanwhile was asked to translate two articles from *Gaceta de Arte* by Eduardo Westerdahl and Alberto Sartoris for Ben Nicholson, and corresponded with Piet Mondrian about the translation of the article that he was contributing.[33] Detailed correspondence between Hepworth and Speight is evidence that the two women were deeply involved in the editing and layout of the resulting volume.[34] It is the three men, however, who are credited with its editing and authorship.[35]

Speight shared her husband's convictions about modernism, but her manner of committing them to print took a more pragmatic form. Whilst work on the production of *Circle* was continuing, Speight began to undertake research for a more practical volume. This was eventually to be published under the joint names of Speight and Martin as *The Flat Book* in 1939. Martin maintained that his wife had undertaken the substantial task of compiling information and the survival of her heavily annotated copy of the book indicates that she continued to do so after the book was published, possibly with the idea of producing a revised edition.[36] A careful reading of the text would suggest a single authorial voice, and it appears that this was primarily Speight's project on which her husband advised and to which he lent his name.

In *The Flat Book* Speight viewed her role as the interpretation of the aims and approaches of modern architects for an interested and educated lay audience. It therefore represents a significant departure from a nineteenth-century tradition in which advice on furnishing the home was often combined with rules of etiquette.[37] She offered advice on all aspects of creating the modern home, from planning and layout, colour schemes, and the arrangement of furniture; through heating, lighting, ventilation and

32   Speight 'Circle Report No. 1', 1936. Martin papers.
33   'Circle Report no. 3', 1 September 1936; letter dated 15 November 1936, Martin papers.
34   Undated pencil sketches and notes, Martin papers.
35   Nicholson's contribution was limited to three quotations, set out on a single page.
36   Interview with Sir Leslie Martin, March, 1993. No second edition was published.
37   See Grace Lees-Maffei, 'From Service to Self-Service; Advice Literature as Design Discourse 1920-1970', *Journal of Design History*, 14:3, (2001), 187–206.

sanitary equipment; to pottery, glass and silverware. The products recommended were all in production at the time and details of designers and/or manufacturers and prices were included.

Speight's selection of products 'strictly on their merit as designs though also with some regard to the reasonable cost of the article' reveals a desire to appeal to a cross section of the population.[38] The range extends from examples designed by some of the great names of international modernism, most of whom were friends of Speight and Martin – Marcel Breuer, Serge Chermayeff, Naum Gabo, Alvar Aalto – to crockery, glassware and cutlery sold at Woolworth's. In the text great emphasis is placed upon the idea that consumer choices should be dictated by the application of a set of elementary rules: in the placing of furniture, the layout of the kitchen and the choice of colour schemes, with several diagrams and charts provided.

It is unclear from the surviving correspondence when the final title of *The Flat Book* was adopted. In a letter to the architect F.R.S. Yorke about illustrations for use in the forthcoming book, retailer Crofton Gane wrote

> I have a request from Miss Sadie Speight MA ARIBA to include illustrations of High Point, Highgate in a book entitled 'How Shall I Finish [sic] My Flat?' which is shortly to be published by Wm. Heinemann Ltd. @ 2/6d.[39]

Speight writing to Yorke a few days later did not specify a title, merely explaining, 'My husband and I are preparing a book on the furnishing of flats for Messrs. Heinemann...'.[40] In a subsequent review of the book, architect Serge Chermayeff admitted to being puzzled as to why the authors had chosen 'so circumscribed a title...[when it is] as valid to the householder in town or country as to the urban flat dweller'.[41] The final title of the publication, however, is significant, since, during the inter-war period, the flat had been identified as *the* modern unit of housing by many contemporary architects and was described as 'a building type peculiar to our own era' by Yorke himself and Frederick Gibberd in their foreword to *The Modern Flat* (1937).[42] Yorke and Gibberd's book was an architectural polemic consisting in the main of an international catalogue of built examples by a range of modernist architects. In its emphasis on the practical tasks of furnishing the home *The Flat Book* did not align itself with architectural texts, nor with more generalised theoretical debate as found in Herbert Read's *Art and Industry*, which Speight and Martin

---

38   Martin and Speight, *The Flat Book*, foreword.
39   Yorke's former partner Marcel Breuer had designed an interior in the Tecton designed block. Letter dated 6 August 1937, file 2/2, FRS Yorke papers, British Architectural Library. I am grateful to Elizabeth Darling for this reference.
40   Letter dated 9 August 1937, file 2/2, FRS Yorke papers.
41   Serge Chermayeff, 'Review', *Focus*, 4, (1939), 80.
42   F.R.S. Yorke and Frederick Gibberd, *The Modern Flat*, London: The Architectural Press, 1937, 8.

claimed to have been its inspiration.[43] Speight's work on this book is most easily positioned within the 'good design' movement then emerging in the 1930s and 1940s.

A further example of complex questions of attribution connected with the partnership of Speight and Martin is revealed through scrutiny of the illustrations in *The Flat Book*. Just before its publication, probably in 1938, they jointly designed the 'Good Form' range of modular furniture for the manufacturer W. Rowntree and Sons, of Scarborough (Figure 8.3). This consisted of a selection of simple ready-made geometric units which were intended to be capable of flexible arrangement within a room and, as Martin later wrote, 'could readily be combined with the early Aalto, Plan and Isokon furniture then becoming available'.[44] On the front of the leaflet, which Rowntree and Sons produced to accompany an exhibition of the 'Good Form' range at their showrooms, the designers are clearly credited as J. L. Martin and Sadie Speight. When they chose to illustrate these same pieces in their book a year later, however, they were attributed solely to Martin. This must have been a joint decision which, years later, Martin was to suggest might have been due to the fact that he was responsible for the drawing up of the original designs.[45] This later attribution was then perpetuated in the catalogue of the exhibition, *Thirties: British Art and Design Before the War*, held at the Hayward Gallery in London in 1979 to 1980. Thus acknowledgement of Speight's contribution to the design of this furniture has been lost, for reasons which remain obscure but appear to have been self-imposed, as will be discussed further below. This is in marked contrast to the more straightforward, and more common, wilful neglect which has been the lot of many female designers. [46]

Post-war Diversification

As can be seen in the examples discussed above, in the inter-war period both Speight and Martin were closely involved not only in architectural projects, but also in other aspects of design. During and after the Second World War, however, Speight continued this diversification into design

---

43 Speight and Martin, *The Flat Book*, 195. 'The authors acknowledge their special debt to Mr Herbert Read, at whose suggestion this book was undertaken and to whose outstanding work on general principles of design, 'Art and Industry', they have made constant reference'.

44 Martin, *Buildings and Ideas*, 204. In this claim Martin is aligning his and Speight's designs with leading modernist designers and manufacturers whose work was being retailed in Britain.

45 Interview with Sir Leslie Martin, March 1993.

46 Interestingly, two pieces of furniture, an easy chair designed for Hull Pioneer Furnishing Stores and cane chairs manufactured by The Blind Institute in Hull, which are directly credited, in *The Flat Book*, to Speight alone, are, like a number of pieces, listed but not illustrated.

practice and criticism, while Martin began to consolidate his architectural career. As with many aspects of Speight's work, the extent of her involvement with, and her position within, DRU is difficult to ascertain precisely. A *DRU Bulletin* from 1968 lists the group of members assembled by its founder as 'Milner Gray, Misha Black, Frederick Gibberd, Felix Samuely *and others*' [author's italics].[47] Whereas in the Unit's own account of its 'Early Origins', Speight is clearly identified as one of the part-time associates of Milner Gray, Misha Black and Kenneth Bayes. The list in which Speight features is suggestive of how women are categorised once they are included in the historical records. Thus we find 'the architect Frederick (now Sir Frederick) Gibberd, the structural engineer, the late Felix Samuely, Sadie Speight (*now Lady Martin, wife of Sir Leslie Martin*), the designers Norbert Dutton and Robert Gutmann, who had trained at the Bauhaus' [author's italics]. [48]

The range of products designed by Speight as a member of DRU included the aforementioned domestic appliances, rugs, a hairbrush and glassware for Pilkington's and Chance Brothers Ltd.[49] This 'hands-on' experience of industrial design, combined with her writings, obviously qualified Speight to become a commentator on contemporary design for *The Architectural Review,* in the eyes of one of its editors, Nikolaus Pevsner. Speight was sufficiently familiar with Pevsner's writings on design to reuse in *The Flat Book* some of the photographic plates published by Pevsner in his 1937 *An Enquiry into Industrial Art in England.*[50] When in 1944 *The Architectural Review* relaunched its monthly Bulletin of Standard Design under the new title 'Design Review', Pevsner invited Speight not only to become a member of its advisory team, which also included Misha Black, Noel Carrington, Milner Gray, Peter Ray and Herbert Read, but also to edit this section of the journal.[51]

'Design Review' appeared at intervals between 1944 and 1946, and detailed correspondence between Speight and Pevsner reveals a fraught working relationship. Some of the problems derived from Pevsner's pedantic, even obsessive, nature which made him difficult to work with; others from tensions between the realities of journalism and magazine production, and the circumstances of Speight's domestic life. Early on she confided to Alastair Morton, 'You probably realise from Nos. 1 and 2 how

---

47   *Design Research Unit Bulletin*, no. 54, Nov. 1968. Misha Black papers, AAD.

48   *Notes on the History of the Design Research Unit 1943–1969*, Misha Black papers, AAD.

49   Tumblers illustrated in 'Industrial Design News, *Scope*, May (1946), 75. The caption reads '...designed...by Sadie Speight...member of Design Research Unit's directorate.'

50   Nikolaus Pevsner, *An Enquiry into Industrial Art in England*, Cambridge: Cambridge University Press, 1937.

51   In a letter dated only January 1944, intended to sent out to manufacturers and designers, Speight announced, '...the Architectural Review is to begin a monthly supplement – a design review, which I am editing for them.' Martin papers.

unsatisfactory it is to work with Pevsner'.[52] At the same time, in a letter to Pevsner, she provided a rare glimpse of family life and the attendant difficulties in juggling responsibilities:

> Here is Design Review no. 5 (October) which I couldn't get off until today as my one reliable cook has gone away with shingles and the house is rapidly filling up with other people's children so that we are a bit under the weather.[53]

Pevsner's letters to Speight are full of demands for tasks to be accomplished immediately and to his specifications, and he was particularly insistent on the writing, and rewriting, of photographic captions.[54] On occasion his interference took on a decidedly patronising if not downright misogynistic tone. His instructions relating to a review of a wallpaper exhibition by the advisory committee read:

> The writing down of what our impressions are will be your job, a journalistic job. But then, you have not had to do the "philosophical" article and you are relieved of the Aluminium feature... It will be needed in a hurry.[55]

There is no record of Speight's reaction to this missive, but she was perfectly capable of mounting a robust defence of her own editorial decisions.[56] Soon, however, her exasperation with Pevsner's behaviour reached a crisis point. In a letter to him which began; 'I think there must be some misunderstanding about this Design Review job', she continued:

> When I took it on I understood that I was to be your "chief scout" to select suitable miscellaneous illustrations to fill "$^1/_2$ to two pages" monthly. ...in order to support this programme I have written articles for each issue compiled by me...you have always changed the text as you thought fit.... your letters seem to suggest that it is part of my job to provide this journalism even to re-writing the issue entirely if my first ideas are opposed to yours. If this is what you feel that I ought to do, I am so sorry but I must resign from the job.[57]

Her letter concluded with a list of conditions under which she would be prepared to continue. These included arranging the programme, making contact with specialists who could write appropriate pieces, collecting material for the areas on which she had specialist knowledge, and to be

---

52   Letter 17 July 1944, Martin papers.

53   Letter 5 July 1944, Martin papers.

54   In a letter dated 8 May 1944 he repeatedly asks her to write captions like an 'uncomic strip', as a consecutive story.

55   Letter 20 April 1945. Martin papers.

56   In response to Pevsner's criticism of the planned inclusion, in one edition, of rugs designed before the war by Jean Finn, Speight wrote, 'They definitely were passed by you and other [committee] members present.' Letter 16 October 1945, Martin papers.

57   Letter 26 April, 1945, Martin papers.

allowed to write under her own name, 'just as Herbert [Read], [John] Gloag
and [Noel] Carrington have done'.[58] In response Pevsner offered to 'discuss
your concrete proposals with my people here', but apart from a more
respectful tone in correspondence, there is little evidence of a change of
policy.[59] Speight nevertheless continued with her work on 'Design Review',
producing a successful Special Issue on American design, on which she was
congratulated by Susanne Wasson-Tucker, of the Museum of Modern Art,
New York.[60]

Problems stemming from the demands of the *Architectural Review* job
resurfaced in a more acute fashion in 1946, when plans were announced for
a special issue devoted to industrial design to link with the 'Britain Can
Make It' exhibition at the Victoria & Albert Museum. Both Pevsner and his
fellow editor, H. de C. Hastings, wrote to Speight stressing that the work
involved on the special issue would amount to a full-time job for six months
and asked her to take it on. She replied that while,

> I should very much like to undertake the work...I am very sorry indeed that I
> couldn't possibly do it owing to my domestic commitments. The only work I am
> able to do is work which in the main I can carry out at home with say one or at
> the very most two days in London per week.[61]

Although Speight made it clear that she would understand if the editors
preferred to employ someone else, there is no evidence that they did so.
When the special issue duly appeared in October, its layout and general
tone very much resembled those of *The Flat Book*. The only instances when
her name was credited related to the illustrations, two of which were of
Speight's kettle and iron for Beethoven Electric Equipment.[62] She still
appeared as a member of the 'Design Review' advisory committee in its
final issue, in December 1946.

Whilst her two years contributing to 'Design Review' do not represent
the easiest episode of her working life, Speight was clearly extremely
interested in researching modern industrial design, as well as working in
the field herself.[63] Her identification, as a female architect and designer,

---

58   Gloag and Carrington were well-known commentators on design. Amongst
     other works, Gloag had edited *Design in Modern Life*, London: Allen and
     Unwin in 1934 and Carrington *British Achievement in Design*, London: Pilot
     Press in 1946.
59   Letter 4 May 1945. In a letter dated 18 May 1945 Pevsner began, 'Please don't
     think I am trying to make things difficult or I am an arch-pedant, but do read
     your captions again'.
60   Letter 6 July 1945, Martin papers.
61   Letter 18 April 1946. Martin papers. Speight and Martin were living in
     Boxmoor, Hertfordshire at the time.
62   *The Architectural Review*, 100 (1946), 111 and 114.
63   In April and May 1946 Pevsner and Speight corresponded about the possibility
     of her being commissioned to design carpets through Pevsner's contacts on the
     Board of Trade's Carpet Working Party.

within the domestic sphere is brought sharply into focus by her essay entitled 'Inside the House', published in *The Practice of Design* in 1946. In contrast to *The Flat Book*, whose tone is didactic and rather impersonal, this piece of writing adopts a more concerned stance. She was anxious that 'new conceptions of space and arrangements within buildings and [explorations] of new materials and techniques', carried out before the war, should be capitalised upon in peacetime reconstruction.[64] She was also keen that scientific research into heating and insulation, for example, should be applied as practical advantages for modern living. In this piece she displayed a more overt identification with a female reader/user. In the caption to an illustration of the 'Kitchen of Tomorrow' exhibition held in Ohio in 1944, Speight wrote 'It is questionable whether the majority of housewives would care to spend so much of their time among so many hard, glittering surfaces'.[65]

In the same year, fellow architect Jane Drew was the only woman speaker at a conference organised by the Council of Industrial Design and the Federation of British Industries. In the subsequent published report, some of her slides were reproduced as illustrations, amongst which were three products designed by Speight. Drew described her iron for Beethoven Electric Company as 'a pleasure to use and a pleasure to look at and a great contribution to a woman's life'.[66] Drew was defined as 'Author, Architect and Industrial Designer', a description which applied just as well to Speight.

The 1940s were a decade when Speight's primary output consisted of writing and criticism, but the early 1950s marked a return to architectural practice, mainly in collaboration with Leonard Manasseh and Partners. This again raises intriguing questions of attribution for the present-day historian. A shop design project which was illustrated in the architectural press provides a revealing case study. Work for 'Gay Kaye', an accessories shop in Bond Street, was described by the *Architects' Journal* as having had 'little external alteration', instead, reliance had been 'placed on good display'.[67] In this instance the work was attributed solely to Sadie Speight. When the same shop was illustrated a year later by *The Architectural Review*, it was termed a reconstruction and the attribution changed accordingly to: 'designed by Sadie Speight in association with Leonard

---

64   Sadie Speight, 'Inside the House', *The Practice of Design*, London. Lund Humphries, 1946, 111.
65   Ibid, 117. Martin also contributed to the volume, with an essay entitled 'Changing Building Methods', perhaps further evidence of their diverging paths.
66   Jane Drew, 'Humanising Industrial Design' in Report *on the Conference on Industrial Design Held at Central Hall 26th–27th September 1946*, London: Council Of Industrial Design and Federation of British Industry, 1946. I am grateful to Lesley Whitworth for this reference. The other products were rugs for Morton Sundour and a kettle for Beethoven Electric Company.
67   Anon, 'Post-war Shop Fronts in London', *Architects' Journal*, 115, (1952), 581.

Manasseh, assistant architect Lois Hutchings'.[68] The implication was clear. A female practitioner was more strongly associated with aspects of layout while structural undertakings required the assistance of a male partner.[69]

After the 1950s, Speight's architectural output seems to have been limited to personal domestic projects and to 'bolstering up' her husband's career, particularly through exhibition design: for example in the planning of the screens for an exhibition, 'Leslie Martin and Associated Architects'.[70] A concern with display and layout featured throughout her career. It has already been noted that Speight and Hepworth planned the layout of *Circle*, and Leslie Martin stated that his wife was responsible for the layout of *The Flat Book* and a later book *Buildings and Ideas 1933–83*.[71] It was further applied to domestic space, in the arrangement of objects in the interiors of Speight and Martin's own house.[72] Commentary on this skill was several times couched in gendered terms as 'feminine flair'. For example, at Martin's memorial service in 2000, a tribute noted Speight's 'sure eye for form and colour... Those of us who enjoyed the Martins' hospitality...will forget neither her gaiety and warmth, nor the wonderful way in which she set out quite ordinary things – whether cups and saucers on a kitchen shelf or vegetables on a cutting board'.[73]

Conclusion: Exclusion and Absorption

As Speight's career began to be written about in retrospect, the process of exclusion continued. In a repetition of earlier excisions, the leaflet accompanying the Lisbon exhibition of Martin's work listed numerous early joint projects, including *The Flat Book*, all of which are credited solely to him. Again, this is a text that Speight was certainly aware of and may well have designed. The absorption of her achievements within those of her husband is nowhere as clearly marked as in Speight's own obituaries, in one of which it was claimed: 'Since this period [the Second World War] her energies were notably injected into the outstanding career of her husband Sir Leslie Martin'.[74]

---

68   Fello Atkinson, 'Post War Shop Display in London', *The Architectural Review*, 109, (1951), 98–105.

69   For a further discussion of women and the practice of 'layout', see below.

70   This phrase was used by Sue Martin Mason, in a telephone conversation with the author, 6 February 2004. The exhibition was held in the Calouste Gulbenkian Foundation building in Lisbon which Martin had designed in 1983–1984.

71   Martin, *Buildings and Ideas*.

72   Interview with Sir Leslie Martin, March, 1993.

73   Speight predeceased Martin in 1992. Peter Carolin, Address, Memorial Service for Sir Leslie Martin held at Jesus College Chapel, Cambridge, 18 November 2000. See <http://www.jesus.cam.ac.uk/college/martin.html>. Accessed 19 September 2003.

74   Michael Parkin, Obituary, *The Independent*, 27 October 1992.

The historian examining Speight's life and work has no hard evidence of how she felt about her role and the treatment of it. It is important, too, to be aware that there is no indication that she was particularly involved in women's issues, or saw herself as a 'trailblazer'. An indication of this is her ambivalence over the ways in which she identified herself and how she wished to be addressed. For example, in the correspondence with Yorke about illustrations for *The Flat Book*, she signs herself Sadie Martin at the end of a letter headed 'J.L. Martin MA PhD ARIBA [and] Sadie Speight MA ARIBA Registered Architects'.[75] Towards the end of her life, her letterhead had become 'Lady Martin MA ARIBA FSIA FRSA Chartered Architect'.

In the context of the 1930s, Speight, as a professional woman, did benefit from a number of advantages. She gained independent employment as an architectural assistant, and was able to work with her husband. This meant that she did not experience the struggle to establish herself that was the lot of some of her contemporary female architects.[76] And while she had experience of pay scales which discriminated in favour of men whilst working as a part-time teacher, this was not uncommon and appears to have been accepted in the grave economic situation of the inter-war period. The RIBA Women's Committee acknowledged that 'women assistants have suffered from the necessary preference given to men with families'.[77] Speight's time spent with DRU provides further evidence of differential scales of fees. In estimates requested by the Council of Industrial Design for work on the *Daily Herald* Modern Homes exhibition, Misha Black's fee was £400, Milner Gray's £300 and Speight's £100.[78] Nor were architects the only professional women to accept lower rates of pay. Enid Marx, the textile and graphic designer, recalled her discovery that a male designer was receiving about four times the amount she did for book jackets: 'On the other hand though, he was keeping a wife and three or four children'.[79] A further advantage enjoyed by Speight derived from the social and professional circles in which she moved. Her working relationships and

---

75   Yorke's secretary replied on his behalf to Mrs J.L. Martin.

76   Incidents of the difficulty of finding work are cited in the Secretary's file, RIBA Women's Committee papers, 1932–1942.

77   Letter from Gertrude Leverkus, to Miss Hughes of the Careers Advisory Bureau, 2 February 1934, RIBA Women's Committee papers. Jean McIntosh's experience was a case in point. She stated that she had called upon 160 architects to try to persuade them to employ her before being taken on by Deane and Braddell, of Portman Square, London. That McIntosh found employment here may have had something to do with the fact that T.A. Darcy Braddell was the husband of Dorothy Braddell whose work as a designer is considered in Darling's chapter.

78   Letter from Mr Weyman to Mrs Tomrley, 8 April 1946, file 383, Design Council Archive, University of Brighton. I am grateful to Lesley Whitworth for this reference.

79   Helen Salter, 'Enid Marx RDI: An Interview', in J. Seddon and S. Worden, *Women Designing: Redefining Design in Britain Between the Wars*, Brighton: University of Brighton Press, 1994, 92.

friendships with influential figures such as critics Read and Pevsner, artists Nicholson, Hepworth and Gabo, and many influential figures, situated her at the centre of the development of British modernism and ensured interesting and worthwhile commissions across a wide range of intellectual and practical pursuits.

Finally, it is appropriate to reflect further on what Speight meant by the phrase 'part-time practice as before'. One reading might convey a downplaying of her achievements and collusion in her own exclusion. It would be simplistic, if not ahistorical, however, to allow this as the sole interpretation. It also acknowledges her ability to maintain a family life without completely surrendering a professional one: a dichotomy only too familiar to many women even now.

Most importantly Speight's phrase is a recognition of the flexibility which she enjoyed in moving in and out of a range of differing practices, from designing buildings to working with an engineer on electrical goods, from design journalism to theoretical writing. Her overriding concern, expressed through all these media, with the myriad ways in which design intersects with people's lives, placed her at the forefront of the social agenda of British modernism, with its strong emphasis on 'everyday things'.[80] From this perspective it becomes possible to assess her achievements in parallel to, as opposed to in unequal competition with, those of her husband. Only in this way is it possible to progress beyond his own touching, but double-edged, appreciation that she had 'made her own very special contribution to my work throughout the whole of my professional career'.[81]

---

[80] See Julian Holder, 'Design in Everyday Things': Promoting Modernism in Britain, 1912–1944', in Paul Greenhalgh (ed.), *Modernism in Design*, London: Reaktion Books, 1990, 123–144.

[81] Anon., 'Obituary', *Building Design*, 30 October 1992.

Figure 9.1
Kitchen-diner, 1932, Bournville Estate
Source: unknown. Every effort has been made to trace the copyright holders of this image

Chapter 9

Workshops Fit for Homeworkers: The Women's Co-operative Guild and Housing Reform in mid-Twentieth-Century Britain

Gillian Scott

This is my mother's childhood memory of washing the dishes in the 1930s, in an old-fashioned scullery in Pontefract, Yorkshire:

> a dank and bleak room, primarily used for the laundry, but the only room in the house with a sink; no table, nowhere to sit, the walls whitewashed, the floor cold stone flags. The sink was low under the window, large but very shallow, an ugly yellow stone contraption, with one large brass tap that violently gushed out cold water. There was a small wooden draining board but no cupboards. Buckets, large enamelled jugs, chamber pots were stacked beneath the sink, with scrubbing brushes and floor cloths.
>
> Water had to be heated in the kettle on the range in the living room; there was never enough of it. There were no detergents; washing-soda dissolved the grease but took the skin off your hands; Lux soap flakes were kinder but less effective. The grease clung stubbornly to every surface: the chipped enamel washing-up bowl, the dish cloth, the sink, hands. The worst thing was trying to clean the pots and pans; they were permanently caked with soot from the open fire of the cooking range, so to wash them inside, the pan had to be held high above the water level with one hand, to keep it clear of the relatively clean but rapidly cooling water in the bowl, while scouring inside with the other. The draining board would soon fill up and there were no work surfaces to hand on which to stack dishes. And the tea towels were always damp and greasy, leaving smears on everything. Washing up was a nightmare.[1]

This account is illustrative of the dirty, hard and sometimes dangerous nature of domestic labour in almost any setting in the first half of the twentieth century. For the majority of women housework had changed little since the Victorian age; still labour-intensive, it seemed closer to Shakespeare's 'greasy Joan doth keel the pot', than to life in a modern,

---

[1] Lorna Scott, 'A Yorkshire Childhood', unpublished memoir in the possession of the author.

industrialised society.[2] Even in the new local authority housing after 1918, cooking was commonly done on ranges in living rooms; back-kitchens or sculleries were cold, cheerless annexes to the home; and wash day involved an immense labour of heating water, scouring, rinsing, mangling and drying.[3]

The primitive nature of domestic labour was emblematic of more general neglect: as Margery Spring Rice observed in her 1939 study, *Working-class Wives*, 'the State is not officially concerned with her physical condition or with the provision of any remedies which may possibly be needed'.[4] She found that the 'standard of health of the average working woman is usually far below what it might be',[5] and identified housing as the largest single contributory factor: there is 'no reform which from the woman's point of view is of greater urgency than the immediate provision of enough decent houses at rents which the working-classes can afford'.[6] Although slum clearance programmes had made some headway by 1939, laissez-faire economic orthodoxies and a deteriorating international situation combined to ensure that comprehensive housing reform remained low on the political agenda.[7]

By 1945 this situation had been radically transformed. Total war, an unlikely midwife to social progress, brought into being a new set of entitlements for the housewife.[8] As well as receiving a family allowance, enacted in 1945, she was now to be included in the envisaged schemes for national health care and social security as set out in the Beveridge Report of 1942.[9] Most importantly from the perspective of domestic labour, she also stood to benefit from new housing regulations, as recommended in the major government report on post-war housing, the 1944 *Dudley Report*.[10] For the Women's Co-operative Guild (WCG, The Guild), a pioneering organisation of working-class wives,[11] all these improvements embodied

---

2   Shakespeare, *Love's Labours Lost*, var. edns.
3   Margaret Forster, *Hidden Lives. A Family Memoir*, London: Penguin, 1996, 99.
4   Margery Spring Rice, *Working-Class Wives* (1939), London: Virago, 1981, xiv.
5   Ibid, xvi.
6   Ibid, 154.
7   Charles Loch Mowatt, *Britain Between the Wars 1918–40*, Cambridge: Cambridge University Press, 1983, 508.
8   Arthur Marwick, *Britain in the Century of Total War. War, Peace and Social Change*, Harmondsworth: Penguin, 1970.
9   William Beveridge, *Social Insurance and Allied Services*, London: HMSO, November 1942, Cmd. 6404.
10 Ministry of Health (GB), Central Housing Advisory Committee, Design of Dwellings Sub-Committee, *Design of Dwellings*, London: HMSO, 1944 (*Dudley Report*), given effect by Housing Manuals (1944 and 1949). See also John Burnett, *A Social History of Housing 1815–1985*, London: Methuen, 2nd edition, 1986, 298.
11 Gillian Scott, *Feminism and the Politics of Working Women: The Womens' Co-operative Guild, 1880s to the Second World War*, London: UCL Press, 1998, chapter 6.

demands for which it had been pressing for decades and were nothing less than 'revolutionary'.[12]

This about turn in the attitude of government to the condition of married women's lives was not simply a 'top-down' application of more enlightened social policies. It also reflected 'bottom-up' pressure from an array of women's organisations, particularly those of the working-class movement. The unusual political circumstances of the Second World War brought a relatively sudden and unprecedented interweaving of these views from below and official policy-making procedures. The purpose here is to explore this process in relation to housing reform through the prism of the WCG. With tens of thousands of members who were married women of the working class, the WCG could claim, with justification, to understand their housing needs. Through the 1920s and 1930s it took a close interest in this subject but found limited opportunities to make a difference. In wartime, however, this situation was transformed as the organised working class became pivotal to the war effort, Labour politicians entered government, and the leaders of the women's labour movement found a new role as advisers on social policy. In this new political environment, the WCG was able to move from a peripheral to a far more influential position in the framing of post-war housing policy.

Between the Wars

The WCG was founded in 1883 as an auxiliary body of the English consumers' Co-operative movement, a large and democratically controlled trading enterprise with deep roots in working class communities.[13] From the outset the WCG recruited widely from the married women who shopped at 'Co-op' stores. With an organisational structure of local branches clustered into districts and sections, a national executive (the Central Committee, henceforth CC), full-time officers headed by a General Secretary, the WCG expanded steadily to 30,000 members by 1913 and a peak of 88,000 in 1,800 branches in 1938.

Alongside its aim to promote Co-operative trade among women, the WCG took up 'Citizenship' questions which concerned its members as working-class wives. This work was underpinned by the conviction that only through collective organisation could reforms be secured: 'the isolation of women in married life', wrote the General Secretary, Margaret Llewelyn Davies, in 1915, 'has, up to now, prevented any common expression of their needs. They have been hidden behind the curtain which

---

12   WCG, *Head Office Monthly Bulletin*, 9:7, July 1948, henceforth HOMB.
13   G.D.H. Cole, *A Century of Co-operation*, London: Allen & Unwin for the Co-operative Union, 1944. For a more recent account see Peter Gurney, *Co-operative Culture and the Politics of Consumption in England, 1870–1930*, Manchester: Manchester University Press, 1996.

falls after marriage, the curtain which women are now themselves raising'.[14]
Operating as a self-styled 'trade union for married women', it thus sought
to increase women's representation in the local and national state, to
inform and educate the membership about the wide range of social issues
that influenced their daily lives, and to apply pressure for progressive
change wherever possible.[15]

In this context, the WCG took a strong interest in housewives' working
conditions. The homes of its members, an early WCG history noted, were
the neglected 'workshops of many trades, where overtime abounds, and
where an eight hours' day would be a very welcome reform [...]. Few men
can realise how much drudgery and lonely effort there is in the everyday
work of a housewife'.[16] There was, wrote Llewelyn Davies, a silence on the
'incessant drudgery of domestic labour. People forget that the unpaid work
of the working-woman at the stove, at scrubbing and cleaning, at the
washtub, in lifting and carrying heavy weights, is just as severe manual
labour as many industrial operations in factories'.[17]

The growth of municipal housing provision between the wars provided
the WCG with a new channel through which such critical insights might be
fed into policy-making. The legislative backdrop to this involvement was
Lloyd George's 'Homes Fit for Heroes' initiative.[18] The 1919 Housing and
Town Planning Act, informed by the *Tudor Walters Report* of 1918,[19]
brought government directly into housing provision with the promise of
reasonable and affordable local authority accommodation for working-class
families. Yet even at the height of these aspirations, limited consultation
with Labour women elicited condemnation of proposed standards as
incompatible with 'the interests of the housewife'.[20] There was official
concern that raising building standards too high would create unrealistic
working-class expectations and emphasise the deficiencies of traditional
housing stock.[21] In the early 1920s the whole project fell victim to public-
spending cuts and a shift to private-enterprise subsidies, which left a huge

---

14   Margaret Llewelyn Davies, *Maternity Letters from Working Women* (1915),
      London: Virago, 1978, 8–9.
15   R.Nash, *The Position of Married Women*, Manchester: CWS Printing Works,
      1907.
16   Llewelyn Davies, *The Women's Co-operative Guild*, Kirkby Lonsdale: WCG,
      1904, 151.
17   Llewelyn Davies, *Maternity*, 5–6.
18   Mark Swenarton, *Homes Fit for Heroes The Politics and Architecture of Early
      State Housing in Britain*, London: Heinemann, 1981.
19   'Report of the Committee appointed by the President of the Local Government
      Board and the Secretary for Scotland to consider the questions of building
      construction in connection with the provision of dwellings for the working
      classes in England and Wales', PP 1918 9191 vii.
20   For more on this, Swenarton, *Homes*, 91.
21   Lawrence F. Orbach, *Homes for Heroes: A Study of the Evolution of British
      Public Housing 1915–21*, London: Seeley Service & Co., 1977, 65.

gap in provision for lower-income families.[22] In 1923, the WCG joined protests against the retreat from more comprehensive working-class provision embodied in the Chamberlain Housing Act,[23] and called for a reinvigoration of the council housing programme.[24] The general tendency of the inter-war years, however, was in the opposite direction and it was the skilled working class which most benefited from new council housing.

Despite its limited reach, the growth of council housing created some openings for the WCG. Town Councils were democratically elected, and women were qualified to vote and stand in such elections. Since the 1890s the WCG had promoted women's election as Poor Law Guardians, to School Boards, and then to councils and to parliament. During the inter-war years it emphasised that Guild members could play a valuable role on housing committees by making the housewife's case for better building standards, and for interior planning and equipment that would improve her working life. By 1931, there were 68 Guildswomen sitting on housing committees in different parts of the country.[25] Although their scope for intervention was usually at the margins, their presence underscored a basic democratic principle, and whatever aspect of the housing question was being discussed in the WCG, the need for more women on housing committees was reiterated.

Alongside this pressure for greater representation ran the WCG's steady insistence through the inter-war period that '[l]abour-saving devices and electrical appliances are long overdue in the homes of the working class'.[26] Its involvement with Co-operative retail trade, and its links with groups such as the Electrical Association for Women (EAW), generated a lively but critical interest in the appliance of new technology to the domestic environment.[27] As a report on the 1920 Glasgow Corporation Exhibition on Housing and Health put it, the many items on show 'designed to save labour' were not 'for us – the workers'.[28] Firstly, they were too expensive. Vacuum cleaners, electric irons and ovens could all cut labour time but were only 'within reach of the well-to-do'.[29] This was to remain the case for several decades: in 1925 an electric carpet cleaner cost £15,[30] and in 1938, at ten guineas, the Co-operative Wholesale Society 'Dudley' vacuum cleaner

---

[22]   Gill Burke, *Housing and Social Justice: The Role of Policy in British Housing*, London: Longman, 1981, 8; see also, Philip Abrams, 'The Failure of Social Reform, 1918–20', *Past and Present*, 24, April 1963.

[23]   Mowatt, *Britain*, 164.

[24]   *Co-operative News*, 3 March 1923, 13.

[25]   Ibid, 4 July 1931, ii, supplement marking 9th Co-operators Day: 'The Fight for the Emancipation of Women'.

[26]   Ibid, 24 January 1925, 12.

[27]   Founded in 1924, James Hinton, *Women, Social Leadership and the Second World War: Continuities of Class*, Oxford: Oxford University Press, 2002, 44.

[28]   *Co-operative News*, 10 January 1920, 12.

[29]   Ibid, 23 May 1925, 13.

[30]   Ibid, 23 May 1925, 13.

was still a luxury item.[31] Secondly, such devices needed electricity which was only slowly becoming available: by 1939 a third of homes still had no supply. Here, there was important work to be done. Electricity was deemed 'one of the greatest aids to the alleviation of drudgery', and branches were urged to press local authorities to secure its supply to working-class homes at a reasonable cost.[32] In some cases, this produced results. In Bolton, for example, a guildswoman's election to the town council and her work on the housing committee resulted in the installation of electric 'power plugs' in corporation houses.[33]

Yet, as the WCG often stressed, for many, perhaps the majority of working-class wives in this period, the problems were more basic: the need was not only for electricity to supplement the more common gas supply but for hot running water as well as cold.[34] Without such amenities, the burden of domestic labour constituted a great impediment to social progress: 'women's emancipation will never be complete', warned one senior guildswoman, 'until the chains of black-leading, war on smoke and the eternal dusting are forever shaken off'.[35] Unless or until large-scale municipal developments made decent housing widely available, and incorporated the benefits of science and technology, working-class wives would continue to pay the price. As Mrs Roe (CC), pointed out at a day school on Housing and Motherhood in 1930: if 'houses for the poor were built at reasonable rents, with labour-saving devices, mothers of the working-class could perform their natural functions without the danger to life and risk of after effects today endured'.[36] That no such improvements were implemented during the 1930s is evident in Spring Rice's verdict, based on material gathered by the Women's Health Inquiry Committee, of which the WCG was a member, that the conditions in which working-class wives lived and worked amounted to 'a devastating indictment of the national housing policy, or lack of it, during the last twenty years'.[37]

By the late 1930s, the WCG was not alone in its concern for housewives. Since 1918 a range of new 'citizenship' organisations had come into being, such as the National Federation of Women's Institutes (NFWI), and the National Union of Townswomen's Guilds.[38] Under the terms of the 1935

---

31   Ibid, 23 May 1925, 13; photograph, 'Modern London Collection', London History Workshop Centre. A guinea was equal to £1 plus 1 shilling.
32   Ibid, 19 April 1924, 13; 4 February 1925, 17.
33   Ibid, 14 February 1942, 8.
34   Ibid, 31 January 1925, 12; WCG, 'Town Planning and the Ideal Home' (1941?, revised 1944), typed MS.
35   *Co-operative News*, 31 January 1925, 12.
36   Ibid, 27 December 1930, 13.
37   Spring Rice, *Working-Class Wives*, 154.
38   Hinton, *Women, Social Leadership,* chapters 3 and 4; see also, Catriona Beaumont, 'Women and Citizenship: A Study of Non-Feminist Women's Societies and the Women's Movement in England, 1928–1950', unpublished PhD thesis, University of Warwick, 1996.

Housing Act, a Women's Advisory Housing Council (WAHC) was established in 1937, whose brief included liaison with organisations with an interest in housewives' needs in the planning of new estates.[39] In 1939 the Women's Group on Public Welfare (WGPW) was formed, with a range of interests including housing, to coordinate 'a broad non-partisan current of social engagement among middle-class women'.[40]

While the WCG was represented on national bodies such as the WAHC, it remained distinctively part of the working-class movement.[41] It followed Labour Party policy on most issues and there was considerable overlap in membership between the leaders of the WCG and of the Labour Party women's sections. Nationally, the WCG's greatest influence came from its membership of the Standing Joint Committee of Working Women's Organisations (SJC). Formed in 1916 to coordinate wartime representation of working-class women, the SJC was made up of senior officials from the Co-operative, trade union and political wings of the women's labour movement, and it operated informally as the Labour Party women's advisory committee on all questions affecting working-class women.[42] While Labour remained in opposition this counted for little, but the formation of a coalition government in 1940, with Labour ministers taking key roles in domestic affairs, changed this situation significantly.

Wartime and the New Consensus

The stasis in housing provision which resulted from the outbreak of war in 1939 was dramatically and painfully shifted by the Blitz, and other exigencies of total war. One effect of aerial bombardment was to create a new 'home front' in which women, as well as men, were military targets. 'Women are in the front line', declared a WCG item in *Co-operative News*, in January 1941.[43] An article by Labour MP, Dr Edith Summerskill, 'Women's Part in the Home Front', spelt out this essential contribution to the war effort:

---

[39]   The WAHC, informally connected to the Ministry of Health (which encompassed Housing), coordinated research and disseminated information to women's political, professional and religious groupings, *Women's Advisory Housing Council*, 1941(?), Women's Forum archive, Women's Library (thanks to James Hinton for this reference).

[40]   Hinton, *Women, Social Leadership*, 177.

[41]   *Co-operative News*, 2 October 1943, 12; 12 February 1944, 13. This relationship is apparent in such special subjects as 'The House that I Want', WCG, *Annual Reports*, 1938–1939, 1939–1940. Mrs K. Shade, who sat on WAHC, joined the WCG in 1921, was prominent in the Labour Party women's section, SJC chair (1944), president of the National Conference of Labour Women (1945), *Co-operative News*, 10 June 1944, 13; 22 August 1945, 12.

[42]   See Scott, *Feminism,* chapter 6.

[43]   *Co-operative News*, 25 January 1941, 12.

Her job is not spectacular, she has no uniform, she has no recognised wages for her work, but nevertheless, if she went on strike she could throw the whole war machine out of gear. She feeds the worker, keeps the home going, deals with ration cards, queues for food, and shows courage in the face of enemy attack equal to any hardened veteran.[44]

Such home-front propaganda, and the large-scale mobilisation of women for voluntary and paid war work, considerably heightened official sensitivity to their needs and their views.

While the initial shock of the Blitz created a sense of hopelessness – as the October 1940 *Guild Bulletin* put it, it was 'difficult to see far into the future' – the news of losses and homelessness soon generated a preoccupation with rebuilding that was indivisible from the emerging national debate about war aims and social reconstruction.[45] This was focused by 1942 on Beveridge's investigation of social insurance and allied services. The WCG's approach reflected a groundswell of feeling that the war effort needed to be buttressed by government commitments to democratic planning, social justice and, crucially, women's participation. Mindful of Beveridge's brief, the 1942 WCG Congress proposed, as 'a basis for fulfilling the terms of the Atlantic Charter',[46] a 'comprehensive programme of social and economic security' covering unemployment, sickness, and education provision.[47] 'It was the guild's task', urged Mrs Ridealgh, a senior guildswoman, in May 1942, to see that any such scheme catered for all classes in the country'.[48]

As an embryonic vision of a welfare state began to take shape, WCG leaders were in the vanguard of those arguing that the acute housing crisis caused by the bombing had major implications for post-war reconstruction, and that women had a vital role to play in this work. In May 1941, at a WCG conference in Bristol, one badly hit city, Ridealgh, asked: 'What sort of a world was going to emerge after the war?'. Slum clearance, as well as rebuilding, had to be tackled; homes in the future must contain 'all that was necessary for a healthy, happy, and vigorous people. Women knew the sort of home they wanted. It must have all the devices for cleanliness, health and beauty'.[49] A Bristol City Council architect, who addressed another Bristol Guild conference in November 1941, made a similar point. We must, he insisted, have 'better homes for our people, not merely houses. You house cattle, but the people who are standing up to this war deserve, and must have, something better'.[50]

---

44 Ibid, 10 January 1942, 8.
45 WCG, HOMB, 1/12, October 1940, 1.
46 A statement of principles for the post-war world agreed in August 1941 by Churchill and Roosevelt.
47 *Co-operative News*, 25 April 1942, 7.
48 Ibid, 16 May 1942, 13.
49 Ibid, 24 May 1941, 9.
50 Ibid, 22 November 1941, 12.

In response to such concerns, in March 1942, the Ministry of Health Central Housing Advisory Committee set up a sub-committee to consider the design of dwellings, chaired by the Earl of Dudley.[51] In the changed conditions of wartime, the Dudley committee engaged with women's experience and specialist knowledge in ways that its predecessors had not.[52] As Margaret Bondfield, of the WGPW, wrote to Mr Symon, Housing Department of the Ministry of Health, in July 1942, they were 'entirely in agreement with the Ministry as to the need for some machinery in obtaining the views of women on a matter which concerns them deeply since the house is largely their workshop'.[53]

The SJC, which had been increasingly successful in influencing social policy in wartime, and had, since its inception, been 'vitally interested in every aspect of Housing', explicitly requested that the new sub-committee should include 'a representative of working-class housewives'.[54] It was duly invited to submit nominees, of whom two – Cecily Cook, WCG General Secretary,[55] and Alderman Mrs E. Gooch (JP), also a Guild member – were subsequently appointed.[56] This brought the female membership of the Dudley committee to seven, out of a total of 18, plus the secretary, Judith Ledeboer.[57]

The Dudley committee also took evidence from a number of bodies including 15 women's organisations.[58] In response to this invitation, the SJC prepared a detailed questionnaire which was circulated through its affiliated organisations.[59] In September 1942, WCG members were encouraged to participate in this survey and reminded of its democratic

---

51   Under the terms of the 1935 Housing Act, the Central Housing Advisory Committee worked through specialist sub-committees.
52   Marion Roberts, *Living in a Man-Made World: Gender Assumptions in Modern Housing Design*, London: Routledge 1991, 81.
53   Bondfield to Symon, 16 July 1942, WF/D18, Women's Forum archive. A former Labour MP, Margaret Bondfield chaired the WGPW.
54   Report of the Standing Joint Committee of Working Women's Organisations and SJC, 'Design of Post-War Houses', in *Report of the Twenty Second National Conference of Labour Women*, 1943, Labour Party, London, 1943, 10–12.
55   Cecily Cook (1887/90–1962). From humble origins, her political career spanned trade unionism, suffrage work, and the Labour Party. In the early 1920s, she worked for Attlee's election campaigns. J.M. Bellamy and J. Saville (eds), *Dictionary of Labour Biography*, vol. II, London: Macmillan, 1974.
56   Report of the SJC, 1943, 12.
57   Ledeboer was an Associate of the Royal Institute of British Architects (ARIBA). The other female members were Miss J.F. Adburgham, Mrs M.M. Dollar, Miss M.E. Haworth, Miss M. Lloyd George, Lady Sanderson.
58   EAW, Mothers' Union, National Board of Catholic Women, National Council of Women, NFWI, NUTG, Society of Women Housing Managers, SJC, Union of Catholic Mothers, WAHC, WCG, Women's Farm and Gardens Association, Women's Gas Council, WGPW, Women's Pioneer Housing, Ltd.
59   SJC, 'Design of Post-War Houses', 13.

significance: 'One of the most important of all tasks in the post-war world will be the re-housing of the people', stated the item in *Co-operative News*. 'When the war ends, over a million houses will have to be built in Britain alone, and it is imperative that BEFORE the war ends, the people themselves should state in emphatic and clear terms precisely what type of houses they require, and insist on getting them'. Guildswomen had an important job to do 'which backs up trade union and organised labour women in their fight for good post-war houses.' The evidence thus compiled would enable the SJC to lay before government 'the collective demands of the ordinary working-class housewife who knows so well the defects of her present house and ... the improvements that should be made'.[60]

The final memorandum submitted by the SJC to the Dudley committee was based on 2,500 completed questionnaires but also on various reports of conferences organised for women to discuss their post-war housing needs.[61] The SJC attached special importance to these 'collective' views, pointing out that it is 'through discussion and the interchange of opinions that new ideas emerge and progress is made'.[62] It is clear from the records of the WCG that it was actively involved in this process at various day schools and conferences prior to the appointment of the Dudley committee. These discussions highlight the WCG's long established practice of member education, and its capacity to make connections between the everyday lives of ordinary housewives and national discussions about post-war reconstruction. That the content of such discussions was to be fed into policy recommendations, through the Guild's involvement in the SJC and through its direct representation on the Dudley committee, makes transparent the 'bottom-up' input into the wartime debate about housing needs.

The WCG adopted 'Town Planning and the Ideal Home' at its 1941 Congress in a resolution which, chiming in with Labour Party policy and the prevalent determination to avoid inter-war housing mistakes, warned against exploitation by 'jerry-builders', and called for planning and land nationalisation as necessary conditions of adequate housing, along with 'controlled rents', and 'modern equipment' in all homes.[63] At a series of regional events, delegates showed themselves 'very definite in their ideas of what was needed for ideal homes'.[64] At the North East Lancashire Conference at Bacup, in August 1941, for example, Guildswomen expressed interest in such 'labour-saving equipment' as 'built-in kitchen cupboards with sliding doors', underlining the absence of such features in many homes. One delegate described 'a cupboard door which she had seen which let down to form a table'; another described a kitchen in which all appliances could be concealed behind panels, and all agreed that it was

---

60   *Co-operative News*, 12 September 1942, 13.
61   SJC, 'Design of Post-War Houses', 12–22.
62   Ibid, 13.
63   *Co-operative News*, 28 June 1941, 12.
64   Ibid, 15 November 1941, 8.

'crazy' to build pantries under the stairs when they should be on an outer wall, out of the sun, well ventilated, and away from the lavatory. Another delegate stressed the desirability of large-paned windows because of the 'great amount of labour' required to clear small panes.[65] At similar events across the country, speakers and delegates restated the importance of a 'good water supply, good windows, and rooms easy to clean, with no dark corners', and 'well-planned' homes which would be 'easy to run'.[66] Above all, as Mrs Cartwright reminded the Bolton District Conference early in 1942, Guildswomen had a responsibility to ensure good quality through town council housing committees.[67]

What the Guild was determined to contribute to the Dudley committee, then, were detailed specifications for labour-saving homes, and the democratic principle that 'those whose daily task is conditioned by the housing accommodation provided for the family' should play a part in planning for post-war reconstruction.[68] 'Town Planning and the Ideal Home', circulated for member education, asserted the housewife's entitlement to a decent working environment because of the 'national importance' of her work.[69] For the married woman, 'home' was a 'workshop or factory where family comfort and happiness is manufactured.' The home-maker did not benefit from an eight hour day, she could not strike, or look forward to promotion or higher pay. Her 'sole reward' was the 'happiness and well-being' of her family. 'Happy, healthy families', furthermore, were not a private indulgence but 'a national asset', so it was a 'national responsibility' to ensure that the 'workshop from which they come is [the] best that modern development can produce'.[70]

The 'FIRST ESSENTIAL' [sic], in this modernisation programme, was to create the conditions for 'EASY HOUSEWORK' [sic]. The work of 'home making', was 'many sided', with so many things to be got through each day that unless each item could be done in the 'easiest way' the 'housewife finds [her] strength exhausted before [the] day's work is completed.' Homes should be 'well planned and equipped to be easy to clean'. They should be light, spacious, fully electric and mechanised: 'fitted with all equipment science has made possible in labour-saving devices including refrigerators', with 'modern conservative-burning fuel stoves or central heating and up-to-date gas appliances as alternatives'.[71] All newly built and re-built houses

---

65   Ibid, 22 August 1941, 9.
66   For example, West Wales District Conference in December 1941, ibid, 6 December 1941, 8; South Manchester District Conference, October 1941, ibid, 25 October 1941, 13; Ashington Society Education Committee Day School in December 1941, ibid, 13 December 1941, 8.
67   Ibid, 14 February 1942, 8
68   Ibid, 13 June 1942, 4.
69   WCG, 'Town Planning and the Ideal Home' (1941, revised 1944), typed MS.
70   Ibid, 4. The wording echoes the ideas expressed by Edith Summerskill (see above).
71   Ibid, 1–2.

should have a hot and cold water supply, bathrooms, windows that could be cleaned from the inside, well-lit passages and staircases, easily guarded fireplaces and stoves. Larders should be hygienically and conveniently located.[72] Instead of sculleries, there should be properly equipped kitchens, planned in every detail for the convenience of the home-worker. The sink should be 'roomy' with adequate draining boards, and 'racks for plates, saucers etc.' to ease washing up, lessen the work of wiping and reduce the labour of tea cloths. Both sink and cooking stove should be convenient to one another, well-lit and easy to clean. Attention should also be paid to materials: 'Kitchen walls should be non-absorbent. Tiled walls in kitchens and bathrooms are proof against steam and moisture which tend to destroy other surfaces. Wall finish everywhere should be of kind to repel dirt and ... washable'.[73]

The basic requirements set out by the WCG, which reflect thorough and first-hand knowledge of housework, were reproduced in the SJC memorandum, 'Design of Post-War Houses'. The 'demand for labour-saving homes', it stated forcefully, 'is universal'.

> This is the expression of an intelligent attitude among working housewives (whose occupation is the largest single occupation in the country) to the organisation of their work, in relation to the well-being of the families for whom they care, and to their own right as workers, citizens, and human beings, to relief from unnecessary physical toil, and leisure to pursue interests and activities outside their work.[74]

A key element of this was the demand for the old-fashioned scullery, and cooking range in the living room to be replaced by decent kitchens, 'arranged for convenience in work'.[75] Most women also wanted upstairs bathrooms and a separate lavatory, with the exception of the mining districts where a stated desire for downstairs facilities was found to relate to the absence of pit-head baths, prompting the SJC to ask that all industrial workers should be able to wash before returning to their homes.[76]

The SJC took the opportunity to circulate 'Design of Post-War Houses' as widely as possible, sending copies to the press, the BBC, Government Departments, Allied and Dominion Government Offices, Municipal Authorities, and Medical Officers.[77] While welcoming the work of the Dudley committee, the memorandum pointed out that many of the demands for reasonable accommodation made by the SJC from 1918 to 1920 had not been met and that many working-class housewives could

---

72   Ibid.
73   WCG, 'Town Planning', 5.
74   Ibid, 16.
75   Ibid, 18.
76   Ibid, 15–17.
77   SJC, 'Design of Post-War Houses', 12.

'speak with some bitterness' of those disappointments. This time, it urged, 'a genuine effort' was needed to improve housing conditions.[78]

Early feedback on the Dudley proceedings indicated that the SJC's demands were similar to those being made by other women's organisations whose submissions also revealed unanimity about basic needs, starting with the abolition of the scullery.[79] The WAHC, for example, wanted kitchens with hot running water, sinks at a height to avoid backache, and deep if there was no separate laundry facility, a well-ventilated cupboard under the sink, two draining boards – well-fitted to avoid grease and dirt in joints, with a tiled and washable surround, a plate rack conveniently nearby – and good natural and artificial lighting. The NFWI reported a 'universal demand' for north-facing larders. The WGPW warned that without a properly planned water supply, laundering was made particularly difficult. The Society of Women Housing Managers made reference to the general desire for kitchens large enough to eat in.[80]

Even more encouraging than this consensus, were signs that 'officials of the Ministry of Health' were sympathetic to the demands of the women's organisations.[81] Housing was undoubtedly accelerating up the political agenda. Home Intelligence reports in the closing years of the war showed it to be a major source of public anxiety and scepticism about reconstruction, and it was to be a deciding issue in the 1945 General Election.[82] 'For several years now', wrote Caroline Haslett, founder of the EAW, 'starting in the darkest days of the blitz on London – interest in the question of Housing has been spreading ... never before have there been so many reports on Housing – from the housewives who have to cook and clean and wash, from the organisations concerned with various aspects of the subject and from the Government itself'.[83]

In these circumstances, it is not surprising that the recommendations of the 1944 *Dudley Report* (1944) incorporated the main demands of the SJC and the other women's organisations. In contrast to the *Tudor Walters Report*, which took little heed of how domestic labour was carried out, *Dudley* started from the premise that the internal planning of modern homes had to centre on the kitchen, to accommodate the supply of

---

78 Ibid, 13.
79 Mrs Mary Millar (London Labour Party), Debate on Housing Resolution, *Report of Labour Women*, 1943, 41.
80 'The Kitchen and Service Rooms', *Housing Digest. An Analysis of Housing Reports 1941–45, prepared for the Electrical Association for Women by the Association for Planning and Reconstruction*, London and Glasgow: Art and Education Publishers, 1946.
81 Millar, Debate on Housing Resolution, 41.
82 Paul Addison, *The Road to 1945: British Politics and the Second World War*, London: Pimlico, 1945, 248. Home Intelligence was a division of the wartime Ministry of Information and concerned itself with sociological investigations into the conditions of daily life in Britain.
83 'Foreword', *Housing Digest*.

electricity, gas and water, and then to take full account of the work of running the home. Starting from a standard semi-detached house for four to five people, it recommended in place of the inconvenient division between sculleries and living rooms with cooking ranges, the integration into the home of a purpose-built kitchen or kitchen/diner. This should be fitted with a sink, two draining boards, a plate rack, work surfaces and cupboards, a larder 'on the shady side of the house', and a utility room, or separate laundry compartment.[84] There should be an ample supply of electrical sockets for 'labour-saving appliances', more efficient plumbing and sanitation systems, 'labour-saving coal-burning grates and stoves', and an upstairs bathroom, with bath, sink, and hot running water, and a separate 'water closet'.[85]

The *Dudley Report* is strikingly sensitive to the daily routines of housework. In tones that are very similar to the WCG paper, 'Town Planning and the Ideal Home', it elaborates on how kitchen/living rooms should be designed for the 'maximum convenience to the housewife'.[86] Kitchen floors, walls and window sills, it recommends, should be 'both easy to clean and attractive in appearance';[87] fittings generally should be of 'a type which will stand heavy wear and which can be easily cleaned'; kitchen units should be designed to eliminate corners and waste spaces 'which are difficult to clean and a source of unnecessary labour to the housewife';[88] windows should be of the 'easy-cleaning type', as should sinks, draining boards, taps, shelves, etc.[89] One-piece kitchen sink units with a splash-back were recommended to 'allow for easy cleaning'; the kitchen window sill should be finished with an 'easily-cleaned surface'.[90] These practical details serve as a reminder that the Guildswomen who represented the SJC on the Dudley committee, Mrs Cook and Mrs Gooch, were well qualified to speak for housewives in general and working-class housewives in particular. Furthermore, they are likely to have been among the small minority of committee members with first-hand experience of cleaning a kitchen.

Conclusion

The WCG strongly endorsed the *Dudley Report*'s advocacy of 'a distinct advance in the type of house and equipment which is recommended' and was satisfied that its members' views had been 'brought well forward'.[91] In an unprecedented manner, its recommendations had incorporated the

---

84   *Dudley Report*, 14, 30, 16.
85   Ibid, 31, 28, 15.
86   Ibid, 14.
87   Ibid, 27–28.
88   Ibid, 30.
89   Ibid, 37, 40–43.
90   Ibid, 41.
91   WCG, 'The Housing Needs of My Area' (revised 1946), typed MS, 2.

views and needs of women, envisaging homes in which the work that fell to mothers and wives would require far less effort than had been the case in older housing stock. The routine chore of washing the dishes, for example, would be transformed from the balancing act of arduous scouring in cooling water by a deep sink, hot piped water and a draining board. In place of 'greasy Joan', the *Dudley Report* presented a new vision of the modern housewife in a sparkling home.

But for the WCG, this was a starting point for continued effort, not the end of the story. Much of what had been achieved in the last twenty-five years, it pointed out in 1944, had been due to the 'work put in by the WCG and similar organisations'. We must, it stressed, 'keep on pegging away'.[92] There was still much to be done. Firstly, there was the continuing need to secure for working-class women a voice in housing policy. The Guild had been particularly gratified by the *Dudley Report's* recognition that while in 'domestic design and equipment the housewife is the expert and local authorities should have constant regard to her views', she was 'still inadequately represented on many local authorities', which should make much fuller use of the powers under Section 85 of the Local Government Act (1933) to co-opt 'suitable women' to their Housing Committees.[93] Yet local authorities were often unwilling to follow such national leads. In 1943 Chelmsford Council was reported once again to have refused to co-opt women onto its Housing Committee.[94] It took another year, and 'long' and at times 'acrimonious' discussions, for representatives from the WCG, the Women's Institutes, the Women's Voluntary Service, the Rotary Club, and the British Legion women's section to be formally invited to discuss new house-building.[95] In December 1944 Warrington Corporation declined the WCG branch's offer of a member to sit on the Town Council Housing Sub-committee, despite a recent statement by the Minister of Health, Conservative MP Henry Willink, urging local authorities to co-opt housewives onto their Housing Committees.[96]

Indivisible from the laborious work of getting women on to housing committees was the need to keep up the momentum of reform. As the WCG paper of 1945, 'Improved Conditions for the Housewife', pointed out, much housing stock was still 'totally inadequate' for healthy family life.[97] The housing problem, explained the 1946 paper, 'Housing a Public Service', had escalated for decades, with the post-1918 failures, the slum clearance deficits, and then the destruction of the Blitz. The new *Dudley* standards were welcome, but 'there will doubtless be a tough fight if the full

---

92   WCG, 'Town Planning', 7; 2.
93   WCG, 'Improved Conditions for the Housewife' (1944, revised 1945), typed MS, 1; *Dudley Report*, 10.
94   *Co-operative News*, 27 November 1943, 13.
95   Ibid, 5 February 1944, 12.
96   Ibid, 16 December 1944, 13.
97   WCG, 'Housing – a Public Service' (1946), typed MS, 2.

equipment specified is to be secured in all post-war houses'.[98] That this fight would be circumscribed by the operations of the market, as well as the budgets of town councils, had already been predicted in the SJC memorandum:

> Mass production and standardisation are the answer to the housewife's demands for labour-saving equipment of a kind that has hitherto been available only for the well-to-do. This need not mean articles of poor design and efficiency. But this is what she may get unless careful thought is given now to the design and efficiency of the main articles of equipment – refrigerators, cookers, stoves, etc.[99]

In fact, *Dudley* ruled out refrigerators as standard provision on grounds of cost; the installation of central heating was also rejected, pending further research.[100] In the longer term, the proliferation of affordable labour-saving commodities brought them within reach of the mass of the population but in the immediate aftermath of the Second World War they continued to be luxury goods.

Quite apart from Conservative town councils and social inequality generally, another factor that would increasingly subvert the Guild's vision of a better life for housewives was the limits of the model itself. The *Dudley Report* proposed a conservative modernisation of the conditions of domestic labour. It provided housing standards devised to ease and make more convenient the routine work – washing, cooking, cleaning – of the 'woman at the sink', while confirming that housework would remain a fundamentally feminine responsibility. The idea that the sexual division of labour itself might be susceptible to reform was not on the agenda, either for *Dudley*, or for the WCG, the SJC and other women's organisations. Yet this was a model of domesticity whose obsolescence was already looming as increasing numbers of women began to take paid employment outside the home. In the second half of the twentieth century, a new generation of female activists was to offer a conception of women's liberation which fundamentally challenged the assumption that domestic labour was women's work, and whose main concern with the kitchen was to get themselves out of it. As the 1970s feminist slogan warned: 'It begins when you sink into his arms; it ends with your arms in his sink'.

Yet the relatively bounded nature of the WCG's conception of how the housewife's life could be made easier should not detract from the importance of its work during this period. For more than half a century the WCG had campaigned not simply for particular reforms in domestic life to improve and dignify the lives of married women, but for the basic principle that the women who worked in the home should have some agency in the re-making of domestic space. The housewife, the WCG continually stressed,

---

98 Ibid.
99 SJC, 'Design of Post-War Houses', 16.
100 *Dudley Report*, 28 and 30.

is the 'practical person on the job and it is her wishes and needs that should be studied and met'.[101] The war effort, with its equality of sacrifice ethos, the emphasis on the Home Front, and on women's participation, brought the needs of married women into the public domain, while the wartime remaking of the political landscape opened up new channels of representation for the working-class women's movement. In these circumstances, reforms for which the WCG had been calling since at least the 1920s – that housewives should have a role in making housing policy, and that working-class wives should benefit, as far as possible, from developments in science, technology and design – now became mainstream and were adopted as national policy.[102] The official ratification of this vision of the modern housewife in the 1940s represented a significant advance on inter-war social norms, and formed an important stepping stone towards greater future liberty for women.

---

[101] WCG, 'Town Planning', 5.
[102] On the Housewives' Committee of the state-sponsored Council of Industrial Design, see Whitworth's chapter in this volume.

Figure 10.1
Portrait of Margaret Allen, 1946
Source: Design Council / Design Archives, University of Brighton
www.brighton.ac.uk/designarchives

Chapter 10

The Housewives' Committee of the Council of Industrial Design: A Brief Episode of Domestic Reconnoitring

Lesley Whitworth

This chapter represents the development of a paper that initially considered the amazingly short duration of a committee of 'Housewives' formed by the Council of Industrial Design (CoID) during its first year of its activity. The CoID was itself propelled into existence in December 1944 by the British wartime coalition government through its Board of Trade. It had as its over-arching remit, the promotion 'by all practicable means' of an 'improvement of design in the products of British industry'.[1] 'Rousing the public to a state of alert sensibility' was one of the practicable means at its disposal, hence the general population constituted one of the Council's several target audiences.[2]

The form of the original paper was determined by the fortuitous survival of the Director's personal copies of minutes from the three earliest meetings of the Housewives' Committee held on 15 and 26 November, and 18 December, 1945. The Council's central copies of these papers were sent to the Victoria & Albert Museum in London, but of these no trace can be found.[3] An accompanying file, 'Papers other than minutes' was destroyed on 9 April 1954. Both of these actions took place as normal elements of the Council's record management process but have tended to heighten the

---

1   Letter dated 19 December 1944, from the Rt Hon. Hugh Dalton, President of the Board of Trade, to Sir Thomas Barlow, first Chairman of the Council of Industrial Design; reproduced in CoID *The Council of Industrial Design: First Annual Report, 1945–1946*, London: HMSO, 1946, 5. See also Lesley Whitworth, 'Inscribing Design on the Nation: The Creators of the British Council of Industrial Design', *Business and Economic History On-line*, 3 (2005) http://www.thebhc.org/publications/BEHonline/2005/whitworth.pdf.

2   Dalton's letter to Barlow identified the others as manufacturers, educators, retailers and government departments.

3   Information from the Archive of Art and Design (AAD), National Art Library, London. The date of deposit is uncertain. In 1994 the Council's substantive archive was deposited in the Design History Research Centre at the University of Brighton and now forms the centre-piece of the Faculty of Arts and Architecture's Design Archives.

impression of a short-lived and possibly tenuously embedded initiative. While the existence of a Housewives' Committee was recorded in the *Council of Industrial Design: First Annual Report, 1945–1946*, which covered the period up to the end of March 1946, the equivalent pages in the *Second Annual Report, 1946–1947* bear no trace of it. The file in which the Director's copies were held was summarily closed in January 1947 and no continuation files were opened.[4]

After an initial ferment of activity, therefore, the Committee seemed to have declined in significance, and, having outlined the Committee's concerns such as they appeared in the various minutes, the paper took as its focus possible reasons why this might have been so. Further research, however, has revealed a kind of half-life endured by the Committee for many further months, during which time some individual members continued to contribute meaningfully to the work of the Council. Moreover, the Committee represented only one aspect of the Council's work with women, and quite other series of records have contributed to the re-formation of this chapter.[5] It now seeks to place the Housewives' Committee of the Council of Industrial Design in a longer trajectory of, firstly, women's emancipatory endeavours in relation to the built spaces of their material environments; and secondly, the efforts of others to foreground women's needs and women's perspectives at a time of considerable national debate about social, spatial and physical reconstruction.[6] It situates the ethos and activity of two key individuals, S.C. Leslie and Margaret Allen (Fig. 10.1 and cover), against the mid-century's ideals of social justice and participatory consumer democracy. Seen from this perspective, the historical moment encapsulating the Housewives' Committee and other like-minded initiatives, seems to embody both the brilliance and the brevity of a meteorite at the highest point in its arc, preparatory to falling to earth.

Identifying the Housewives' Committee: Then and Now

The creation of the new Committee was considered at a meeting of Council held in late summer 1945, and was part of a wider reconfiguration of committee structures based on six months' formative experience.[7] It was to

---

4   DCA File 295 (originally H1). The original file 295 was the one recorded as having been sent to the Victoria & Albert Museum.

5   These are discussed below.

6   See also Matthew Hilton, *Consumerism in Twentieth-Century Britain: The Search for a Historical Movement*, Cambridge: Cambridge University Press, 2003, Ina Zweiniger Bargielowska, *Austerity in Britain: Rationing, Controls and Consumption, 1939–1955*, Oxford: Oxford University Press, 2000, and James Hinton, 'Militant Housewives: The British Housewives' League and the Attlee Government', *History Workshop Journal*, 38 (1994), 129–156.

7   The paper was delivered by Barlow; C(45)30 'Committee Organisation: Note by the Chairman' within the papers of the seventh meeting of the Council, in DCA

be appointed 'with a Council Chairman and outside members, to keep touch with women's organisations, and consider questions of design in the home from the woman's point of view'.[8]

This was not, in fact, the Council's first explicit overture to women. While discussions concerning the membership of the Committee were still ongoing, a booklet entitled *New Home* was said to be in preparation. This was to give 'concrete practical advice to housewives in the lower income groups about furnishing and equipping their houses in the conditions of the transitional period'.[9] It was hoped that it would be available in November and would be on sale priced sixpence; it was envisaged that it would be distributed in association with a number of show-houses being furnished for display purposes by the Council.[10]

By mid-September, Mrs Margaret Allen, pre-existing Council member and newly appointed Chairman of the Housewives' Committee, was said to have had 'discussions with the Director and Staff and [was] working out suitable lists and holding preliminary discussions with intended members'.[11] In November the membership was announced to Council and the date of the first meeting set for the fifteenth of that month.[12] The other members were Mrs Barbara Castle MP, Mrs M. Hill, Mrs A.R. Nilson, Lady Railing and Mrs M. Murdoch, a staff member and the Committee's Secretary. Castle attended only one meeting, the first. Unsurprisingly no trace of her modest exposure has found its way into published biographical or autobiographical writings; meanwhile, the personal papers including diaries which may be revelatory of her impressions are presently closed to scholars.[13] Mrs Nilson (Fig. 10.2) was Head of the Experimental Kitchens Section of the Ministry of Food, where her work was associated with the Food Advice Division of the Ministry. As Council member Francis Meynell had a pivotal role in delivering the Ministry's wartime 'Food Facts' series for the advertising agency Mather & Crowther, it seems reasonable to

---

File 1/1945, 'Council Meetings – 1945'. All Design Council Archive (DCA) material is held within the Design Archives of the University of Brighton.

8   Ibid.

9   C(45)32, Report by the Director to the Meeting of the Council of 14 September 1945 in DCA File 1/1945.

10   Interestingly there seems to have been no suggestion that the Housewives' Committee should review the content of the *New Home* publication, even retrospectively, or contribute to the evolution of any revised editions (there was one in 1948). Leslie, however, made known his objection to editing by committee, in response to an enquiry from Council member Francis Meynell (see C(45)28, Report by the Director to the Meeting of Council of 13 July 1945, in DCA File 1/1945).

11   DCA File 1/1945; C(45)32, Report by the Director to the Meeting of the Council of 14 September 1945.

12   DCA File 1/1945; C(45)40, Report by the Director to the Meeting of the Council of 9 November 1945.

13   They will not be made available until cataloguing is complete. Information from the Bodleian Library.

surmise that Nilson might have been his suggestion.[14] Of Hill and Lady Railing little is known.

Figure 10.2
A.R. (Bee) Nilson participating in the Council of Industrial Design Domestic Equipment Selection Committee for 'Britain Can Make It', 1946
Source: Design Council / Design Archives, University of Brighton
www.brighton.ac.uk/designarchives

Of Margaret Allen we have a much fuller picture. A resident of Kenton in Harrow in Middlesex, Allen was described in a Council press release as a member of the Women's Co-operative Guild (WCG), of the Management Committee of Watford Co-operative Society Ltd., and of the Central Board of the Co-operative Union. Her experience may or may not support Gillian Scott's contention that the WCG was increasingly dominated by career-minded activists from the 1920s onwards; it would take quite different kinds of sources to substantiate such a claim.[15] It remains true, however, that her energetic investment in semi-official activity – the kinds of activity that are minuted and archived – makes her infinitely more accessible to us as a historical entity.[16] For these were not her only commitments. In the

---

[14] Nilson went on to become a highly regarded and prolific author of cookery books.
[15] Gillian Scott, *Feminism and the Politics of Working Women*, London: UCL Press, 1998.
[16] Which is not, of course, to claim that she is entirely accessible to us.

year ending 30 November 1946, coterminous with her membership of the Council of Industrial Design, Allen was one of two Co-operative members of the Standing Joint Committee of Working Women's Organisations (SJC) serving on its General Purposes Committee (GPC). Whilst it is noteworthy that her connection to the SJC was not fore-grounded in Council statements, it is also the case that she was not formally appointed to the Council to *represent* the views of any of the bodies to which she belonged, but rather in a personal capacity for which she appeared eminently suitably qualified to those who selected her.[17] Similarly, when the Council of Industrial Design's activities were deliberated by the SJC, Allen was under no obligation to divulge her opinions, though what went unminuted we can only speculate. What intrigues, therefore, are two sets of parallel records with both of which Allen was intimately connected, but within which the interplay of her dual roles remains somewhat opaque.

The Committee's Deliberations

A mere three months after Victory in Japan day, Mrs Allen welcomed members of the new Housewives' Committee and thanked them for their readiness to co-operate.[18] She invoked a mood of optimism, assuring them that they would find their involvement as stimulating as it was valuable. A previously circulated note had set out preliminary information about the proposed 1946 exhibition, soon to be named 'Britain Can Make It', and the women were asked to identify items of household equipment which would benefit from re-design. The committee named sinks, plate racks, vacuum cleaner attachments, wardrobes, dirty linen disposal and plate heating arrangements, and undertook to give the matter further consideration. More substantially, there followed an in-depth consideration of the relative merits of different methods of information collection, for it had been suggested that this might be 'one of their first and most important tasks'.

> Mrs Murdoch said that of the various ways in which this might be done, consumer research surveys carried out among a controlled sample of the population by trained interviewers were regarded as the most reliable and the results of such survey [sic] would carry weight with manufacturers. On the other hand there was much to be said for giving an unlimited number of women the opportunity to answer questions about design.

The choice of forms over interviews, Hill wisely observed, would narrow the field of responses to those who felt most able to express themselves in this

---

[17]   No details of the selection process for the Housewives' Committee have survived; such a small body was clearly not intended to be representative in any sense.

[18]   Unless indicated otherwise, all quotations are taken from papers in DCA File 295. In the UK, VJ Day was celebrated on 15 August 1945.

format. Railing and Nilson raised practical concerns over the efficacy of photographic 'prompts' where actual objects would be so much better. A hope was expressed that samples of some items might be carried in mobile displays. Castle feared that housewives' expectations might be unhelpfully raised when many fittings for prefabricated and temporary homes were due to be standardised: the Committee determined to discover by the following week's meeting whether it might still be possible to have an impact on the work then being undertaken by the British Standards Institute (BSI). Lastly Hill reminded the meeting that an overwhelming majority of the population lived in older housing, and means of improving their convenience should be at the forefront of members' minds.

At the next meeting it was explained that preparation of certain British Standards was already far advanced, while work on others had yet to begin. The Committee's wish to contribute to their framing had been conveyed to the relevant Board of Trade section, then transferred to the Ministry of Supply. This section was responsible for working closely with BSI on component specifications. While the response to their offer was muted, a further means of influencing the process through the Council's own collaboration with BSI was also identified. The Committee decided to examine standards for equipment connected with cooking, dishwashing, laundry, space heating and water heating as soon as possible, in order to ascertain whether their own consumer surveys might yet influence them.

In further consideration of the scope of those same surveys, it was suggested by a member of Council staff that a great deal of attention had already been given to 'mechanical devices', whereas furniture and floor coverings would benefit from scrutiny and the Board of Trade and Utility Furniture Panel would be grateful for the information.[19] There followed a preliminary debate about headings for inclusion, and the possible form of questions.[20] To the spectre of findings that revealed housewives to be poor judges, Allen asserted that such data could still inform the shaping of future educational policy by the Council's Training Committee, which was oriented towards consumers just as much as designers.

At the third meeting the Secretary reported that various BSI specifications had been received but it had not been possible to transcribe them fully into a suitable format for Committee discussion. Attention therefore reverted to the proposed suite of consumer surveys. A Board of Trade representative had urged that findings on furniture design should be accelerated to meet the needs of the forthcoming Furniture Working Party report, but it was felt that meeting this deadline would involve too great a

---

[19]   For more on the Utility scheme see Judith Attfield (ed.), *Utility Re-assessed: The Role of Ethics in the Practice Of Design*, Manchester: Manchester University Press, 1999; and Harriet Dover, *Home Front Furniture: British Utility Design, 1941–1951*, Aldershot: Scolar Press, 1991.

[20]   The questionnaire would be actioned by Wartime Social Survey. On Wartime Social Survey see Ian McLaine, *Ministry of Morale: Home Front Morale and the Ministry of Information in World War II*, London: George, Allen & Unwin, 1979.

sacrifice of longer term goals.[21] In reaching this decision, the Committee was undoubtedly influenced by the views of visiting Council member and designer, Gordon Russell, himself the author of the idea that a 'more deliberate approach' should be taken. Russell thought it essential to prioritise the collection of 'fundamental information about people's living habits'.

In all of its deliberations, the account of which is necessarily curtailed here, the Committee showed itself to be thoughtful, practical and pro-active in response to the broad range of issues with which it concerned itself. In particular, its sensitive engagement with the question of best research practice aligned it with debates then ongoing amongst professionals in the emerging fields of consumer and market research. It showed through its determination to retain a focus on domestic appliances as an area of interest that as a collectivity it was independently minded, and its willingness to deal with the labyrinthine technical detail of British Standards augured well for the future. Its perceptive recognition of the need for concrete examples to focus discussion with respondents was also enlightened.[22]

Nevertheless, in the minutes of the last meeting it is possible to deduce more clearly than with previous meetings, the guiding hand of the parent body. Russell's framing of a research project concerned with 'How People Live' was predicated on a view that 'without background information about the kind of lives people led, ... any study of design for household equipment lost its value'. Whilst the argument he was clearly positioned there to make was accepted, the women of the Housewives' Committee were evidently resistant to the survey's conceptual breadth. Hill and Railing were unconvinced by questions they feared would yield endlessly diverse data. To Russell's assertion that the most important question of all was 'whether or not the great changes caused by the war had made people less conservative and more receptive to new ideas', the Committee thought 'it would be difficult to find a formula that would express such a question but agreed that an effort should be made to do so'. In the following paragraph, the tensions underlying the debate are even more apparent and the firm direction of the Chairman, Allen, is palpable:

> Against [Russell's] view it was pointed out that even if habits of living altered, firmly rooted tradition and prejudice operated against any radical changes in design of furniture and equipment to meet the new situation; but the Committee

---

21 One of a series of industry-specific working parties established by the government. The Furniture Working Party reported in 1946. Great Britain Board of Trade, *Furniture Working Party Report*, London: HMSO, 1946.

22 This was in advance of later Council policy, which frequently contented itself with the consideration of two-dimensional representations. See Catherine Moriarty, 'A Backroom Service? The Photographic Library of the Council of Industrial Design, 1945–1965', *Journal of Design History*, 13:1 (2000), 39–57.

agreed in discussion that it was undoubtedly their work to find where unreasonable prejudice lay and to counter it by any means at their disposal.

It was proposed that from the New Year meetings would be held on the third Monday in each month, but for sixteen months the Minutes of full Council meetings reveal a consistent pattern: 'There have been no meetings of the ... Housewives Committee during the past month'.[23] The situation was not unique, for the Design, Training, Exhibition Policy, and Finance and General Purposes Committees were similarly affected, and this was reflective of nothing more sinister than the strains experienced by an embryonic organisation charged with the orchestration of Britain's first major post-war exhibition. The event, which displayed several thousand items painstakingly gathered from the country's re-emerging manufacturing base, to more than a million and a half people by the time of its closure, was staged by a body with copious other responsibilities and which had a staff base in mid-1945 of just 28, including secretarial, clerical and junior grades. This number rose only slowly to 35 in September, and by year's end stood at 65 permanent staff and 11 temporary appointments in association with the exhibition.[24] A discussion in autumn 1946 concerning a possible extension to or relocation of the exhibition noted 'the great burden already imposed on the Council's staff'. This was not merely 'a matter of personal strain and weariness... , but of interference with, amounting in some respects to almost complete obstruction of, the Council's long term programmes'.[25] An accompanying document referred to the need to fully constitute and set to work the Council's Committees, which had been 'inactive of late for various reasons'.[26]

The last reference to the Housewives' Committee appeared in April 1947.[27] In May the Director, S.C. Leslie, resigned to take up a leadership role in the Treasury's new Economic Information Unit, and by July the Deputy Director had proposed that 'the purpose and utility of some of the existing committees should be reviewed with a view to either disbanding them, or resuscitating and re-energising them'.[28] This appears to have been the moment when the irrevocable step to abandon the Housewives was taken. In between the Committee's last mention and the May resignation, however, an intriguing additional meeting was orchestrated and directed by Leslie. Held on 23 April 1947, the 'Conference with Women's Organisations' brought together a broad range of representatives, including those from the Electrical Association for Women, BSI, Good Housekeeping Institute,

---

23   DCA File 1/1946 Minutes of 22nd meeting of the Council, 13 December 1946. A similar formulation of words appeared every month.
24   Figures taken from CoID *First Annual Report, 1945–1946*, 7–8.
25   DCA File 1/1946 Document dated 4 October 1946 on 'The Future of Britain Can Make It'.
26   Ibid, 'The Council's Forward Programme: Note by the Director' C(46)29.
27   DCA File 1/1947 Minutes of the meeting of Council held on 11 April 1947.
28   DCA File 1/1947 Memorandum on Future Policy by the Deputy Director C(47)28.

National Union of Townswomen's Guilds, National Federation of Women's Institutes, and Women's Group on Public Welfare. Allen was not present, although her SJC colleague, Cecily Cook, was there representing the Women's Co-operative Guild. Although a Trades Union Congress (TUC) representative was present, the absence of anyone from the Women's Labour League or the SJC is, perhaps, striking.

The meeting appears to have been lengthy but may not have proceeded in the way Leslie intended. In opening proceedings he referred to the 'important common interests' which the Council shared with these organisations, and of the significance of housewives as an audience for its message. He wished to discover their impressions of the teaching aids that were currently under development. The second and, one suspects, more crucial part of the discussion attempted to establish common ground between them on the value of information flows between housewives and manufacturers, a flow which, as gradually became apparent at the meeting, would in fact be instigated by the Council and mediated through the organisations represented there. Just as administrative procedures for the loan of equipment, photographs, and educational box sets had proved a stumbling block in the earlier part of the conference, the suggestion being that the Council might take advantage of pre-existing circuits and structures within the various organisations, the distribution of Council questionnaires now also proved contentious. Leslie appeared unable to satisfy the women's questions concerning the exact nature, scope and purpose of such material. The discussion was laboured and protracted, but appeared unresolved when the meeting was drawn to a close. One guest referred to the 'weariness of spirit' prevalent among women who needed to be convinced that 'what they really want they will eventually have'. Of this meeting, no mention was made by the Director in his report to Council.[29] By the time that a meeting concerned with the organisation of the Council's Public Relations Section determined to recruit a Woman Press Officer in the autumn, seeming thereby to circumvent more laborious ways of reaching women, Leslie was deeply immersed in his new role, and trying hard to reach another female target audience.

Having served on the Furniture, Carpets, Radio Cabinets and Wallpaper Selection Committees for 'Britain Can Make It', and the Finance and General Purposes Committee of the Council itself, Allen completed her three years' membership of the CoID and departed. Although the provision existed for the President of the Board of Trade to extend membership beyond the allotted period, this did not happen in Allen's case.

Having remained a busy and active member of its GPC throughout 1946, Allen was elected SJC Chair in 1947. The following year she returned to the GPC, and, beyond her SJC responsibilities, was elected Chair of the Watford Co-operative Union. In 1948 she presided over a rally attended by

---

[29]   The report of the conference with women's organisations, 23 April 1947 appears in DCA File 189 on 'Public Relations Policy'.

3,000 Co-operative, Trade Union and Labour women at which Chancellor Sir Stafford Cripps spoke on the country's economic situation. In 1949 the rally's guest was the Rt Hon. Herbert Morrison, MP, Lord President of the Council, and Allen was one of the accompanying speakers. She served a further period on the GPC, from 1949 to 1950. Her death was reported in the Biennial Report for 1954 to 1956 of the, now, National Joint Committee of Working Women's Organisations.

S.C. Leslie and the Standing Joint Committee of Working Women's Organisations

Evidence of a continuing instrumental engagement by the Council of Industrial Design with a significant women's organisation of the Left, one with which the former Chair of its Housewives' Committee was closely associated, is provided by the SJC's own records. The SJC Annual Report for 1946 to 1947, which covered the period of the CoID Conference described above, reported that its Secretary had 'agreed to co-operate with the Council of Industrial Design in securing local interest and publicity among members of affiliated organisations in exhibitions being arranged in a number of provincial centres'.[30] Over the following two years further co-operation with CoID Design Weeks was reported, and representatives of local branches of affiliated organisations were said to have taken part in the Housewives' Forums which were a feature of these events.[31] Minutes of the SJC's General Purposes Committee reported on the Council's preparations, as well as its own steps to promote attendance at the Cardiff and Manchester Weeks, especially their open forums.[32] In 1950 the Council invited SJC representatives to attend the closed exhibitions it was organising in association with its selection of items to be shown at the forthcoming 'Festival of Britain'. A small party of members arranged to visit the Home Furnishings event at 2.15 pm on Thursday, 8 June.[33] When, soon afterwards, a discussion of the viewing was prompted by a CoID request for addresses of London-based SJC affiliates to whom it could notify future

---

[30]   Documents held in the Modern Records Centre of the University of Warwick (hereafter MRC) MRC MSS 292/62.14/1 SJC SJCWWO Annual Report 1.12.1946–1930.11.1947, 15.

[31]   MRC MSS 292/62.14/1 SJC Annual Reports December 1947–November 1948, and December 1948–November 1949. See Lesley Whitworth, 'Anticipating Affluence: Skill, Judgement and the Problems of Aesthetic Tutelage', in L. Black and H. Pemberton (eds), *An Affluent Society? Britain's Post-Ware 'Golden Age' Revisited*, Aldershot: Ashgate, 2004, 167–183.

[32]   Labour History Archive & Study Centre, People's History Museum, Manchester (hereafter LHASC), Minutes of Meetings of the General Purposes Committee of the Standing Joint Committee of Working Women's Organisations, 8 January 1948, 11 March 1948, 13 May 1948.

[33]   LHASC Minutes of Meetings ... 11 May 1950.

events, the view was taken that those already seen had been very small scale and were liable to disappoint. Whilst the restricted space of the Council's premises was acknowledged to have played a part, what irked the visitors most was the absence of a CoID representative who could explain the organisation's remit and the purpose of the displays.[34]

During these years the Council's overtures to the SJC were overshadowed by debates concerning the country's parlous economic position: it may hardly have seemed a propitious moment for national design reform. The apparent mismatch between CoID aims and the country's predicament does not seem to have been commented on in the same way that it had been at the 'Conference with Women's Organisations'. Oddly enough, though, the same energetic proselytizer was busy at work. As Head of the government's newly established Economic Information Unit (EIU), Leslie, the former CoID Director, now renewed his efforts to reach the country's womenfolk.

Against the backdrop of a country facing conditions of significant privation, the SJC framed a resolution to the National Conference of Labour Women which pledged its support to the government and urged 'the adoption of any further controls necessary to ensure fair shares of scarce goods for all'. The Committee also added a plea that the public be kept 'fully informed regarding the reasons for any measures adopted to meet the crisis'.[35] It must therefore have been delighted to begin receiving the steady stream of invitations emanating from Leslie's Unit. Annual Reports for the period 1946 to 1950 show SJC representation at a large number of conferences called by the Unit to discuss aspects of the economic situation with women's organisations, and 'to consider methods of publicity and ways in which women could assist in the recovery drive'.[36] Stafford Cripps, the Chancellor of the Exchequer and Leslie's boss, was fully committed to any impetus which built upon women's support, proposing the formation of Women's Recovery Committees in every borough and urban district, and outlining specific matters with which such Committees could assist.[37] Naturally the SJC sent a letter to affiliates urging participation in, if not initiation of, such work.[38] It also suggested ways in which the usefulness of the EIU's periodic conferences could be increased; for example, by arranging for an official from the Ministry of Food to make a statement on the food position.[39]

---

34   LHASC Minutes of Meetings ... 6 July 1950. A letter was written suggesting the usefulness of a short talk from a Council representative.
35   MRC MSS 292/62.14/1 SJC Annual Report 1.12.1946–30.November.1947.
36   Ibid. And Annual Reports 1 December 1947–30 November 1948, December 1948–November 1949 and December 1949–December 1950. The quotation is taken from the second of these.
37   MRC MSS 292/62.14/1 SJC Annual Report 1 December 1947–30 November 1948. The conference took place in July 1948.
38   LHASC Minutes of Meetings ... 29 July 1948.
39   Ibid. Using the press to communicate food policy changes was difficult because of space restrictions. The SJC's idea was accepted. It initially suggested the

The SJC was, then, far from a passive conduit of information. It regularly operated as a vehicle for criticism of the EIU too. The Unit's 'Conference of Women's Organisations' held on 11 September 1947 covered the nature of the economic crisis, the salvage campaign, domestic fuel economy, the recruitment of women for industry, and food problems, but the SJC felt that a large part of the discussion had been 'useless and irrelevant'. It also expressed disquiet about anomalies in the range of national and local groups who were represented. These included the National Union of Conservative and Unionist Associations and the Liberal Women's Federation, but not the Women's Advisory Committee of the TUC nor the Women's Sections of the Labour Party: it was agreed to record 'strong dissatisfaction' with this.[40] Allen and her co-representative, Mrs Martin, also expressed 'grave dissatisfaction with the inefficient arrangements and doubts about the value of the Conference' held on 5 March 1948. A lengthy discussion followed their report, and it was agreed that the Secretary would take the matter up with the appropriate Department.[41] Allen and Martin next reported on the Unit's conference on 'Economic Information' held on 16 April. Both felt that events of this type were 'serving no useful purpose', as the information they supplied was 'largely a repetition of that given at a previous Conference'. Their view was endorsed by another SJC member. It was again agreed that representations should be made in the appropriate quarter.[42] At the same meeting, however, the Secretary related that a meeting on 22 April had been well attended, and there had been 'a lucid and objective talk on the background to the present economic situation, and a short summary of the Economic Survey for 1948'. She felt that the 'factual information given though familiar to a number of organisations was appreciated by the majority', as was an 'account of a successful experiment in Halifax to recruit women for part-time work in industry', which had followed discussion of the main address. Of a conference held on 6 October Allen was able to report that it had been 'the most useful one yet held'. On this occasion the GPC decided to obtain copies of the hand-out given to the meeting, and of the leaflet 'Sharing the Power', for circulation to members.[43] Allen was again in attendance at the Unit's event entitled 'The Intelligent Woman's Guide to ERP' on 24 November,[44] but what really garnered praise was the opening of the Exhibition 'On Our Way' in the following spring. In stark contrast to the disappointment generated by the CoID exhibition, this one elicited a letter

---

reconstitution of the Women's Advisory Committee which had functioned during the early part of the war, but was told that this was not practicable.

40   LHASC Minutes of Meetings ... 16 October 1947.
41   LHASC Minutes of Meetings ... 11 March 1948.
42   LHASC Minutes of Meetings ... 13 May 1948.
43   LHASC Minutes of Meetings ... 7 October 1948. The Ministry of Fuel and Power appears to have been a co-organiser.
44   LHASC Minutes of Meetings ... 25 November 1948. ERP stands for European Recovery Programme.

of praise to its co-creators, the Central Office of Information (COI), expressing the hope that it would tour provincial centres, while the GPC wrote in similar vein to Mrs Horton of the Economic Information Unit, expressing appreciation of the exhibition and strong satisfaction with its organisation.[45] Allen and the SJC Secretary were present at 'Dollars and Sense' on 6 December, which was felt to provide a 'comprehensive background' to the current situation, and at that month's GPC meeting the publication of the Unit's 'For Women Only' leaflet about devaluation was welcomed.[46] All members were sent a copy, and affiliates wishing to secure their own supplies were to be directed to the COI.

Clearly the Standing Joint Committee had a deep regard for the importance and accessibility of information. It had, for example, regularly published and disseminated its own pamphlets. And when it was dissatisfied with the quantity or quality of information being made available to women, it strove to reform those information flows through an engagement in dialogue with source bodies. The SJC wrote to Herbert Morrison, impressing the need for 'a continuing flow of publicity' on the country's finances, and suggesting 'a series of informative broadcasts ... on the lines of the "Can I Help You?" talks', plus the inclusion of items on the BBC's 'Woman's Hour' radio programme in summer 1947.[47] It also sought broadcasts on aspects of the food situation.[48] The following year there was appreciation of the EIU's 'Talking Points' notes to assist speakers of women's organisations. These covered, for example, the export drive and important facts about key industries.[49] When in 1952 the Treasury reported the likely cessation of the monthly 'Report to Women' as an economy measure, the SJC wrote to the Treasury expressing regret that 'such a valuable and informative publication should be suspended'.[50]

Shortly after this Allen died. The biennial report which announced her death bore for the first time a section heading, 'Consumer Questions', marking the arrival of a new, though not necessarily unproblematic, national sensibility.[51] In 1953 the GPC considered a report from BSI outlining the work it was undertaking to define guaranteed standards of quality in consumer goods, in substitution of those embodied in the wartime (and immediate post-war) Utility scheme. It agreed to send copies

---

45   See MRC MSS 292/62.14/1 SJC Annual Report December 1948–November 1949, LHASC Minutes of Meetings ... 14 April 1949, and 10 February 1949. 'On Our Way' ran for six weeks from 21 March at the COI exhibition hall in Oxford Street. The GPC wrote drawing the attention of all SJC members to it.
46   LHASC Minutes of Meetings ... 8 December 1949.
47   LHASC Minutes of Meetings ... 14 August 1947.
48   LHASC Minutes of Meetings ... 12 June 1947.
49   MRC MSS 292/62.14/1 SJC Annual Report December 1947–November 1948.
50   LHASC Minutes of Meetings ... 12 June 1952.
51   MRC MSS 292/62.14/1 SJC National Joint Committee of Working Women's Organisations Report for Two Years, December 1954–December 1956.

of BSI leaflets to all Committee members.[52] It was in regular contact with BSI, and later when the BSI Associate Scheme was launched 'to assist consumers with advice and information', it took up Associate membership, poring over the quarterly *Shopper's Guide* and making suggestions for future reports. Later in the decade they also decided to take out a subscription with Consumers' Association Ltd, and its own monthly magazine *Which?* was given similar 'close attention'.[53]

Conclusion: The SJC and the Council of Industrial Design

The SJC's engagement with the project of consumer empowerment was neither straightforward nor streamlined. Its interest in determining 'The [kind of] House the Working Woman Wants' dated back to the pre-war period when it was also represented on the Women's Advisory Housing Council (WAHC).[54] It was instrumental in achieving wartime representation of 'working-class housewives' on the Ministry of Health's Central Housing Advisory Committee, its Committee on the Design of Dwellings, and its Committee on Rural Housing, yet in 1946 it determined, after discussion, not to send a representative to a WAHC conference set for November.[55] In 1948 a request from the Board of Trade's Committee on Resale Price Maintenance for SJC assistance with consumer representation was also declined. Predicated on the perceived difficulty of 'giving useful evidence in view of the complex issues covered by the Committee's Terms of Reference, on which, as consumers, they had no information', the SJC's rejection of the invitation remained firm despite further pleading from the Committee's Mrs Malone.[56] As women and housewives however, the SJC unlike CoID, had an involvement in debates across the full spectrum of consumer concerns. In 1947, for example, it was represented on the Board of Trade's Weights and Measures Committee, and more than a decade on, when the recommendations of the resulting report had still to be implemented, its location as a focal point for working-class representation enabled it to protest strongly that 'there was no reason to believe that

---

52 LHASC Minutes of Meetings ... 10 September 1953.
53 MRC MSS 292/62.14/1 SJC Minutes of the Biennial Meeting of the National Joint Committee of Working Women's Organisations for the period ending 10 January 1957, and for the years 1959–1960.
54 MRC MSS 292/65.2/2 Draft report of the year's work of the Labour Party in Women's Interests at Home and Abroad, May 1936–March 1937. MRC MSS 292/62.14/1 SJC Annual Report November 1936–November 1937. It is not intended to suggest here that the home was necessarily conceptualised as a site for new consumption practices by the SJC at this time.
55 MRC MSS 292/65.2/2 Report of the Chief Woman Officer on the Year's Work of the Labour Party in Women's Interests, May 1942–April 1943. LHASC Minutes of Meetings ... 19 September 1946.
56 LHASC Minutes of Meetings ... 8 January 1948.

housewives today were more willing to be cheated in regard to weights and measures than they were ten years ago'.[57] Ironically its involvement with a number of bodies brought into being to address the fuel crises of the later 1940s gave it a better platform from which to debate the design of optimally efficient fires than the Council, which appears to have taken little part.

The SJC's predominant concern throughout the period under discussion was with issues of necessitous consumption, and the shift to a new and more conventionally 'consumerist' perspective was slow to take place, as has been indicated. Yet its determination to secure the availability to working women of good quality food, clothing and shelter, should have made it a natural ally of the CoID after that body's formation in 1944, that is, above and beyond the happenstance of Margaret Allen's dual membership. Housing *per se* was beyond the Council's remit, it is true, but the achievement of improved standards of design in all household goods was at the heart of its mission. Furthermore, the government's 1959 interest in 'a social survey to explore the habits and needs of consumers in present conditions' (in relation to its 'Weights and Measures' Agenda) shows how prescient the investigative work proposed by the Housewives' Committee in 1945 was. That CoID chose not to sustain its Housewives' Committee, nor indeed its contact with SJC after 1950, is indicative of a change of emphasis in its orientation following the departure of S.C. Leslie.

For his own part Leslie continued, through his work in the EIU, to invest in the provision and dissemination of information. Surviving correspondence between him and John Beavan of *The Manchester Guardian* newspaper, dating from spring 1948, reveals his absolute determination that the Unit reach out to women, 'because we have repeatedly had evidence that ... women citizens feel that altogether insufficient pains are taken to explain economic problems and policies in their terms'.[58] The series of conferences for women's organisations that resulted from this determination has been alluded to above. On this occasion the conference in question had been called for women journalists, and the text also betrays some frustration: 'If the conference revealed nothing new that must principally be the fault of the questioners. Every question was answered fully and fairly.' In the following letter he repeated his assertion that the questions had been 'for the most part ... futile', but went on to suggest, in a more positive tone, that this and a string of successor conferences would be 'worth while for the education of women journalists apart from anything else'.[59] At CoID, just as at EIU, Leslie had been utterly committed to the encouragement of critical engagement. Teaching materials and pamphlets produced by the Council and intended

57   MRC MSS 292/62.14/1 SJC Annual Report December 1947–December 1948, and Report for two years 1959–1960.
58   Letter from S.C. Leslie to John Beavan, 12 March 1948, B/L140/12a-c. *Guardian* Archive, John Rylands University Library of Manchester.
59   Letter from S.C. Leslie to A.P. Wadsworth, 15 March 1948, B/L140/13. *Guardian* Archive, John Rylands University Library of Manchester.

for popular consumption were meant to inculcate the habit of asking questions.

It is unclear whether Allen was alive at the time of the opening of the Council's Haymarket Design Centre in London in 1956. What is certain is that the SJC and CoID had much to learn from one another, and the continuance of interaction between the two bodies could have been mutually beneficial. Most especially, the formation by CoID of a Housewives' Committee was prescient given the conditions of Britain in the immediate post-war period. Its leadership by a member of the Women's Co-operative Guild who was also a leading member of the SJC ran counter to the prevailing trend of increasingly conservative domination of consumer representation roles.[60] Furthermore, its capacity to champion the emergent consumer needs of the ordinary housewife within a body answerable to the Board of Trade would have been invaluable after 1951, when the country's Labour administration was succeeded by a Conservative one that viewed consumer protection issues rather differently. The simultaneous struggles of bodies like BSI to achieve an effective engagement between itself and the various formations of women who sought to represent the consumer voice, made manifest both the importance of the endeavour, and the difficulty of making it work well.

It is through the confluence of Leslie's and Allen's careers that this particular episode in the history of women's making of space is revealed. The fortunate triangulation of three sets of records, the archives of the CoID, SJC, and *Guardian* newspaper, allows an interpretation of an apparent moment of opportunity. Some tensions in the account remain unresolvable. We can never know whether, or in what terms, Allen talked informally to the SJC about her CoID experiences, or how exhausted the SJC and other groups were by the ever-more frequent recourse to their 'good offices' to generate findings about women's 'needs'. It remains the case, however, that the CoID's decision to create a Housewives' Committee was made as a result of a growing inter-war and wartime consensus that women's presence within decision-making forums was both necessary and valuable. The abandonment of the Committee by the Council reminds us that the claim to that space requires continual re-making.

---

[60] See Matthew Hilton, 'The Female Consumer and the Politics of Consumption in Twentieth-Century Britain', *The Historical Journal*, 45:1 (2002) 103–128, and Elizabeth Darling, 'A Citizen as well as a Housewife: new spaces of femininity in 1930s London', in Hilde Heynen and Gulsum Baydar (eds), *Negotiating Domesticity: Spatial Productions of Gender*, London: Routledge, 2005, 49-64.

Bibliography

Archival Sources

British Library of Political and Economic Science (BLPES) Archives
Papers of Beatrice and Sidney Webb (Passfield).
Miscellaneous records relating to Katherine Buildings.

Bromley Public Libraries, Local Studies and Archives, Bromley
MS Diary of Emily Hall, Hall Family Diaries [Hall family of West Wickham, Kent].

Design Archives, University of Brighton
Design Council (Council of Industrial Design) Archive.

Girton College, Cambridge
Papers of the exhibition committee of the Loan Exhibition of Women's Industries, Bristol, 1885, within the Helen Blackburn Collection.

Harry Simpson Memorial Library, University of Westminster
Elizabeth Denby papers.

John Rylands University Library, Manchester
Manchester Guardian Archive.

Kensington Central Library Local Studies Collection.
Linley Sambourne Archive.

Labour History Archive and Study Centre, People's History Museum, Manchester
Papers of the Standing Joint Committee of Working Women's Organisations.

Max Lock Centre, University of Westminster Archive
Max Lock papers.

Modern Records Centre, University of Warwick
Papers of the Standing Joint Committee of Working Women's Organisations.

The National Archives of the UK, Public Record Office, Kew
Board of Trade.
BT 57 Council for Art and Industry: Minutes and Papers, 1934-1940.

Royal Institute of British Architects (RIBA) Archives
Sir Leslie Martin papers.
FRS Yorke papers.
RIBA Women's Committee papers.

University of Bristol
D.J. Carter, 'The social and political influences of the Bristol Churches 1830–1914'. Unpublished MS.

Victoria & Albert Museum, National Art Library, Archive of Art and Design
Misha Black papers.
Design Research Unit (DRU) papers.

Women's Library, London Metropolitan University
Records of the Women's Forum.

Newspapers and Periodicals

Architectural Review
Art at Home (12 vols.) London: Macmillan 1876-1883
Bristol Times
Clifton Chronicle
Co-operative News
Daily Herald
Englishwoman's Review
Forward
Labour Leader
Labour Woman
League Leaflet (Women's Labour League)
New Age
Pall Mall Gazette
Queen
Western Daily Press
Women's Union Journal

Unpublished Theses

Beaumont, Catriona, 'Women and Citizenship: A Study of Non-Feminist Women's Societies and the Women's Movement in England, 1928–1950', unpublished PhD thesis, University of Warwick, 1996.

Darling, Elizabeth, 'Elizabeth Denby, Housing Consultant: Social Reform and Cultural Politics in the Inter-War period', unpublished PhD Thesis, Bartlett School of Architecture, University College London, 2000.

Dehaene, M., 'A Descriptive Tradition in Urbanism: Patrick Abercrombie and the legacy of the Geddesian survey', unpublished PhD Thesis, Katholieke Universiteit Leuven, 2002.

Ferry, Emma, 'Advice, Authorship and the Domestic Interior: an Interdisciplinary Study of Macmillan's "Art at Home Series"', 1876–83, unpublished PhD thesis, Kingston University, 2004.

Stevens, Fiona, 'Open Spaces for the People; The Aims and Achievements of Octavia Hill in Nineteenth-Century London', unpublished MA Dissertation, University of Leicester, 1993.

Electronic Resources

The National Trust
Accessed 22 February, 2005.

Max Lock Centre, University of Westminster Archive
<http://www.wmin.ac.uk/builtenv/maxlock/HISTORY.HTM>
Accessed 22 May 2006.

[Leslie Martin funeral address]
Peter Carolin, Memorial Service for Sir Leslie Martin held at Jesus College Chapel, Cambridge, 18 November 2000,
<http://www.jesus.cam.ac.uk/college/martin.html>
Accessed 19 August 2003.

Published Sources

A Correspondent, 'An All-Europe House, a Pocket Ideal Home', *The Times*, 28 April, 1939, 21.
Abercrombie, Patrick, *Greater London Plan 1944*, London: HMSO, 1945.
Abercrombie, Patrick, Sydney Kelly and Arthur Kelly, *Dublin of the Future: the New Town Plan*, London: Hodder and Stoughton, Liverpool: University of Liverpool Press, 1922.
Abrams, Philip, 'The Failure of Social Reform, 1918-20', *Past and Present*, 24:1 (1963) 43-64.
Adam, Jill, 'Humanity House', *News Chronicle*, 14 April 1939
Adams, Peter, *Eileen Gray: Architect/Designer*, London: Thames & Hudson, 2000.
Addison, Paul, *The Road to 1945: British Politics and the Second World War*, (rev. ed.) London: Pimlico, 1994.
Aldridge, Meryl, 'Garden Cities: the disappearing 'Woman Question'' in S. Zimmerman (ed.), *Urban Space and Identity in the European City 1890s to 1930s*, Budapest: Central European University, 1995.
Anon. 'The birth of the council tenants movement. A study of the 1934 Leeds rent strike', <http://freespace.virgin.net/labwise.history6/1934.html>, accessed 20 May 2006.
Anon. 'Cottage Homes for Artisans', *London*, 4, (1895), 336–337
Anon. 'Industrial Design News', *Scope*, May (1946), 75.
Anon. 'Events and Comments', *Architect and Building News*, 158, (1939), 25.
Anon. 'The Glorified Spinster' *Macmillan's Magazine*, 58, (1888), 371–376.
Anon. 'Homes and Ideals', *Architect and Building News*, 158, (1939), 25–26.
Anon. 'Live Architecture Down at Poplar', *The Sphere*, June 2, (1951), 381.
Anon. Obituary [Sadie Speight], *Building Design*, 30 October 1992.
Anon. 'On Art and Archaeology', *The Academy*, 2 March 1878, 197.
Anon. 'Post-war Shop Fronts in London', *Architects' Journal*, 115, (1952), 581.
Anon. 'Red Cross Hall, Southwark', *The Builder*, 30 (1889), 333.

Anon. Review of '*A City Girl*', *Charity Organisation Review*, August 1887, 317.

Anon. 'The All-Europe House designed by Elizabeth Denby', *Journal of the Royal Institute of British Architects*, 46, (1939), 813–819.

Anscombe, Isabella, *A Woman's Touch: Women in Design from 1869 to the Present Day*, London: Virago, 1984.

Arts Council of Great Britain, *Thirties: British art and design before the war* [an exhibition organised by the Arts Council of Great Britain in collaboration with the Victoria & Albert Museum at the Hayward Gallery, 25 October 1979–13 January 1980], London: Arts Council of Great Britain, 1979.

Association for Planning and Reconstruction, *Housing Digest. An Analysis of Housing Reports 1941–45, prepared for the Electrical Association for Women*, London and Glasgow: Art and Education Publishers, 1946.

Atkinson, Fello, 'Post War Shop Display in London', *The Architectural Review*, 109, (1951), 98–105.

Attfield, Judith, 'What does History have to do with it? Feminism and Design History', *Journal of Design History*, 16:1, (2003), 77–87.

Attfield, Judith, 'Inside Pram Town', in Judith Attfield and Patricia Kirkham (eds), *A View from the Interior*, London: The Women's Press, 1989.

Attfield, Judith and Pat Kirkham (eds), *A View from the Interior, Feminism, Women and Design*, London: the Women's Press, 1989.

Attfield, Judith (ed.), *Utility Re-assessed: The Role of Ethics in the Practice of Design*, Manchester: Manchester University Press, 1999.

Banks, Olive, *The Biographical Dictionary of British Feminists*, Volume 1: 1800–1930, Harvester Press, 1985.

Bannon, Michael J., (ed.), *The Emergence of Irish Planning 1880–1920*, Dublin: Turoe Press, 1985.

Bannon, Michael J., 'Dublin town planning competition: Ashbee and Chettle's 'New Dublin – A study of Civics', *Planning Perspectives* 14:2 (1999) 145–163.

Barrett-Browning, Elizabeth, *Aurora Leigh*, London: Chapman & Hall, 1857.

Barrington, Mrs Russell, 'The Red Cross Hall', *English Illustrated Magazine*, 117, (1893), 610.

Bartley, Paula, *The Changing Role of Women 1815–1914*, London: Hodder & Stoughton, 1996.

Beach, Abigail, 'The Idea of Neighbourhood 1900–50', *History Today*, 45:9 (1995), 8.

Bell, Gwen and Jacqueline Tyrwhitt (eds), *Human Identity in the Urban Environment*, Harmondsworth: Penguin, 1972.

Bellamy, Joyce and H.F. Bing, 'Cecily Cook (1887/90–1962)', Joyce M. Bellamy and John Saville (eds), *Dictionary of Labour Biography*, vol. II, London: Macmillan, 1974.

Berkeley, Ellen Perry, (ed.), *Architecture: a Place for Women*, London and Washington: Smithsonian Institution Press, 1989.

Beveridge, William, *Social Insurance and Allied Services*, London: HMSO, November 1942, Cmd. 6404.

Binghan, Amy, Lise Sanders and Rebecca Zorach (eds), *Embodied Utopias:Gender, Social Change and the Modern Metropolis*, London: Routledge, 2002.

Birch, Eugenie Ladner and Deborah S. Gardener, 'The Seven-Percent Solution: A Review of Philanthropic Housing, 1870–1910' *Journal of Urban History*, 7, (1981), 403–436.

Boardman, Philip, *Patrick Geddes: Maker of the Future*, Chapel Hill: University of North Carolina Press, 1944.

Boardman, Philip, *The Worlds of Patrick Geddes: Biologist, Town Planner*, London: Routledge and Kegan Paul, 1978.

Bock, Gisela, and Pat Thane, *Maternity and Gender Politics: Women and the Rise of European Welfare States 1880s–1950s*, London: Routledge, 1994.

Bosanquet, Bernard, *Aspects of the Social Question*, London: Macmillan, 1895.

Bourdieu, Pierre, *Distinction. A Social Critique of the Judgement of Taste*, London: Routledge & Kegan Paul, 1984.

Bozovic, Miran (ed.), *Jeremy Bentham: The Panoptican Writings*, London: Verso, 1995.

Braddell, Dorothy, 'The Interior, Kitchens, Bathrooms etc', in Patrick Abercrombie (ed.), *The Book of the Modern House*, London: Hodder and Stoughton, 1939, 337–360.

Bradley, Quintin, 'The Leeds Rent Strike of 1914', http://freespace.virgin.net/labwise.history6/rentrick.htm, 1 February 2005.

Breward, Christopher, *Fashioning London. Clothing and the Modern Metropolis*, Oxford: Berg, 2004.

Brion, Marion and Anthea Tinker, *Women in Housing, Access and Influence*, London: The Housing Centre Trust, 1980.

Broome, M.A., Lady, *Colonial Memories*, London: Smith, Elder & Co., 1904.

Brown, Denise Scott, 'Sexism and the Star System', in Jane Rendell, Barbara Penner and Iain Borden (eds), *Gender, Space, Architecture: An Interdisciplinary Introduction*, London: Routledge, 2000, 258–265.

Burke, Gill, *Housing and Social Justice: The Role of Policy in British Housing*, London: Longman, 1981.

Burnett, John, *A Social History of Housing*, (2nd Edition) London: Routledge, 1986

Callen, Anthea, 'Sexual Division of Labour in the Arts and Crafts Movement' in Judith Attfield and Pat Kirkham (eds.), *A View from the Interior: Women and Design*, London: The Women's Press, 1995 (rev. edition), 151–164.

Callen, Anthea, *Angel in the Studio: Women in the Arts and Crafts Movement 1870–1914*, London: Astragal, 1979.

Carrington, Noel, *British Achievement in Design*, London: Pilot Press, 1946.

Chadwick, Whitney and Isabelle de Courtivron (eds), *Significant Others: Creativity and Intimate Partnership*, London, Thames & Hudson, 1993.

Chase, Ellen, *Tenant Friends in Old Deptford*, London: Williams and Norgate, 1929.

Chermayeff, Serge, [Review of *The Flat Book*], *Focus*, 4, (1939), 80.

Cherry, Deborah, *Beyond the Frame: Feminism and Visual Culture, Britain 1850–1900*, London: Routledge, 2000.

Cherry, Gordon E. (ed.), *Pioneers in British Planning*, London: The Architectural Press, 1981.

Cherry, Gordon E., *The Evolution of British Town Planning: a History of Town Planning in the UK during the Twentieth Century and of the Royal Town Planning Institute 1914–74*, Leighton Buzzard. L. Hill, 1974.

Cieraad, Irene (ed.), *At Home, an Anthropology of Domestic Space*, Syracuse: Syracuse University Press, 1999.

Clarke, David B., *The Consumer Society and the Postmodern City*, London; Routledge, 2003.

Cole, G.D.H., *A Century of Co-operation*, London: Allen & Unwin for the Co-operative Union, 1944.

Coleman, Alice, *Utopia on Trial, Vision and Reality in Planned Housing*, London: Hilary Shipman, 1990.

Coleman, Debra, Elizabeth Danze and Carol Henderson (eds), *Architecture and Feminism*, Princeton: Princeton Architectural Press, 1996.

Collette, Christine, *For Labour and for Women: the Women's Labour League, 1906–1918*, Manchester, Manchester University Press, 1989.

Collette, Christine, 'An Independent Voice. Lisbeth Simm and Women's Labour Representation in the North West, 1906–14', *North West Labour History*, 12, 1987, 79–86.

Collini, Stefan, *Public Moralists: Political Thought and Intellectual Life in Britain, 1850–1930*, Oxford: Clarendon Press, 1991.

Colomina, Beatriz (ed.), *Sexuality and Space*, Princeton: Princeton Architectural Press, 1992.

Corr, Helen, 'Helen Crawfurd (1877–1954)', *Oxford Dictionary of National Biography*, Vol. 14, Oxford: Oxford University Press, 2004, 88–90.

Corr, Helen, 'Agnes Johnston, Lady Dollan (1887–1966)', *Oxford Dictionary of National Biography*, Vol. 16, Oxford: Oxford University Press, 2004, 472–473.

Cowell, Ben, 'The Commons Protection Society and the Campaign for Berkhamstead Common 1866-70', *Rural History*, 13, (2002), 145–162.

Council for Art and Industry, *The Working Class Home, Its Furnishing and Equipment*, London: HMSO, 1937.

Crawford, Elizabeth, *Enterprising Women, the Garretts and their Circle*, London: Francis Boutle Publishers, 2002.

Creedon, Alison, 'A benevolent tyrant? The principles and practices of Henrietta Barnett (1851–1936), social reformer and the founder of Hampstead Garden Suburb', *Womens' History Review* 11:2, (2002), 231–52.

Critic, 'A London Diary', *New Statesman and Nation*, 6 May 1939, 675.

Cullingworth, J. Barry. and Vincent Nadin, *Town and Country Planning in the UK*, London: Routledge, 13th edition 2002.

Curtis, Lionel, *Octavia Hill and Open Spaces*, London: Association of Women House Property Managers, 1930.

Daily Mail Ideal Home Exhibition, *Ideal Home Exhibition Catalogue*, London: DMIHE, 1939.

Darke, Jane, 'Women architects and feminism' in Matrix, *Making Space. Women and the Man Made Environment*, London: Pluto, 1984.

Darley, Gillian, *Octavia Hill*, London: Constable, 1990.

Darley, Gillian, 'Octavia Hill (1838–1912)', *Oxford Dictionary of National Biography*, Vol. 27, Oxford: Oxford University Press, 2004, 164–167.

Darling, Elizabeth, 'Enriching and enlarging the whole sphere of human activities': the Work of the Voluntary Sector in Housing Reform in Inter-War Britain' in C. Lawrence and A-K. Mayer (eds), *Regenerating England: Science, Medicine and Culture in inter-war Britain*, Amsterdam: Rodopi, 2000, 145–172.

Darling, Elizabeth, '"To induce humanitarian sentiments in prurient Londoners": the Propaganda Activities of London's Voluntary Housing Associations in the Inter-war Period', *London Journal*, 27, (2002), 42–62.

Darling, Elizabeth, 'Elizabeth Denby or Maxwell Fry? A Matter of Attribution', in Brenda Martin and Penny Sparke (eds), *Women's Places: Architecture and Design 1860–1960*, London: Routledge, 2003, 149–169.

Darling, Elizabeth 'A Citizen as well as a Housewife: new spaces of femininity in 1930s London', in Hilde Heynen and Gulsum Baydar (eds), *Negotiating Domesticity: Spatial Productions of Gender*, London: Routledge, 2005, 49-64.

Darling, Elizabeth, '"The Star in the Profession she created for herself": A Brief Biography of Elizabeth Denby, Housing Consultant,' *Planning Perspectives*, 20:3, (2005) 271–300.

Darling, Elizabeth, *Re-forming Britain: Narratives of Modernity before Reconstruction*, London: Routledge, 2007.

Daunton, Martin (ed.), *The Cambridge Urban History of Britain* Vol 3, 1840–1950, Cambridge: Cambridge University Press, 2000.

Davidoff, Leonore, and Catherine Hall, *Family Fortunes. Men and Women of the English Middle Class 1780–1850*, London: Hutchinson, 1987.

Davies, Margaret Llewelyn, *The Women's Co-operative Guild*, Kirkby Lonsdale: WCG, 1904.

Davies, Margaret Llewelyn, *Maternity, Letters from Working Women* (1915), London: Virago, 1978.

Davin, Anna 'Imperialism and Motherhood', *History Workshop Journal*, 5, (1978) 9–65.

Dawson, J., 'Why Women Want Socialism', *Clarion*, 30 April 1909.

De Certeau, Michel, 'Walking in the City' repr. in Graham Ward (ed.), *The Certeau Reader*, Oxford: Blackwell, 2000.

Denby, Elizabeth. 'Oversprawl' in Ian Nairn (ed.), *Counter Attack against Subtopia*, London: Architectural Press, 1957, 427–434.

Denby, Elizabeth, *Europe Rehoused*, London: George Allen & Unwin, 1938.

Denby, Elizabeth. 'Rehousing from the Slum Dwellers' Point of View', *Journal of the Royal Institute of British Architects*, 44, (1936), 61–80.

Design Research Unit, *The Practice of Design*, London: Lund Humphries, 1946.

Dover, Harriet, *Home Front Furniture: British Utility design, 1941–1951*, Aldershot: Scolar Press, 1991.

Drew, Jane, 'Humanising Industrial Design', in *Report on the Conference on Industrial Design Held at Central Hall 26th–27th September 1946*, London: Council Of Industrial Design and Federation of British Industry, 1946, 41–46.

Dunnett, H. McG, *Guide to the Exhibition of Architecture, Town-planning and Building Research*, London:HMSO, 1951.

Durant, Ruth, *Watling: A Survey of Social Life in a New Housing Estate*, London: P.S. King, 1939.

Dyhouse, Carol, *Girls Growing Up in late Victorian and Edwardian England*, London: Routledge, 1981.

Eastlake, Charles L, *Hints on Household Taste in Furniture, Upholstery and Other Details*, London: Longmans, Green & Co, 1868.

Englander, David, *Landlord and Tenant in Urban Britain 1838–1918*, Oxford: Clarendon Press, 1983.

Englander, David, (ed.), *The Diary of Fred Knee*, Coventry: Society for the Study of Labour History, 1977.

Fagg, C.C., 'The History of the Regional Survey Movement', *South-Eastern Naturalist and Antiquary* (1928) 32, 71–94.

Ferry, Emma, '"Decorators May be Compared to Doctors": An analysis of Rhoda and Agnes Garrett's Suggestion for House decoration in Painting, Woodwork and Furniture', in *Journal of Design History*, Vol. 16:1, (2003), 15–33.

Fletcher, Ian, 'Some Aspects of Aestheticism', in O.M. Brack (ed.), *Twilight of Dawn: Studies in English literature in Transition*, Tucson: University of Arizona Press, 1987, 1–33.

Forster, Margaret, *Hidden Lives. A Family Memoir*, London: Penguin, 1996.

Foucault, Michel, *Discipline and Punish: The Birth of the Prison*, Harmondsworth: Penguin, 1977.

Fowler, Bridget, *Pierre Bourdieu and Cultural Theory. Critical Investigations*, London: Sage, 1997.

Friedman, Alice, *Women and the Making of the Modern House, A Social and Architectural History*, New York: Harry N. Abrams, 1998.

Furniss, Averil D. Sanderson, and Marion Phillips, *The Working Woman's House*, London: Swarthmore Press, n.d. [1919].

Garside, Patricia, 'Central Government, Local Authorities and the Voluntary Housing Sector 1919-1939' in Alan O'Day (ed), *Government and Institutions in the post-1832 UK*, Lampeter: Edwin Meller Press, 1995, 82–105.

Gauldie, Enid, *Cruel Habitations: a History of Working Class Housing*, London: Allen & Unwin, 1974.

Geddes, Patrick and Colleagues, *The Masque of Ancient Learning and its many meanings: a Pageant of Education from Primitive to Celtic times, devised and interpreted by Patrick Geddes*, Edinburgh: Outlook Tower, 1912.

Geddes, Patrick, 'The City Survey: a first step – I', *Garden Cities and Town Planning* 1, 1911, 18.

Geddes, Patrick, 'Civics: as Applied Sociology' Lectures delivered to the British Sociological Society Parts I and II 1904 reprinted with notes in H. Meller (ed.), *The Ideal City*, Leicester: Leicester University Press, 1979.

Geddes, Patrick, *City Development: a study of parks, garden, and culture-institutes, a report to the Carnegie Dunfermline Trust*, Bournville: St George Press and Edinburgh: Geddes and Co., 1904.

Geddes, Patrick, and J. Arthur Thomson, *The Evolution of Sex* London: Walter Scott, 1889.

Geddes, Patrick, *Cities in Evolution*, new and revised edition edited by the Outlook Tower Association Edinburgh, and the Association for Planning and Regional Reconstruction, London: Williams and Norgate, 1949.

Glasier, Katharine B., *Socialism and the Home*, London: ILP, 1909.

Glass, Ruth, 'Urban Sociology in Great Britain: a trend report', *Current Sociology* 4:12 (1955).

Glendinning, Miles, and Stefan Muthesius, *Tower Block*, London: Yale University Press, 1994.

Glennie, Paul D. and Nigel J. Thrift, 'Modernity, urbanism and modern consumption', *Environment and Planning D: Society and Space*, 10, (1992), 423–443.

Gloag, John, (ed.), *Design in Modern Life*, London: Allen and Unwin, 1934.

Grazia, Victoria de and Ellen Furlogh (eds), *The Sex of Things, Gender and Consumption in Historical Perspective*, Berkeley: University of California Press, 1996.

Great Britain Board of Trade, *Furniture Working Party Report*, London: HMSO, 1946.

Great Britain Board of Trade, *Carpet Working Party Report*, London: HMSO, 1947.

Great Britain Ministry of Health [and] Ministry of Works, *Housing Manual, 1944*, London: HMSO, 1944.

Great Britain Ministry of Health, Central Housing Advisory Committee, Design of Dwellings Sub-Committee, *Design of Dwellings*, London: HMSO, 1944 (*The Dudley Report*).

Great Britain Ministry of Health, *Housing Manual, 1949*, London: HMSO, 1949.

Greed, Clara, *Surveying Sisters: Women in a Traditional Male Profession* London: Routledge, 1991.

Greed, Clara, *Women and Planning: Creating Gendered Realities*, London: Routledge, 1994.

Greenhalgh, Paul, *Ephemeral Vistas: The Expositions Universelles, Great Exhibitions and World's Fairs, 1851–1939*, Manchester: Manchester University Press, 1988.

Gregg, Pauline, *A Social and Economic History of Britain 1760–1980*, 8th Edition, London: Harrap, 1982.

Grier, Katherine, *Culture and Comfort: People, Parlours and Upholstery 1850–1914*, Rochester and New York: The Strong Museum, 1988.

Griffiths, C.V.J., 'Ethel Bentham (1861–1931)', *Oxford Dictionary of National Biography*, Vol. 5, Oxford: Oxford University Press, 2004, 215–216.

Gurney, Peter, *Co-operative Culture and the Politics of Consumption in England, 1870–1930*, Manchester: Manchester University Press, 1996.

Hannam, June, 'An enlarged Sphere of Usefulness: the Bristol Women's Movement, c.1860–1914' in Madge Dresser and Philip Ollerenshaw (eds), *The Making of Modern Bristol*, Tiverton: Redcliffe Press, 1996.

Hannam, June and Karen Hunt, *Socialist Women. Britain, 1880s to 1920s*, London: Routledge, 2002.

Hardy, Dennis, *From Garden Cities to New Towns*, London: E. & F.N. Spon, 1991.

Harris, Jose, *Private Lives and Public Spirit, a Social History of Britain, 1870–1914*, Oxford: Oxford University Press, 1993.

Harrison, Brian, 'Marion Phillips (1881–1932)', *Oxford Dictionary of National Biography*, Vol. 44, Oxford: Oxford University Press, 2004, 126–128.

Harrison, Brian, *Prudent Revolutionaries: Portraits of British Feminists between the Wars*, Oxford: Clarendon Press, 1987.

Harrison, Brian, *Separate Spheres – The Opposition to Women's Suffrage in Britain*, London: Croom Helm, 1978.

Hayden, Dolores, *The Grand Domestic Revolution: A History of Feminist Designs for American Neighbourhoods and Cities*, Cambridge, Mass.: MIT Press, 1981.

Hebbert, Michael, 'The daring experiment – social scientists and land use planning in 1940s Britain', *Environment and Planning B*, 10, (1983), 3–17.

Hewitt, Martin, 'District Visiting and the Construction of Domestic Space' in Inga Bryden and Janet Floyd (eds), *Domestic Space: Reading the Nineteenth-Century Interior*, Manchester: Manchester University Press, 1999, 121–141.

Heynen, Hilde, and Gulsum Baydar, *Negotiating Domesticity: Spatial Productions of Gender*, London: Routledge, 2005.

Hill, Octavia, 'Blank Court: Or, Landlords and Tenants', *Macmillan's Magazine* 24 (1871), 456–465.

Hill, Octavia, 'The Work of Volunteers in the Organization of Charity', *Macmillan's Magazine* 26 (1872), 441–449.

Hill, Octavia, *Charities Organisation Review*, 1905, 315.

Hill, Octavia, *Homes of the London Poor*, London: Macmillian & Co., 1875.

Hill, Octavia, *Letter to My Fellow Workers*, London: Houseboy Brigade, 1883.

Hill, Octavia, *Letter to my Fellow Workers*, London: Houseboy Brigade, 1879.

Hill, Octavia, 'Report of an Attempt to Raise a Few of the London Poor without Gifts', London: G Meyer, n.d.

Hill, Octavia, 'Trained Workers for the Poor', *The Nineteenth Century*, 33, (1893), 36–43.

Hill, Octavia, 'Colour, Space and Music for the People', *The Nineteenth Century*, May 1884, 745.

[Hill, Octavia],'The Kyrle Society', *The Magazine of Art*, 1880, 210.

Hill, Octavia, *The Importance of Raising the Poor Without Almsgiving*, repr. from Transactions of the Social Science Association, 1869.

Hill, Octavia, 'The Influence of Model Dwellings on Character' in Charles Booth (ed.), *Life and Labour of the People of London* Vol II, London: Williams and Norgate, 1891, 262–270.

Hilton, Matthew, 'The Female Consumer and the Politics of Consumption in Twentieth-Century Britain', *The Historical Journal*, 45:1 (2002) 103–128.

Hilton, Matthew, *Consumerism in Twentieth-Century Britain: The search for a historical movement*, Cambridge: Cambridge University Press, 2003.

Hinton, James, 'Militant Housewives: The British Housewives' League and the Attlee Government', *History Workshop Journal* 38 (1994), 129–156.

Hinton, James, 'Women and the Labour Vote, 1945–1950', *Labour History Review* 57:3 (1992), 59–66.

Hinton, James, *Women, Social Leadership and the Second World War: Continuities of Class*, Oxford: Oxford University Press, 2002.

Hitchcock, Henry-Russell and Philip Johnson, *The International Style*, New York: W.W. Norton and Co., 1932, 19.

Holder, Julian, 'Design in Everyday Things': Promoting Modernism in Britain, 1912-1944', in Paul Greenhalgh (ed.), *Modernism in Design*, London: Reaktion Books, 1990, 123–144.

Hollis, Patricia, *Ladies Elect: Women in English Local Government 1865–1914*, Oxford: Clarendon Press, 1987.

Howard, Ebenezer, *Tomorrow: a peaceful path to real reform*, [1898] facsimile edition, London: Routledge, 2003.

Hughes, Ann and Karen Hunt, 'A Culture Transformed? Women's Lives in Wythenshawe in the 1930s' in Andy Davies and Steven Fielding (eds), *Workers' Worlds. Cultures and Communities in Manchester and Salford, 1880–1939*, Manchester: Manchester University Press, 1992, 74–101 .

Hunt, Karen, 'Negotiating the boundaries of the domestic: British socialist women and the politics of consumption', *Women's History Review*, 9:2 (2000), 389–410.

Jacobs, Jane, *The Death and Life of Great American Cities*, London: Jonathan Cape, 1962.

John, Angela V. (ed.), *Unequal opportunities: Women's Employment in England 1800–1918*, Oxford: Blackwell, 1986.

Jones, Gareth Stedman, Outcast London: A Study in the Relationship between the Classes in Victorian Society, Oxford: Oxford University Press, 1971.

Joyce, Patrick, *Democratic Subjects: the Self and the Social in Nineteenth Century England*, Cambridge: Cambridge University Press, 1994.

Keeble, Trevor, 'Creating "The New Room": The Hall Sisters of West Wickham and Richard Norman Shaw', in Brenda Martin and Penny Sparke (eds), *Women's Places: Architecture and Design 1860–1960*, London: Routledge, 2003, 23–46.

Kitchen, Paddy, *A Most Unsettling Person: an Introduction to the Life and Ideas of Patrick Geddes*, London: Victor Gollancz, 1975.

Koven, Seth, *Slumming: Sexual and Social Politics in Victorian London*, Princeton: Princeton University Press, 2004.

Koven, Seth and Sonya Michel, 'Womanly duties: maternal politics and the origins of the welfare state in France, Germany and the United States 1880–1920', *American Historical Review* 95:4 (1990), 1076–1108.

Koven, Seth and Sonya Michel, (eds), *Mothers of a New World: Maternalist Politics and the Origin of Welfare States*, London: Routledge, 1993.

Lanchester, Henry V., *Town Planning in Madras: A Review of Conditions and Requirements of City Improvement and Development in the Madras Presidency*, London: Constable, 1918.

Langland, Elizabeth, *Nobody's Angels: Middle Class Women and Domestic Ideology in Victorian Culture*, Ithaca and London: Cornell University Press, 1995.

Law, Cheryl, 'The old faith living and the old power there: the movement to extend women's suffrage' in Maroula Joannou and June Purvis (eds), *The Women's Suffrage Movement. New Feminist Perspectives*, Manchester: Manchester University Press, 1998.

Law, John, [Margaret Harkness], *A City Girl*, London: Vizetelly, 1887.Lees-Maffei, Grace, 'From Service to Self-Service; Advice Literature as Design Discourse 1920–1970', *Journal of Design History*, 14:3, (2001), 187–206.

Lewis, Jane, *Women and Social Action in Victorian and Edwardian England*, Aldershot: Edward Elgar, 1991.

Lindsay, Thomas Martin, *The Kyrle Societies and their Work*, Glasgow: McLaren & Son, 1883.

Lipovetsky, Gilles, *The Empire of Fashion. Dressing Modern Democracy* (Translated by Catherine Porter), Princeton: Princeton University Press, 1994.

Livesey, Ruth, 'Reading for Character: Women Social Reformers and Narratives of the Urban Poor in Late Victorian and Edwardian London', *Journal of Victorian Culture* 9:1, (2004), 43–67.

London County Council, *London Housing*, London: LCC, 1937.

Maasberg, Ute and Regina Prinz (eds), *Die Neue Kommen! Weibliche Avantgarde in der Architektur der zwanziger Jahre*, Hamburg: Junius Verlag, 2004.

McBrinn, Joseph, '"Decoration should be a common joy": The Kyrle Society and Mural Painting', *The Acorn, Journal of the Octavia Hill Society*, forthcoming.

Mackenzie, Norman, (ed.), *The Letters of Beatrice and Sidney Webb* I, Cambridge: Cambridge University Press, 1978.

Mackenzie, Norman and Jeanne Mackenzie (eds), *The Diary of Beatrice Webb vol. 1*, London: Virago, 1982.

Maguire, Patrick J. and Jonathan M. Woodham, *Design and Cultural Politics in Post-war Britain: The Britain Can Make It Exhibition of 1946*, Leicester: Leicester University Press, 1992.

Malpass, Peter, The Work of the Century, the Origins and Growth of the Octavia Hill Housing Trust in Notting Hill, London: Octavia Hill Housing Trust, 1998.

Manchester Women's History Group, 'Ideology in bricks and mortar. Women and housing in Manchester between the wars', *North West Labour History*, 12 (1987), 24–48.

Markus, T.A., *Buildings and Power: Freedom and Control in Modern Building Types*, London: Routledge, 1993.

Marsh, Jan, and Pamela Gerrish Nunn, *Pre-Raphaelite Women Artists*, London: Thames & Hudson, 1997.

Martin, Leslie and Sadie Speight, *The Flat Book. A Catalogue of Well-designed Furniture and Equipment*, London: William Heinemann, 1939.

Martin, Leslie, Buildings and Ideas 1933–1983: From the Studio of Leslie Martin and His Associates, Cambridge: Cambridge University Press, 1983.

Marwick, Arthur, *Britain in the Century of Total War. War, Peace and Social Change*, Harmondsworth: Penguin, 1970.

Massey, Doreen, *Space, Place and Gender*, Cambridge: Polity, 1994.

Matrix, *Making Space: Women and the Manmade Environment*, London: Pluto Press, 1984.

Meacham, Standish, *Toynbee Hall and Social Reform, 1890–1914*, London:Yale University Press, 1982.

Meller, Helen, *Leisure and the Changing City: a Study of Bristol 1870–1914*, London: Routledge and Kegan Paul, 1976.

Meller, Helen, Patrick Geddes: Social evolutionist and city planner, London: Routledge, 1990.

Meller, Helen, *Town, Plans and Society in Modern Britain*, Cambridge: Cambridge University Press, 1997.

Melling, J., *Rent Strikes. Peoples' Struggle for Housing in West Scotland 1880–1916*, Edinburgh: Polygon, 1983.

Middlesbrough Corporation, *The County Borough of Middlesbrough Survey and Plan* [directed by Max Lock], Yorkshire: Middlesbrough Corporation, 1946.

Milicevic, Aleksandra S., 'Radical Intellectuals: what happened to the New Urban Sociology?', *International Journal of Urban and Regional Research* 25:4, (2001), 759–783.

Miller, Daniel, *Material Culture and Mass Consumption*, Oxford: Basil Blackwell, 1987.

Miller, Mervyn, *Raymond Unwin: Garden Cities and Town Planning*, Leicester: Leicester University Press, 1992.

Milton, Nan, *John Maclean*, London: Pluto Press, 1973.

Ministry of Health (GB), Central Housing Advisory Committee, Design of Dwellings Sub-Committee, *Design of Dwellings*, London: HMSO, 1944.

Moberley Bell, Enid, *Octavia Hill*, London: Constable, 1942.

Morrell, Caroline, 'Octavia Hill and Women's Networks in Housing Management' in *Gender, Health and Welfare* Ann Digby and John Stewart (eds), London: Routledge, 1996, 90–118.

Mowat, Charles Loch, *Britain Between the Wars 1918–40*, Cambridge: Cambridge University Press, 1983.

Mumford, Lewis, *The Culture of Cities*, London: Secker and Warburg, 1938.

Nash, Rosalind, *The Position of Married Women*, Manchester: CWS Printing Works, 1907.

Nava, Mica, 'Modernity's Disavowal. Women, the City and the Department store', in Mica Nava and Alan O'Shea (eds), *Modern Times. Reflections on a Century of English Modernity*, London: Routledge, 1996, 38–76.

Nevinson, Margaret, *Life's Fitful Fever: A Volume of Memories*, London: A & C Black, 1926.

Newton, Stella M., *Health, Art & Reason – Dress Reformers of the Nineteenth Century*, London: John Murray, 1974

Nicholson, Shirley, *A Victorian Household*, London: Barrie and Jenkins, 1988.

Nord, Deborah Epstein, *The Apprenticeship of Beatrice Webb*, Amherst: University of Massachusetts Press, 1985.

Nord, Deborah Epstein, *Walking the Victorian Streets, Women, Representation and the City*, New York: Cornell University Press, 1995.

Nunn, Pamela Gerrish, *Victorian Women Artists*, London: The Women's Press, 1987.

O'Day, Rosemary, 'How Families Lived Then: Katherine Buildings, East Smithfield, 1885–1890', in Ruth Finnegan and Michael Drake, ed., *Studying Family and Community History* Vol. I, Cambridge: Cambridge University Press, 1994, 129–165.

O'Day, Rosemary, *The Family and Family Relationships, 1500–1900*, Basingstoke: Macmillan, 1994.

Orbach, Lawrence F., *Homes for Heroes: A Study of the Evolution of British Public Housing 1915–21*, London: Seeley Service & Co., 1977.

Owen, David, *English Philanthropy*, Cambridge, Mass: Belknapp Press of the Harvard University Press, 1964, 496.

Pankhurst, E. Sylvia, *The Home Front*, London: Hutchinson, 1932.

Pankhurst, E. Sylvia, *The Suffragette Movement*, London: Virago, 1977.

Parker, Julia, *Women and Welfare: Ten Victorian Women in Public Social Service* London: Macmillan, 1989.

Parkes, K., 'The Leek Embroidery Society', *Studio*, 1, (1893), 136–40.

Parkin, Michael, Obituary [Sadie Speight], *The Independent*, 27 October 1992.

Peel, Dorothy Constance, *The Art of Modern Housekeeping*, London: Warne, 1935.

Perry, Ruth and Martine Watson Brownley (eds), *Mothering the Mind: Studies of Writers and their Silent Partners*, New York and London: Holmes and Meier, 1984.

Pevsner, Nikolaus, *An Enquiry into Industrial Art in England*, Cambridge: Cambridge University Press, 1937.

Plummer, Raymond, *Nothing Need Be Ugly, the first Seventy Years of the DIA*, London: DIA, 1985.

Pollock, Griselda and Rozsika Parker, *Old Mistresses: Women, Art and Ideology*, London: Women's Press, 1981.

Ponsonby, Margaret, 'Ideals, Reality and Meaning. Homemaking in England in the First Half of the Nineteenth Century,' *Journal of Design History* (special issue: 'Anxious Homes' edited by Lesley Whitworth), 16:3, (2003), 201–214.

Pope, Alexander, 'Moral Essays, III: Of the Uses of Riches', in John Butt (ed.), *The Poems of Alexander Pope*, London: Methuen & Co, 1963, 582.

Potter, Beatrice, 'A Lady's View of the Unemployed at the East', *Pall Mall Gazette*, 18 February 1886.

Prochaska, Frank, *Women and Philanthropy in Nineteenth Century England*, Oxford: Clarendon Press, 1980.

Prunty, Jacinta, *Dublin Slums 1800-1925: a Study in Urban Geography*, Ballsbridge: Irish Academic Press, 1998.

Rappaport, Erika, *Shopping for Pleasure, Women in the Making of London's West End*, Princeton: Princeton University Press, 2000.

Ravetz, Alison, *Council Housing and Culture, the History of a Social Experiment*, London: Routledge, 2001, 29.

Read, Herbert, *Art and Industry: The Principles of Industrial Design*, London: Faber & Faber, 1934.

Rendall, Jane, (ed.), *Equal or Different?: Women's Politics 1800–1914*, Oxford: Basil Blackwell, 1987.

Rice, Margery Spring, *Working-Class Wives* (1939), London: Virago, 1981.

Richter, Melvin, *The Politics of Conscience: T.H. Green and his Age*, London: Weidenfield and Nicholson, 1964.

Roberts, Elizabeth, 'Women and the domestic economy, 1890–1970: the oral evidence' in Michael Drake (ed.), *Time, Family & Community. Perspectives on Family and Community History*, Oxford: Blackwell, 1994.

Roberts, Marion, *Living in a Man-Made World: Gender Assumptions in Modern Housing Design*, London: Routledge 1991.

Rose, Gillian, *Feminism and Geography: The Limits of Geographical Knowledge*, Cambridge: Polity, 1993.

Rose, Michael E. and Anne Wood, *Everything went on at the Round House: 100 years of Manchester University Settlement*, Manchester: Manchester University Press, 1995.

Rothschild, Joan and Victoria Rosner, 'Feminisms and Design: A Review Essay', in Joan Rothschild (ed.), *Design and Feminism, Re-visioning Spaces, Places and Everyday Things*, New Brunswick: Rutgers University Press, 1999, 7–33.

Rowntree, Diana, [Leslie Martin Obituary], *The Guardian*, August 2, 2000.

Ruskin, John, 'Of Queens' Gardens', in *Sesame and Lilies: Two Lectures*, London: Smith and Elder, 1864.

Ruskin, John, *The Seven Lamps of Architecture*, [1849] London; George Allen and Unwin, 1925.

Ryan, Deborah, *The Ideal Home through the 20th Century*, London: Hazar Publishing Ltd, 1997.

Saint, Andrew, 'Sir Raymond Unwin (1863–1940)', *Oxford Dictionary of National Biography*, Vol. 55, Oxford: Oxford University Press, 2004, 911–914.

Salmon, Nicholas, *The William Morris Chronology*, Bristol: Thoemmes Press, 1996.

Scott, Gillian, *Feminism and the Politics of Working Women: The Womens' Co-operative Guild, 1880s to the Second World War*, London: UCL Press, 1998.

Seddon, Jill and Suzette Worden (eds), *Women Designing: Redefining Design in Britain between the Wars*, Brighton: University of Brighton Press, 1994.

Seddon, Jill, 'Mentioned, but Denied Significance: Women Designers and the "Professionalisation" of Design in Britain c. 1920-1951', *Gender & History*,12:2 (2000), 426-447.

Silkin, Lewis, 'Continental Housing Lessons for Municipalities', *The Town and County Councillor*, 1 (1936), 11.

Simey, M.B., *Charitable Effort in Liverpool*, Liverpool: Liverpool University Press, 1951.

Simey, Margaret, *The Disinherited Society: a Personal View of Social Responsibility in Liverpool during the Twentieth Century*, Liverpool: Liverpool University Press, 1996.

Slater, Helen, 'Enid Marx RDI: An Interview', in Jill Seddon and Suzette Worden, *Women Designing: Redefining Design in Britain Between the Wars*, Brighton: University of Brighton Press, 1994, 89–93.

Smith, Harold L., *The British Women's Suffrage Campaign, 1866–1828*, London: Longman, 1998.

Spain, Daphne, *Gendered Spaces*, Chapel Hill: University of North Carolina Press, 1992.

Speight, Sadie, 'Inside the House' in Design Research Unit, *The Practice of Design*, London: Lund Humphries, 1946, 111–122.

Srebrnik, H., 'Class, Ethnicity and Gender Intertwined: Jewish women and the East End Rent strikes, 1935–40', *Women's History Review*, 4:3 (1995), 283–299.

Standing Joint Committee of Working Women's Organisations, 'Design of Post-War Houses', in *Report of the Twenty Second National Conference of Labour Women*, 1943, Labour Party, London, 1943.

Summerson, John, *London Building World of the 1860s*, London: Thames & Hudson, 1973.

Sutcliffe, Anthony, *Towards the Planned City: Germany, Britain, the US and France 1780–1914*, Oxford: Basil Blackwell, 1981.

Swenarton, Mark, *Homes Fit for Heroes The Politics and Architecture of Early State Housing in Britain*, London: Heinemann, 1981.

Tanner, Andrea, *Bricks and Mortals, 75 Years of the Kensington Housing Trust*, London: Kensington Housing Trust, 2001.

Tanner, S.J., *How the Suffrage Movement began in Bristol Fifty Years Ago*, Bristol: The Carlyle Press, 1918.

Tarn, John Nelson, *Five Percent Philanthropy: An Account of Housing in Urban Areas between 1840 and 1914*, Cambridge: Cambridge University Press, 1973.

Tennyson, Alfred Tennyson, Baron, *The Princess: A Medley*, London: Edward Moxon, 1847.

Thiele, Beverly, 'Vanishing Acts in Political and Social Thought, Tricks of the Trade', in Linda McDowell and Rosemary Pringle (eds), *Defining Women: Social Institutions and Gender Divisions*, Cambridge: Polity Press, 1992, 26.

Tomrley, Cycill, 'The Designer and her Problem', *Design for Today*, 1, (1933), 175–184.

Tomrley, Cycill, *Furnishing your Home*, London: Allen and Unwin, 1939.

Torre, Suzanne (ed.), *Women in American Architecture: A Historic and Contemporary Perspective*, New York: Whitney Library of Design, 1977.

Tosh, John, *A Man's Place. Masculinity and the Middle-Class Home in Victorian England*, New Haven and London: Yale University Press, 1999.

Tyrwhitt, Jacqueline (ed.), *Patrick Geddes in India*, London: Lund Humphries, 1947.

Veasey, Christine, 'Lighting the Home of To-day', *The Studio*, 108, (1934), 199–202.

Veasey, Christine, (ed.), *Good Furnishing*, London: Times Publishing Co. Ltd, n.d.

Veblen, Thorstein, *The Theory of the Leisure Class*, [1899] New York & London: Dover, 1994.

Vicinus, Martha, *Independent Women, Work and Community for Single Women, 1850–1920*, Chicago, University of Chicago Press, 1985.

Vickery, Amanda, 'Golden Age to Separate Spheres? A review of the Categories and Chronology of English Women's History', *The Historical Journal*, 36:2, (1993), 383–414.

Vickery, Amanda, *The Gentleman's Daughter. Women's Lives in Georgian England*, London: Yale University Press, 1998.

Vincent, Andrew, and Raymond Plant, *Philosophy, Politics and Citizenship*, Oxford: Blackwells, 1984.

Wait, Vincent, *Bristol Civic Society: The First Sixty Years*, Bristol, 1966.

Walker, Linda, 'Helen Blackburn (1842–1903)', *Oxford Dictionary of National Biography* Vol. 5, Oxford: Oxford University Press, 2004, 927–928.

Walker, Lynne, ' Concrete Proof: Women, Architecture and Modernism', *Feminist Arts News*, 3, (1986), 8.

Walker, Lynne, *Women Architects, their Work*, London: Sorella Press, 1984.

Walker, Lynne, (ed.), *Drawing on Diversity, Women, Architecture and Practice*, London: RIBA Drawings Collection, 1997.

Walkowitz, Judith, *City of Dreadful Delight: Narratives of Sexual Danger in Late-Victorian London*, Chicago: University of Chicago Press, 1992.

Ward, Stephen V., *Planning and Urban Change*, London: Sage, 2nd edit, 2004.

Webb, Beatrice, *My Apprenticeship*, Harmondsworth: Pelican, 1938.

Weiner, Deborah, *Architecture and Social Reform in Late-Victorian London*, Manchester: Manchester University Press, 1994.

Whelan, Robert, (ed.), *Octavia Hill's Letters to Fellow Workers*, London: Kyrle Books, 2005.

Whitworth, Lesley, 'Anticipating Affluence; Skill, Judgement and the problems of Aesthetic Tutelage', in Lawrence Black and Hugh Pemberton, *An Affluent Society? Britain's Post-War 'Golden Age' Revisited*, Aldershot: Ashgate, 2004, 167–183.

Whitworth, Lesley, 'Inscribing Design on the Nation: The Creators of the British Council of Industrial Design', *Business and Economic History On-line*, 3 (2005) http://www.thebhc.org/publications/BEHonline/2005/whitworth.pdf

Whitworth, Lesley (ed.), *Journal of Design History* (special issue: 'Anxious Homes'), 16:3, (2003).

Williams, Raymond, *Keywords. A Vocabulary of Culture and Society*, London: Fontana Press, 1976.

Williamson, Philip, 'Margaret Grace Bondfield (1873–1953)', *Oxford Dictionary of National Biography*, Vol. 6, Oxford: Oxford University Press, 2004, 524–526.

Willsden, Clare A.P., *Mural Painting in Britain 1840–1940: Image and Meaning*, London: Clarendon Studies in the History of Art, Oxford University Press, 2000.

Willsden, Clare A.P., 'Scotland's Mural Renascence', *The Scottish Review*, 29, (1983), 15–22.

Wilson, Elizabeth, *The Sphinx in the City: Urban Life, the Control of Disorder and Women*, Berkeley: University of California Press, 1991.

Wilson, J.M., 'The Progress of Christian Church life during the last 25 years', *Sermons at Redland Park Congregational Chapel, Bristol* Bristol: privately published, 1886.

Winslow, Barbara, *Sylvia Pankhurst. Sexual politics and political activism*, London: Routledge, 1996.

Wolff, Janet, 'The Culture of Separate Spheres: the Role of Culture in Nineteenth-century Public and Private Life', in Janet Wolff and John Seed (eds), *The Culture of Capital: Art, Power and the Nineteenth-century Middle Class*, Manchester: Manchester University Press, 1988, 117–134.

Wolff, Janet, 'The Invisible Flaneuse: Women and the Literature of Modernity' in Andrew Benjamin (ed.), *The Problems of Modernity. Adorno and Benjamin*, London; Routledge, 1989, 154.

Woodham, Jonathan, 'Dorothy Adelaide Braddell (1889–1981)', *Oxford Dictionary of National Biography*, Vol. 7, Oxford: Oxford University Press, 2004, 170–171.

Wright, H. Myles, and Robert Gardner-Medwin, *The Design of Nursery and Elementary Schools*, London: The Architectural Press, 1938.

Wrigley, Chris, 'Katherine St John Bruce Glasier, (1867–1950)', *Oxford Dictionary of National Biography*, Vol. 22, Oxford: Oxford University Press, 2004, 441–442.

Yeo, Eileen Janes, *The Contest for Social Science: relations and representations of gender and class*, London: Rivers Oram, 1996.

Yorke, F.R.S. and Frederick Gibberd, *The Modern Flat*, London: The Architectural Press, 1937.

Young, Linda, *Middle Class Culture in the Nineteenth Century: America, Australia and Britain*, London: Palgrave, 2002.

Zweiniger-Bargielowska, Ina, *Austerity in Britain: Rationing, Controls and Consumption, 1939–1955*, Oxford: Oxford University Press, 2000.

Index